Growing Young Leaders

Australian College of Theology Monograph Series

SERIES EDITOR EDWINA MURPHY

The ACT Monograph Series, generously supported by the Board of Directors of the Australian College of Theology, provides a forum for publishing quality research theses and studies by its graduates and affiliated college staff in the broad fields of Biblical Studies, Christian Thought and History, and Practical Theology with Wipf and Stock Publishers of Eugene, Oregon. The ACT selects the best of its doctoral and research masters theses as well as monographs that offer the academic community, scholars, church leaders and the wider community uniquely Australian and New Zealand perspectives on significant research topics and topics of current debate. The ACT also provides opportunity for contributors beyond its graduates and affiliated college staff to publish monographs which support the mission and values of the ACT.

Dr Edwina Murphy
Series Editor and Deputy Dean

Growing Young Leaders

Faith, Freedom, Failure, and Flourishing

DONALD SMITH

WIPF & STOCK · Eugene, Oregon

GROWING YOUNG LEADERS
Faith, Freedom, Failure, and Flourishing

Copyright © 2025 Donald Smith. All rights reserved. Except for brief quotations in critical publications or reviews, no part of this book may be reproduced in any manner without prior written permission from the publisher. Write: Permissions, Wipf and Stock Publishers, 199 W. 8th Ave., Suite 3, Eugene, OR 97401.

Wipf & Stock
An Imprint of Wipf and Stock Publishers
199 W. 8th Ave., Suite 3
Eugene, OR 97401

www.wipfandstock.com

PAPERBACK ISBN: 979-8-3852-4145-3
HARDCOVER ISBN: 979-8-3852-4146-0
EBOOK ISBN: 979-8-3852-4147-7

VERSION NUMBER 01/09/25

Scripture quotation marked (MSG) are taken from *The Message*. Copyright © 1993, 1994, 1995, 1996, 2000, 2001, 2002. Used by permission of NavPress Publishing Group.

Scipture quotations marked as (NIV) are taken from the Holy Bible, New International Version, NIV® Copyright © 1973, 1978, 1984, 2011 by Biblica, Inc.™ Used by permission. All rights reserved worldwide.

Scripture quotations marked (NLT) are taken from the Holy Bible, New Living Translation, copyright © 1996, 2004, 2007 by Tyndale House Foundation. Used by permission of Tyndale House Publishers, Inc., Carol Stream, IL 60188. All rights reserved.

To young men and those who intergenerationally serve with them in ministry, particularly those who move into the background, empower youth to lead, and thus *do it together*.

To the memory of Peter Garlick, a graduate of *Leadership*. Peter died pursuing his dreams in a climbing accident in April 2021 when he was on the cusp of joining the *Leadership* staff. His legacy lives on as a contributor to the research on which this book is based through his completion of the survey and participation in an interview. His unique and candid comments often stimulated significant and deeper insights.

Contents

Illustrations | ix

Acknowledgments | xiii

Glossary | xv

Abbreviations | xvii

Preface | xix

1 Introduction | 1

Part I: Program Elements and Key Concepts | 13

2 Program Elements and Key Concepts—Stage 1 | 19

3 Program Elements and Key Concepts—Stage 2 | 45

4 Program Elements and Key Concepts—Stage 3 | 68

Part II: Lenses | 85

5 *Communitas* | 87

6 Liminality | 97

7 Rites of Passage | 106

8 Wilderness | 123

CONTENTS

9   Lenses of Infilling: Communitas, Liminality, Rites of Passage, Wilderness | 128

10   Servant Leadership | 140

11   Masculine Spirituality | 164

12   Lenses of Outpouring: Servant Leadership and Masculine Spirituality | 178

Part III: Uniqueness Characterization | 183

13   Uniqueness of *Leadership* | 185

Part IV: Theory Development | 205

14   The Substantive Theory | 208

15   Acceptance | 215

16   Imperfection | 224

17   Freedom and Empowerment | 231

18   Spiritual Dimension (Mystery) | 236

Part V: Implications, Conclusions and Contextualization | 245

19   Beyond *Leadership* | 247

20   Conclusions and Youth Ministry as Context | 258

Appendix I: Excerpts from Reports of Three Participants | 277

Appendix II: Research Methodology and Methods | 283

Appendix III: Doing It Together | 288

Appendix IV: The Theory as a Symphony Metaphor | 291

Bibliography | 297

Illustrations

Tables

Table 1. Significance of Overall *Leadership* Community | 15

Table 2. Significance of Specific Characteristics of Overall *Leadership* Community | 15

Table 3. Significance of *My Group* | 21

Table 4. Stimulus to Group Becoming a Well-Functioning Team | 28

Table 5. Most Significant Characteristics Identified in Group Facilitators | 28

Table 6. Significance of Overnight Expedition | 32

Table 7. Significance of Music Workshop | 35

Table 8. Other Stage 1 Activities Nominated as Significant | 38

Table 9. Additional General Comments from Participants about Stage 1 | 41

Table 10. Significance of Solo | 46

Table 11. Most Significant Solo Experiences | 47

Table 12. Significance of Solo Celebration | 49

Table 13. Significance of Becoming a Man Theme | 56

Table 14. Significance of the Panel | 59

ILLUSTRATIONS

Table 15. Other Stage 2 Experiences of Significance | 61

Table 16. Significance of Mission Statement | 69

Table 17. Significance of Duo | 73

Table 18. Significance of *7 Habits* | 76

Table 19. Other Stage 3 Activities in Order of Significance | 78

Table 20. Pivotal Moments in Achieving *Communitas* | 93

Table 21. Occasions Most Felt in Liminal Space | 99

Table 22. Statements Explaining Experience of Liminal Space | 103

Table 23. Experiences Contributing to Rites of Passage in Order of Significance | 116

Table 24. Events Significant to Becoming a Man | 118

Table 25. Wilderness Experiences | 125

Table 26. Servant Leadership Characteristics Most Noted in Staff—List 1 | 152

Table 27. Servant Leadership Characteristics Most Noted in Staff—List 2 | 155

Table 28. Leader Roles Exercised Post-*Leadership* | 157

Table 29. Respondents' Descriptions of Their Current Leadership Style | 160

Table 30. Indicators of the Spirituality of a Christian Man | 173

Table 31. Indicators of the Spirituality of a Christian Man—Comparison of Choices | 174

Table 32. Unique Characteristics of *Leadership* | 186

Table 33. Summary of Theory Narrative | 213

Table 34. What Participant Respondents and Staff Respondents Consider Was Most Taught at *Leadership* | 247

Table 35. Categorization of Additional Comments | 250

Table 36. Comparison of Elements of *Leadership* with *Best Practice* in Youth Ministry | 269

Table 37. The Tasks of Practical Theology and Book Framework | 287

ILLUSTRATIONS

Figures

Figure 1. Sample Mission Statement | 71

Figure 2. Joe and Al—Duo Partners | 75

Figure 3. Movement through Liminal Space in Stage 1 | 101

Figure 4. Movement through Liminal Space in Stage 2 | 101

Figure 5. Movement through Liminal Space in Stage 3 | 102

Figure 6. Properties of Uniqueness | 192

Figure 7. Theory Development—Core Category, Subcategories, Contextual Category, Properties, Dimensions, and Themes | 207

Figure 8. Substantive Grounded Theory | 208

Figure 9. Grounded Theory Design Framework | 285

Figure 10. *Leadership* as an Orchestra/a Symphony | 292

Acknowledgments

Jesus looked at them intently and said, "Humanly speaking, it is impossible. But with God everything is possible." (NLT)

Firstly, I acknowledge the permission given by the Boys' Brigade Queensland to undertake this study of a program conducted by the organization for forty years, including access to documents and people.

I share the experience of many, that while a PhD program necessarily focuses on the individual, it is a team effort, involving family, friends, academic colleagues, and supervisors (advisors), and often those who contribute data through surveys, interviews, focus groups, and reference/advisory groups. Then there are the many authors who have walked a similar or related path previously and whose work is shared in their publications, many of which are referenced in a work such as this.

I acknowledge the contributions of these others who have contributed to the completion of this work. In particular, I thank my academic supervisors, Rev. Dr. Ian Hussey, Dr. Robert Hershell, and Dr. Ruth Lukabyo. Your contributions to the final thesis have been not only valuable, but unique, sharing from your own experience and expertise. I also warmly acknowledge my host college, Malyon Theological College, and the support and assistance of Jill Walker, Librarian at Malyon Theological College. I am yet to find a reference that Jill is not able to produce for me.

ACKNOWLEDGMENTS

Importantly, as without them, this publication would never have been birthed, I acknowledge the participants of *Leadership*, both the young men who have completed the program and the many staff over the years who have served them in various roles, bringing your youth ministry experience, including your innovations and energies to bear on the development and continuation of the program for forty years. You have all taught me much. In particular, thanks to those who shared your experiences and memories through completing surveys and joining me in interviews and focus groups.

Special thanks to two *Leadership* graduates for your contributions: to Mitch Smith for designing figures 6 and 8 and to emerging composer. Alexander Voltz, for your assistance and expertise in describing the content of Appendix IV: The Theory as a Symphony Metaphor.

Thank you to those who I was able to engage with as sounding boards and those who read and gave feedback on parts of the manuscript, in particular Dr. Pamela Condie who was in the unique role of having had sons and grandsons complete the course as well as being the Course Director for the companion course for young women.

My thanks too to the Australian College of Theology for its support of this publication based on my thesis and contextualizing it into a youth and young adult ministry framework. I appreciate the assistance of my ACT contact persons in the task of bringing a thesis into publication, Rev. Dr. Megan Powell du Toit, Publication Manager, and Dr. Louise Gosbell, Research Manager. Having journeyed the editing phase with editor, Greta Morris, I am pleased to add her name to the list of those who have given their time and expertise.

Most importantly, I acknowledge that while it was me that God gave the privilege of studying this program for young men, it was something that was brought to fruition only through the grace of God and his enabling.

Glossary

Grounded Theory Terms[1]

Advanced Coding	Techniques used to facilitate integration of the final grounded theory
Category	A higher-level concept that represents a group of codes
Code	A form of shorthand that researchers repeatedly use to identify conceptual reoccurrences and similarities in the patterns of participants' experiences
Concept	An idea or notion that encapsulates a descriptive explanation of a phenomenon or characteristic of a phenomenon
Core category	A concept that encapsulates a phenomenon apparent in the categories and sub-categories constructed and the relationships between these
Dimensions	Variations of a property
Initial coding	The process of fracturing the data in order to compare incident with incident, name apparent phenomena or beginning patterns, and begin the process of comparison between the codes applied. Also referred to as open coding

1. Birks and Mills, *Grounded Theory*.

GLOSSARY

Intermediate coding	The identification of properties, dimensions, patterns and relationships during the process of category development
Memoing	A fundamental analytical process in grounded theory research that involves the recording of processes, thoughts, feelings, analytical insights, decisions, and ideas in relation to a research project
Metaphor	A figure of speech that can be used as a theoretical code where there is sufficient fit between a metaphor and the grounded theory
Properties	Characteristics of a category
Storyline	A strategy for facilitating integration, construction, formulation and presentation of the research findings through the production of a coherent grounded theory
Substantive codes	Taken from the language of the data. Usually assume the form of gerunds or *in vivo* codes
Substantive grounded theory	Theory that aims to address a studied phenomenon in a specific situation
Theoretical coding	The use of advanced abstractions to provide a framework for enhancing the explanatory power of a grounded theory
Theoretical integration	The pulling together of the abstract theoretical scheme into a final grounded theory
Theoretical saturation	Occurs when no new codes are identified pertaining to a particular category. Categories are clearly articulated with sharply defined and dimensionalized properties
Theoretical sensitivity	The ability to recognise and extract from the data elements that have relevance for the emerging theory
Theory	An explanatory scheme comprising a set of concepts related to each other through logical patterns of connectivity

Abbreviations

General Abbreviations

BB	Boys' Brigade—a parachurch organization which operates as a ministry of local churches, supported with resources, activities, and leader training through regional, state, and national structures
CISD	Critical Incident Stress Debriefing
HSTP	High School Theology Program (USA)
Leadership	The Boys' Brigade Queensland leadership development program for young men
ANZAC	(Australia and New Zealand Army Corps) Originally a military partnership between Australia and New Zealand, which developed into an ethos that became an identity for those who fought in war together. The ethos extended beyond war and became synonymous with the spirit shared by those who experienced combat together; it is also extended to other joint experiences shared between people from the two countries

ABBREVIATIONS

Biblical Book Quotations and Abbreviations

All quotations of the Bible are from the NIV unless otherwise indicated. MSG refers to The Message and NLT to the New Living Translation.

See below for abbreviations used for biblical books. For other books, when referenced, full titles are used.

OLD TESTAMENT		NEW TESTAMENT	
Book Name	**Abbreviation**	**Book Name**	**Abbreviation**
Genesis	Gen	Matthew	Matt
Exodus	Exod	Romans	Rom
Deuteronomy	Deut	1 Corinthians	1 Cor
Joshua	Josh	2 Corinthians	2 Cor
Judges	Judg	Galatians	Gal
2 Samuel	2 Sam	Ephesians	Eph
2 Chronicles	2 Chr	Philippians	Phil
Psalm	Psa	Colossians	Col
Isaiah	Isa	1 Timothy	1 Tim
Zephaniah	Zeph	2 Timothy	2 Tim
		Hebrews	Heb
		James	Jas
		1 Peter	1 Pet
		2 Peter	2 Pet
		Revelation	Rev

Preface

THIS BOOK IS BASED on a PhD thesis that examined the factors contributing to the apparent success of a leadership development program for young men.[2] That research is referred to throughout this book as a case study in one specific youth ministry. The program (*Leadership*) commenced in 1981 and has run continuously since, apart from a one-year gap in 2020, because of the COVID-19 pandemic.

Leadership refers to a leadership development course of the Boys' Brigade Queensland.[3] Over time, participants began referring to the program simply as *Leadership*. This term has continued and is used in this publication.

The findings of the research have been shared with staff of the program and various insights have been incorporated into the program. The evaluation of this program is now offered to the wider youth ministry audience, presenting insights that may be an encouragement and of general application.

Leadership, the Program

Because *Leadership* is a unique program, relevant contextual characteristics are stated:

    2. Smith, "Theory of What Factors."

    3. A corresponding program for girls and young women is run by the Girls' Brigade Queensland.

- It is a program for fifteen- to nineteen-year-old young men.
- It runs over three stages, a year apart.
- It is progressive, with built in cross-stage themes.
- Each stage is residential, over eight or nine days.
- Small groups are the key medium of program delivery and for the emergence of *communitas*.
- Each stage involves a wilderness experience.
- It is staff-intensive.
- Its staffing model is described as multigenerational, nonhierarchical, and servant-led, not placing a high value on differentiation of status.

As examples of participants' feedback between 2008 and 2014, brief excerpts from detailed reports of three participants are included as Appendix I.

While program content has changed to maintain a contemporary focus and introduce new resources, the overall ethos and goals have been maintained. The course structure is that participants are members of three different groups—the whole course community, their stage cohort, and in Stages 1 and 2, their small group with one or two facilitators (in Stage 3, the stage cohort remains the operational group). Generally, over time, the spiritual focus has become more specifically young-man focused, something that is recognized in their participation in worship.

Purpose of the Research

The purpose of the research was to develop an understanding of the elements of an effective leadership development program for young men incorporating spiritual and personal development. By abstracting the concepts and program elements, it was anticipated that there would be a level of generalizability of the findings, adding to knowledge as well as leading to enhancement in both practice and policy of youth and young adult ministry.

Research Question

In 2017, *Leadership* staff were surveyed and from their responses a set of goals and indicators of goal-attainment was developed.[4] These were adopted as indicators of program effectiveness. There is more than adequate evidence in the data from a 2018 research project,[5] which is confirmed from other sources to support the finding of a high level of goal attainment: for example, overwhelmingly positive responses, testimony of spiritual challenge and growth, frequent mention of the uniqueness of the *Leadership* community, and participants' acceptance into the community, modeling by the adult staff, references to increasing spiritual and masculine maturity, learning of new leadership and other skills, transformation experienced, and close, lasting friendships formed. This was confirmed in documented feedback offered by parents and participants.

Based on the evidence from staff, participants, and parents, the effectiveness of the program on a measure of goal attainment was established. Foundational to this new research was the recognition that *Leadership* has been successful in achieving its goals.

The research question in this study is: *What factors contribute to the apparent success of the Boys' Brigade Leadership program?* The research question was addressed by examining the dynamics of key program elements and by approaching it through several theoretical lenses: *communitas*, liminality, servant-leadership, masculine spirituality, rites of passage, and wilderness, and how these perspectives coalesce into a leadership pedagogy.

The study is contextualized in a practical theological paradigm. The grounded theory methodology and the methods utilized in the research are summarized in Appendix II. Grounded theory terms continue to be used in the text to outline processes (see glossary). The primary data collection method used was the administration of a questionnaire to participants who had completed at least one stage of *Leadership* during a ten-year period. The responses of those who later joined the staff were bracketed and collated separately—this group are referred to as staff respondents and the main group as participant respondents. A further group of experienced staff completed a separate questionnaire and where comparisons of difference

---

4. Leadership Queensland, *Goals of Leadership*.
5. Smith, "Theory of What Influences."

PREFACE

are indicated, they are referred to as experienced staff. A research collaboration group of a range of staff was also formed.

Explanations for the Reader

Young men are the focus of the research that led to this book. *Leadership* is usually commenced in school years ten or eleven (ages fifteen or sixteen) and runs for three years, so participants in the program are generally aged between fifteen and nineteen years. However, the research, conducted in 2020, was directed at those who had completed the course over a ten-year period, so at the time were aged up to twenty-six years. Quotations from participants, using their actual words, often include the year of completion to give timeline context.

The reference to *young men* should be taken to mean those between fifteen and approximately twenty-four years, incorporating the years of participation in *Leadership* and the following five to seven years.

Repetition will be observed throughout, including the direct quotes from participants if it illustrates more than one observation. This places intentional emphasis on the *voices of youth* and adds meaning and a sense of completeness for readers who choose to read by selected chapter topic.

Readers are reminded throughout that when *Leadership* is capitalized and in italics it is referring to the program being evaluated.

There is reference throughout to Stages 1–3. These are the three stages of the *Leadership* program, usually completed a year apart.

1

Introduction

HAVING OPENED THIS BOOK, you are now between the covers. You have opened a door. You are invited into an imperfect liminal community; into the shared story of participants of *Leadership*,[1] doing it together in an experience where they are fully accepted, such that they discover they are in a safe place and have the freedom and empowerment to say:

> I can talk about anything, share my personal story, or ask any question I want to, and I know my secrets are safe. I can talk about those things and ask those questions that never get talked about in church; that I can't raise at Youth or with my parents.
>
> I would say it's some of the most significant worship ever in my life. The worship at leadership feels like we're not singing for ourselves. We're singing to God. Like, I can't sing. A lot of the boys next to me can't sing. You can really lean into that and not worry about anyone else. It's all worship when we all sing together, there's something really beautiful about that. It feels intentional and from God.

In the preface, the program upon which the research is based is introduced, the purpose of the research is described, and the research question stated: *What factors contribute to the apparent success of the Boys' Brigade Leadership program?* This chapter summarizes the justification and importance of the research in the context of youth ministry, and the leadership development of young men.

---

1. A reminder, as explained in the preface, *Leadership* (when italicized) refers to the program that has been researched and upon which this book is based.

INTRODUCTION

Justification and Importance of the Research

Leadership is acknowledged as a program that deals with issues confronting young men and builds resilience and personal and spiritual health, thus equipping young men to deal with the life issues they and their friends face.

The justification of the research is that a program that holds itself out as a significant youth ministry should be evaluated for the sake of those whom it serves and for what the findings may offer others. The importance of the research reflects the importance of God's plan for youth as people with issues and as people in transition. Its importance is reinforced in recognizing the status of children (including young men), the importance of family for young men, the capacity of youth, and their readiness for ministry.

In a 2020 survey by Mission Australia,[2] young people were asked to respond to a series of questions which provide a picture of their concerns and other life matters. The most important issues for Queensland males were found to be COVID-19 (41.2%), equity and discrimination (31.7%), mental health (24.7%), and the environment (21.8%). Issues of personal concern (extremely or very concerned) among males were coping with stress (19.9%), school or study problems (18.7%), physical health (16.6%), and mental health (16.6%). Young males in Queensland identified race/cultural background as the highest reason for being treated unfairly (34.1%). This was followed by gender (23.8%), mental health (20.9%), and age (20.0%).

In response to a question on what they value, Queensland males identified that friendships (other than family) were either extremely or very important (80.3%), followed by family relationships (74.7%), physical health (63.5%), school or study satisfaction (61.1%), mental health (55.8%), financial security (49.0%), and getting a job (40.6%). All these issues were impacted by the COVID-19 pandemic, creating mental health concerns for youth.

The significance of these issues for young men today is acknowledged, in particular, concerns about the issue of mental health. Almost a quarter of young men are concerned about coping with stress. Of importance in the research is that participants say that *Leadership* is where they can raise their pressing issues,[3] even the issues that are taboo elsewhere. That their significant life issues are real, and that they feel they can deal with them at

---

2. Tiller et al., *Youth Survey Report*.
3. Smith, "Theory," 85.

Leadership, may be a factor contributing to their positive experience and the apparent success of the program.

Leadership is focused on the period of transition between immaturity and maturity, between boyhood and manhood. The Bible, and specifically Jesus's actions, recognize children/young men and their needs and status. This is the contextual backdrop to the examination of *Leadership*.

Biblical sources justify an acknowledgment that children and youth, including young men who are the focus of *Leadership*, are in need of, even entitled to, protection (Exod 22:22; Deut 10:18; Isa 1:17; Matt 18:6, 10; Mark 9:42; Luke 17:2), training and mentoring (Deut 6:6–7), encouragement, guidance, and advice (Titus 2:6; 1 Pet 5:5), teaching (Deut 6:4–9), and discipleship (the example of Jesus).

God's plan for children, including youth, who are not yet adults, has been violated. For example, from a review of several studies, the Australian Institute of Family Studies[4] reported (in 2017) the prevalence of physical abuse of children in Australia (5–16%), emotional maltreatment (9–14%), exposure to family violence (4–23%), sexual abuse of boys (5.2–12%), and sexual abuse of girls (14–26.8%). This indicates that for a substantial number of children, their need for protection is not being met. Many are growing up with abuse and neglect, parental separation, emotional detachment, and poverty.[5] This has, or should have, a substantial impact on the nature of effective contemporary youth ministry, an important understanding supporting the value of programs such as *Leadership*.

Jesus's dealings with the disciples, particularly Peter, through naming him "the rock" (Matt 16:17–18), then later, through mentoring strategies of forward prediction, challenge, and affirmation, with restoration and a renewed trust (John 21:15–19), stand as exemplars of training and mentoring. Young men are not yet mature adults. They will make mistakes. Barnabas is an example of a man who provided encouragement, guidance, and advice to John Mark (Acts 15:36–39), despite mistakes and even in the face of opposition from Paul.

Teaching children is the primary responsibility of parents (Deut 6:4–9), but the church (and as a part of the church, *Leadership* and like programs) also has a responsibility towards children, as observed by May et al., "God does not intend for one man and one woman to carry the full

---

4. Australian Institute of Family Studies, "Families in Australia."

5. Australian Institute of Family Studies, "Parenting Arrangements"; St. Vincent de Paul Society, "Two Australias."

responsibility for their children's spiritual formation. God's plan, seen in Deuteronomy 6, is that the faith community supports the family and together they nurture the children."[6] The responsibility of the church is to bring others into their fellowship, often through a discipleship strategy. This responsibility continues with succeeding generations, so that at any one time, the church is a dynamic intergenerational body.

Status of Children/Young Men

Children and youth have a recognized status in God's plan. They belong to the kingdom of heaven; they are ready and able to serve; and they are sharers in the life of faith. Jesus welcomed children and recognized their status as having a belongingness in the "kingdom of heaven" (Matt 19:13–15; Mark 10:13–16; Luke 18:15–17). Jesus called young men, most commonly thought to be still in their teens or early twenties[7] to serve with him in a group who would change the world. *Leadership* is a ministry to youth and emerging adult men. Jesus and his disciples provide a model for *Leadership*. Youth and young adults have a right and expectation to receive training. This is so, both as part of God's plan reflected in Jesus's relationship with his disciples, and as the responsible approach of the church, including *Leadership*, towards children as they move towards physical, intellectual, and spiritual maturity.

> Young men are recognised as being strong and capable of having the word of God living within them (Prov 20:29; 1 John 2:14), as capable of sincere commitment and devotion evidenced in their overcoming the evil one (1 John 2:13), of ministering to and setting a positive example and teaching others (1 Tim 4:12), and to be treated as brothers (1 Tim 5:1).[8]

6. May et al., *Children Matter*, 34.

7. It is considered based on the available evidence of Jewish custom concerning ages of learning, following a rabbi, marriage, and paying taxes; Jesus's age, the biblical record; and the disciples' characters, that: Peter was the oldest, certainly under thirty and most likely in his early twenties; Matthew may have been the next oldest, most likely under twenty; John was the youngest, aged between fifteen and twenty, most likely under eighteen, and possibly as young as sixteen; the others were younger than Peter and older than John, therefore, most likely between sixteen and twenty and probably under eighteen; or, generally, that all the disciples were between fifteen and their early twenties (Luke 3:23; Matt 4:21–22; Matt 8:14; Matt 17:24–27; Acts 12:2; Cary and Cary, nd.; Cox, "How Old?"; Got Questions Ministries, "Jesus' Disciples."

8. Smith, "Leadership Development Program," 74.

God did not wait for full maturity, for example, with Joseph, Daniel, David, and Timothy. Jesus chose young men for the role of disciples, despite their immaturity. As McGarry notes, "Jesus could have called any group of people to become His disciples, but He chose a group of teenagers and young adults who were overwhelmingly ordinary."[9] Then he set about bringing them to maturity; training them for the leadership roles they would take on. *Leadership* and the young men who attend *Leadership* are in a similar position—at the junction of the child/adult threshold, but not yet fully mature. Jesus called the disciples, he appointed them to leadership roles, and he taught them about servanthood. *Leadership* is located within the church as an agent of advancing God's kingdom in the world, so it is timely and appropriate that the program's effectiveness be examined to consider whether it can be viewed as an effective intense period of training, mirroring the model Jesus used.

Family

Family and friendships outside the family remain very significant for young men.[10] But domestic and family violence continue to be a serious concern. By 2017 the divorce rate in Australia stabilized to around 50 percent,[11] but many children and youth are living in violent situations, often with at least one absent parent.

The work of scholars and the experience shared at *Leadership* combine to reinforce the continuing importance of families to youth and emerging adult men, though the communication of this reality is not always clear. Of particular interest is the application in relation to boys and their fathers, as illustrated by this comment from a *Leadership* participant, in an anonymous letter to his father:

> I wish we could be able to spend more time together because you're always doing work or giving us work. I know you say you've got a lot to be done but we should still spend more time together doing fun stuff like 4 x 4 driving or shooting.[12]

---

9. McGarry, *Biblical Theology*, 55.
10. Tiller et al., *Youth Survey Report*.
11. White et al., *Youth and Society*, 171.
12. Leadership Queensland, *Dear Dad*.

INTRODUCTION

The challenge for the church, and for youth ministries such as *Leadership*, is to "create a caring place where adolescents can talk about changes in their parents' abilities to bless the persons they are becoming"[13] and to communicate participants' wishes to their parents. The opportunity for this research was to see if the experience of participants confirms these observations. As a place where personal issues, including family concerns, are openly shared, *Leadership* has a potential role in being a two-way conduit for this communication between parents and sons.

Capacity of Youth and Readiness for Ministry

There is a developing thrust that youth ministries in all forms, including *Leadership*, need to understand that while they are dealing with persons in transition at a critical developmental time of their lives, youth are more competent and more able than they are sometimes given credit for; that their heroic acts are recognized and highly regarded; and that they are capable of running their own programs. Youth in the community and in the church are teachers as well as learners.

Youth ministries in succeeding generations have demonstrated the sometimes unrecognized capacity of youth.[14] It is a common observation of those who reflect academically and practically on youth ministry that both personally and theologically, youth are capable and ready for ministry leadership *now*—not at some time in the future. For example, "The truth is that teenagers are capable of far more disciplined theological reflection, far holier lives, and far more courageous leadership than most adults assume or practice."[15]

There is a continuing theme in the US High School Theology Program (HSTP)[16] that youth should be respected and dealt with as persons of competence, including theological competence, ready to understand difficult concepts and to lead *now*, not at some ill-defined future time. Proffitt

13. Stancil, "Genesis," 399.
14. Lukabyo, *Ministry for Youth*.
15. Dean and Hearlson, "Taste Tests and Teenagers," 25.
16. The HSTP is extensively funded by the Lilly Endowment. It commenced in 1993, located in theological colleges. High school young people are invited onto campuses for a live-in experience of "a longer, broader, more diverse church than most of them have ever known or imagined" (Dykstra, "Foreword," xi), providing them with theological teaching (which we would probably describe as biblical or Christian teaching rather than using the term *theology* in this context).

and Young refer to the collegial learning practice of mutual respect. They continue to say that youth respond to being treated with dignity and when they are enabled to exercise leadership, and that their opinions are asked for and valued—being treated "like full-on adults" and "fellow theologians"[17]—backing up a similar observation by Dean and Hearlson that HSTP participants appreciated being treated as competent theologians.[18]

The lack of recognition of the capacity of youth and their readiness for ministry is expanded by youth ministry specialists. Dean observes that "we are more likely to consider youth as *objects* of ministry than *agents* of ministry; people to be ministered *unto* rather than people Jesus has called into ministry in their own right."[19] Dean continues, "Youth ministry that emphasizes evangelism, without simultaneously giving adolescents opportunities to serve in substantive ministry eviscerates discipleship." They should be invited "to jump into the Christian community alongside us."[20] Rahn suggests that churches are making "a grave mistake [by] forcing kids to wait until post-adolescence to begin to use their gifts and energy in the church and in the world."[21] If youth are not being appointed into Christian leadership roles, we are neglecting the strategy and example of Jesus who explicitly chose mostly young men as his disciples.[22] Root suggests that if we delay, "youth ministry . . . becomes the place where we are *preparing* young people to be vital participants in their churches in the future—not participants and members *now*."[23] Dever encourages the appointment of young men to leadership roles, which he sees as exercising "advance trust," even if that is taking a risk. In his words: "If you wish to see leaders raised up, your general posture should be characterized by a willingness to advance trust." "I do definitely take risks in leadership. It's worth it. God is sovereign. Christ will build his church. So, let's lean in and take some risks."[24] He follows these words with a particular reference to young men:

> Congregations, for their part, need to be patient with young men in leadership as they make young-man mistakes. I often tell

---

17. Proffitt and Young, "Catalyzing Community," 71–72.
18. Dean and Hearlson, "Calling as Creative Process," 52.
19. Dean, "Fessing Up," 30.
20. Dean, "Fessing Up," 33.
21. Rahn, "Focusing Youth Ministry," 173.
22. Cox, "How Old?," 24.
23. Root, *Taking the Cross*, 46.
24. Dever, "9 Ways," para 4.

churches not to be afraid of nominating a young lion cub. He may scratch the floors or damage some furniture, but if you're patient with him, you'll have a lion who loves you for life.[25]

Lawless makes the point that "At a time when young men are often most open to being challenged and stretched, churches aren't ready for them."[26] As an observation and an explanation, Lawless continues: "Their churches have sometimes forgotten them after their teen years."[27] Investigating the identified research question will assist those who provide such programs in their ministry with emerging young adults, emerging young leaders, as they take up the challenge of preparing others to receive the baton of Christian leadership.

Hine has commented that "young people are often judged to be less able than they are."[28] He summed up the American cultural creation of teenager by listing a series of negative characteristics, which he detailed as "A messy, sometimes loutish character who is nonetheless capable of performing heroically when necessary." As a further reversal of the usual way of seeing youth, adults need to recognize that there are lessons to learn from those who are not yet adults. Beckwith states that "what the experts do agree on is that children of this generation have the potential for living unselfish lives. We would do well to expose them to areas of service and mission in our churches."[29] *Leadership* sets out to do this in its invitation to participants to exercise leadership at any time.

Youth themselves are often disappointed that their gifts and readiness are not understood, acknowledged, or utilized. Dean compares and contrasts youth ministry in churches with farm teams in Major League Baseball, preparing emerging players to be ready for leadership in the main game. Church farm teams include "confirmation programs, church camps, volunteer corps, and denominational youth leadership organizations." Camp is particularly mentioned, contrasted with what happens in local churches: "Thousands of young people find Christian community more palpable—and their gifts, more utilized—in the course of summer camp than in their congregations or youth groups, and for these young people, camp becomes 'the new church.'" Dean continues: "nor is it clear whether

25. Dever, "9 Ways," para 4.
26. Lawless, "7 Reasons," para 3.
27. Lawless, "7 Reasons," para 3.
28. Hine, *Rise and Fall*, 7.
29. Beckwith, *Postmodern Children's Ministry*, 33.

the 'Major Leagues' of Christian vocational formation—congregations, denominations, and theological schools—are prepared to make room for this young talent when it appears."[30] This is a challenge for the local church and for camps/retreats such as *Leadership*.

Equipping youth for leadership and letting them loose runs risks, but not equipping and empowering them runs greater risks. Dean offers a look into the future of youth ministry and theological education, something which, if true, sounds a warning and is important for churches to consider. Two of her predictions are considered:

> *Missional communities.* As youth ministry moves away from youth fellowship models, young people longing for community are finding it in missional communities. Among the important changes this signals is a movement away from creating ministries for young people to participate in, toward supporting young people in ministries that they themselves create—a significant step toward the vocational formation of spiritually motivated teenagers.[31]

> *Early leadership experience.* Early leadership experience begets adult leadership. Young people who are participants—not spectators—in Christian leadership, and who have received primary experiences of service, witness, and stewardship (accompanied by theological reflection on these experiences) are the most likely to emerge as Christian leaders.[32]

Contrasting baseball farm teams and HSTPs, Dean suggests that HSTPs

> do not view themselves as preparatory holding tanks for future players. High School Theology Program leaders are steadfast in their insistence that young people are the church of *right now* and not just tomorrow: every HSTP impresses on teenagers that the church requires their leadership *immediately*, and that youth, not their managers, decide when they are ready to enter the game. Second, unlike farm teams that prepare players for baseball's established roles, High School Theology Program leaders encourage switch-hitting and experimentation; the roles their alumni will play in the church are unknown, and "hacking"[33] the system is encouraged.[34]

30. Dean, "Hitting It Out," 266–67.
31. Dean, "Hitting It Out," 284.
32. Dean, "Hitting It Out," 285.
33. Hacking: devising shortcuts through existing structures that are no longer culturally useful for the church to make them more useful.
34. Dean, "Hitting It Out," 268–69.

INTRODUCTION

All this begs the question of what HSTP (and therefore, *Leadership*) will look like in the future—not to mention, what youth ministry (including the ministry that offers *Leadership*) will look like in the future. Motivated teenagers, as emerging adults, may either change these ministries and programs, or take it into their own hands and walk somewhere else with a fresh entrepreneurial flair. If for no other reason, this realization is sufficient justification for the research.

Young Men and Leadership Development

Leadership development for young men is defined as a positive movement towards personal and spiritual maturity, including adoption of a servant leadership style, dealing with *roadblocks*, moving towards authentic manhood, and preparation for serving in Christian ministry.

Having considered the justification and importance of the research through contemporary youth issues, the status of youth, the importance of family, their capacity and readiness for ministry, I now turn to consider the leadership development of young men. Much of the literature on leadership development has focused on adults. This gap in the literature, linking youth and leadership development, was identified by Karagianni and Montgomery, pointing out that studies have generally been of adult leadership.[35] Mortensen et al. also noted that most studies of leadership have adopted adult perspectives and theories, and these have been applied to youth.[36] Their findings were that youth perspectives were more closely aligned with contemporary and developing general theories: "transformational, servant, shared/relational, social exchange, authentic." The ethos and philosophy of *Leadership*, which emphasizes servant leadership, modeling and mentoring, is consistent with the perspectives and narratives outlined by Mortensen et al.[37]

The limited inclusion of certain characteristics in secondary college-based programs has been critiqued by Eva and Sendjaya who in their review of a number of leadership development programs applied a servant leadership framework.[38] Servant leadership is a helpful lens through which to examine *Leadership* because it is frequently referred to as one of the key principles

---

35. Karagianni and Montgomery, "Developing Leadership Skills," 86.
36. Mortensen et al., "Leadership," 447.
37. Mortensen et al., "Leadership," 447.
38. Eva and Sendjaya, "Creating Future Leaders," 584, 588, 595.

of the program. This is explored in chapter 10. A question for *Leadership* is whether the identified characteristics are included in the program.

Organization of Chapters

In part I, chapters 2–4, key *Leadership* program elements, generic and stage-specific, are identified from the research findings and the emerging categories/themes are highlighted. Part II, chapters 5–12, considers the six lenses. The lenses of *communitas*, liminality, rites of passage, and wilderness are each considered separately in chapters 5–8, from a theoretical perspective and presentation of findings. They are then grouped into a coalescence of lenses—the lenses of infilling in chapter 9, where a mutual critical correlation approach is adopted to bring together the findings, including insights drawn from social science, with theological reflection. Chapters 10 and 11 deal with the lenses of servant leadership and masculine spirituality, which are then grouped in chapter 12—the lenses outpouring—following a similar pattern as with the first grouping of lenses. Part III, chapter 13, presents an analysis of the characterization of *Leadership* as unique. Part IV, chapters 14–18, draw the major findings into a substantive grounded theory, which explains the transformational experiences of young men through acceptance, imperfection, freedom and empowerment, and the spiritual mystery. Part V, chapters 19–20, deals with the issue of what happens beyond *Leadership* and contextualization of the study into a youth ministry framework, including recognition of the tensions (theory and practice), the expectations on those who practice youth ministry (church expectations, own expectations, etc.)—and finally, presents the conclusions.

Summary of Chapter

This chapter has considered the justification and importance of the research and the role of leadership development for young men. The organization of chapters has then been outlined, as they deal with consideration of the findings across the program elements and a series of key lenses, presentation of a substantive grounded theory, looking beyond *Leadership*, locating the study in the context of youth ministry, and presenting conclusions. Part I now follows, examining program elements, where the themes from which the foundational categories of the grounded theory begin to emerge.

Part I

Program Elements and Key Concepts

HAVING INTRODUCED AND CONTEXTUALIZED the research in chapter 1, part I presents the basic research findings in relation to program elements and key concepts.

Findings and analysis that incorporate the overall *Leadership* community are presented here. Then, each of the three stages is presented and considered in turn, in chapters 2–4, following the sequence of topics in the survey questionnaire. The value of these chapters (dealing with the content of the three stages) is that they present activities that resonate with young men and place them on a trajectory towards strong Christian manhood. It will be noted that certain themes run across stages—beginning in Stage 1, at times intentionally (e.g., servant leadership), and, as will be seen, emerging from the data (e.g., the impact of personal story sharing and worship). These themes and experiences are consolidated later in chapter 14 (the substantive theory).

Frequently in the questionnaire, knowledge of the relative significance of program elements and themes was desired. To measure this, a five-point Lickert scale was applied to questions where respondents were asked to rate significance of each component, compared to other components of the program. Descriptions and their numerical values are:

1. Not at all significant
2. Slightly significant
3. Moderately significant
4. Very significant

5. Extremely significant.

Ratings were averaged across respondents. A rating of three or more is regarded as indicating a high level of significance; a rating of four or more, very highly significant.

The *Leadership* Community

> One of the highlights for me from leadership was the family feeling between friends and [leaders]; the feeling that everyone was there for each other and loved and supported one another. (Stage 1, 2008)

There are three distinct groupings at *Leadership* to which all participants belong: the whole course community, their stage cohort (1, 2, or 3), and their designated small group of approximately eight participants and one or two facilitators (Stages 1 and 2). The first group encountered is the whole course intergenerational community. This group becomes very significant.

Experiencing a sense of community is a common desire, even need, of all people. People were made for community (Gen 2:18; Acts 2:44–46; 1 Cor 12; 27; Heb 10:24–25). God himself desires community with his followers and the Trinity models living in community. People search for community in many ways. God has "put within this heart of those who were created in his image" an "awareness . . . of the need for community."[1] "Coming individually to know Jesus means being introduced into community."[2]

The effectiveness of the *Leadership* program may be because of its communal aspects. *Leadership* is regarded as a closed, somewhat liminal community, similar to the American summer camp and retreats.[3]

The *Leadership* community is different to other experiences in participants' lives; in their churches; their schools; their clubs; even their families. Increasingly, some long for and see the *Leadership* community as providing a close father relationship.[4]

Participants join the *Leadership* community as soon as they arrive at the venue to commence Stage 1. This initial introduction occurs

---

1. Beckwith, *Postmodern Children's Ministry*, 47.
2. Beckwith, *Postmodern Children's Ministry*, 48.
3. Kendellen et al., "Facilitators and Barriers"; Bialeschki et al., "Camp Experiences"; Garst et al., "Growing without Limitations"; Nagy, "Lens of Liminality."
4. Leadership Queensland, *Dear Dad*.

spontaneously. It becomes a long-term community that one remains a member of beyond Stage 3, whether or not one takes on any staff role, for example, an ongoing Facebook group formed by the 2013 Stage 1 cohort, most of whom have never served on staff. The community is made up of all participants and all staff—past and present. As reported from a 2018 study: "There is an atmosphere around the unique *Leadership* community/environment, which is motivational, remembered and the impact continued in the long-term, even up to 12 years or longer."[5]

Respondents were asked how significant the overall *Leadership* community was for them, *compared to the other components of the (Stage 1) program*. Results are summarized in table 1.

Not at all significant	Slightly significant	Moderately significant	Very significant	Extremely significant
0%	1.5% (2)	16.0% (21)	49.6% (65)	32.8% (43)

Table 1. Significance of Overall *Leadership* Community

Respondents rated the overall *Leadership* community as very highly significant.[6] The average measure of significance on the five-point Likert scale was 4.1. Respondents were then asked to identify up to three characteristics of the overall *Leadership* community that were most significant to them. The eighteen potential characteristics of the overall *Leadership* community put to survey respondents were drawn from a variety of sources, in particular from participant feedback. The list was supplemented by several random possibilities to enable a greater level of discrimination in level of significance. All eighteen possibilities presented were selected at least once. Their choices are presented in table 2.

CHARACTERISTIC	%
Uniqueness of the experience	34.3
There was a strong spiritual presence	33.6
Staff presented themselves authentically through openly sharing information and feelings	32.8
Felt supported	29.9

5. Smith, "Leadership Development Program."

6. As explained above, a rating of three or more is regarded as indicating a high level of significance; a rating of four or more, very highly significant.

PART I: PROGRAM ELEMENTS AND KEY CONCEPTS

CHARACTERISTIC	%
All there for one another	29.1
Felt accepted	26.1
It triggered a new sense of personal direction	22.3
Older and younger men together	18.7
Family feeling	17.9
The staff acted as a united team, which I felt invited to join	16.4
Staff demonstrated understanding of their own strengths and weaknesses	14.9
Felt loved	14.4
We were allowed to give input	13.4
The attitude of the staff	13.4
That many staff were not much older than me and had done *Leadership* themselves	12.7
The behaviour of everyone seemed regulated by internal moral standards	11.9
It gave me an anchor	8.2
The welcome	7.5

Table 2. Significance of Specific Characteristics of Overall *Leadership* Community

The uniqueness of the experience was rated most highly (providing an early indication of a key characteristic fully reported and discussed in chapter 13), followed closely by characteristics emphasizing the importance of the spiritual dimension and authenticity. A strongly emerging theme was the feelings of support and acceptance, incorporating the characteristics identified by survey respondents of one another, family, and love, and the observation of a research collaboration group member that "groups that welcome new members are a rare experience," linking this into the "uniqueness of the experience."

Other characteristics are identified to a lesser extent, all significant for many participants. Certain themes continue beyond Stage 1 as all staff and all participants across stages interact together in a unique, authentic, and supportive/accepting manner within an overtly spiritual context. That is part of what makes the program unique, but it also undergirds its apparent successes as an effective and transformational experience for young men. Comments from participants, particularly one who completed Stage 3 in 2013 and is now aged twenty-four, illustrate the key components of the *Leadership* community and its longevity.

> The atmosphere of just being able to be you while being supported unconditionally, being able to be open, and be with a group of boys from very different backgrounds . . . However, I believe I appreciate what leadership has done for me even more now than it did back then, and I believe I will continue to appreciate it more and more the years I experience and the older I get. (Stage 3, 2013)

Interviews confirmed that the overall *Leadership* community took on a particularly real meaning during worship and the formal dinner.

To further explore the impact of the *Leadership* community experience, respondents were invited to comment on what contact they had maintained post-*Leadership*. Completing the survey drew some relevant comments. It reminded them of people and experiences, and even stimulated a link at the time:

> I am still in contact with my group since Stage 1, but I was privileged to be with the same group again in Stage 2, and I am actually getting messages from them as I do this survey. (Stage 2, 2019)

Some said the survey has prompted in them a desire to renew specific contacts, particularly with their Stage 3 Duo partner:[7]

> Up until the end of last year I remained in regular (weekly/fortnightly) contact with my Duo Partner and because of this survey, I'm planning to talk to him again soon. (Stage 3, 2019)

Some respondents are part of a local community at their local Boys' Brigade (BB) groups or churches, which includes others who have done *Leadership*, not necessarily in the same year. This becomes a shared experience that provides a unique bond, even within the broader youth or church group to which they belong. And though many may no longer be in regular contact, *Leadership* is a community to which they believe they belong, that is revived when they meet one another, even casually and unexpectedly. Some mentioned that they keep in contact through church; they renew friendships when they meet by accident or at other events (e.g., a BB national event; even a funeral). One interviewee, commenting on what stands out in his memory, in his case ten years after completing Stage 3, said: "most of all it was the friendships. I built up a couple of friendships that I still have to this day, guys called O and T, who ended up being the best man at my wedding" (Stage 3, 2010). Another two interviewees (Stage 2, 2019) referred to the significance of their local group (*the Leadership boys*).

---

7. See chapter 4.

Many stayed in touch with a mix of staff and fellow participants. The only real trend was those who said it was their Stage 3 Duo partner with whom they were or still are in contact. Social media is the most common form of contact: for example, the 2013 Stage 1 cohort, referenced earlier, who have a Facebook group which is maintained to this day and posts attract a sizeable response.

Summary of Overall Leadership Community

The overall *Leadership* community, significant from Stage 1, continues to have a long-term significance for some, the data pointing towards enduring relationships, even when not active. The staff/participant relationships are also significant in this. These relationships also endure. As one interviewee shared: by the time one is finishing Stage 3, "the leaders felt less like leaders and more like friends, it's much easier to converse with the leaders more as equals." "There's still respect there, but you can have a real conversation." In one sense, Stage 3 participants have already become role models and pseudo-staff or peer mentors to other participants.

The overall *Leadership* community is unique, has a strong spiritual presence, highlights authenticity experienced in staff, and demonstrates support and acceptance. Membership of the *Leadership* community extends beyond Stage 3 through enduring relationships. A quality of the community of staff and participants is the perception of it being nonhierarchical and a relationship of equality between staff and participants, especially with Stage 3 participants. This invites a seamless transition to ongoing friendships and brotherliness, which is likened to the *Anzac Phenomenon*, an *in vivo* code that emerged in interviews.

Chapters 2–4 now deal with the findings from the research, taking each of the three stages in turn and highlighting cross-stage themes that emerged. A range of cross-stage themes will be identified; first, uniqueness, then acceptance and freedom which quickly emerge in Stage 1, and which continue in Stages 2 and 3. They are accorded category status in the developing grounded theory outlined in chapter 14. Other emerging themes that will be identified after considering the research results from all the stages, are the importance of worship, transformation and celebration, the formal dinner, and the spiritual dimension.

2

Program Elements and Key Concepts—Stage 1

IN STAGE 1, PARTICIPANTS are placed in a small group of around eight. The critical impact of the group is recognized. The introductory session for Stage 1 establishes and explores the opportunity for the impact of dissonance or liminal space (see chapter 6). It includes sitting in their new groups, drawing out what is important to operate as a community for the week ahead, challenges for full participation and being open to change, recognition that they are not too young (e.g., boys their age and even as young as thirteen enlisted to serve in the Australian Army in World War I), and teamwork in the context of servant leadership. Each group has its own cabin, and they share a table for meals. Many activities are undertaken in their group, and they have a key group time every evening. An overnight expedition[1] provides the group with opportunity to work together without the presence or constraints of the whole course community.

The three most significant Stage 1 program elements are My Group, Overnight Expedition, and Music Workshop.[2] These are each dealt with in detail, followed by reference to other program elements.

---

1. This is a group activity, in their own small group, involving planning, navigation, and journeying in the bush to an overnight campsite, returning on the following day.

2. Music Workshop is intentionally a confusing name for the session. A song is used, with the session facilitator leading participants through a silent, reflective time based on the lyrics and leading into a spiritual and personal challenge to reflect on where one is with God and what is getting in the way of full commitment. Participants are invited to

PART I: PROGRAM ELEMENTS AND KEY CONCEPTS

My Group

> The company of my group. I especially enjoyed the encouragement and compassion they showed me. I liked it that I could provide my faults and failures to them without fear of being judged. The moral support they gave me when I was having trouble or when I was telling them about my troubles encouraged me to be a better friend to everyone around me because I wanted others to feel the way that my group made me feel.[3]
>
> It was a group of young men who would be there, despite the challenges we faced during the week or challenges we may face in the future. It was a group of boys who were willing to go with us. (2019)[4]

Living in community—and in particular *my community* is important and is lived out through the small groups we belong to. *Leadership* provides participants with a unique small group. In the face of what some perceive as antigroup and antisocial challenge to relationship development, namely the rise of technology and social media and their imposition on time, Zirschky has undertaken a study which he relates to youth ministry.[5] This study is relevant to retreat experiences, including *Leadership*, where the impact of the mobile phone and all its applications is generally removed by requiring participants not to access this technology during the program, providing opportunity for face-to-face relationships and communication as a primary focus.

Developments in technology and social media present a challenge for those involved in ministry. Relating this observation to youth ministry, Zirschky proposes that teenagers use technology "in a desperate bid for intimacy that is largely absent from face-to-face society—and the church."[6] This presents a new challenge to the group—or a significant opportunity. The social media revolution has made the group even more significant.

---

share in their group if they wish, and in this experience of *communitas*, spiritual and personal struggles are often shared (spiritual questions, sexuality issues, suicidal thoughts, family distress, etc.).

3. Smith, "Leadership Development Program," 87.

4. In this chapter, when participant quotes are included, the year is the year they completed Stage 1.

5. Zirschky, "Beyond the Screen."

6. Zirschky, "Beyond the Screen," back cover.

Zirschky considers the development of the social media obsession among teenagers as illustrative of their need and desire for connection and community; their hunger for "relationships of presence."[7] Connection in a group, sometimes a gang, is a hallmark of adolescent boys. Zirschky concludes that in the absence of other opportunities, including within most churches, youth are drawn to connect through their screens, in what becomes a "networked individualism," which "leaves young people searching for intimacy amidst a sea of technology."[8] He adds that "despite their longing to escape from partial and transitory relationships, the demand to grow the network pulls teenagers away from the presence and intimacy they desire. Instead, they find themselves in faceless relationships where they are not deeply known."[9] This issue became more widespread with the COVID-19 pandemic requiring more online activity for youth (and everyone). For young people—working, doing school, even doing youth group from home—the pandemic created mental health problems.[10]

Survey respondents were asked how significant their group was for them, *compared to the other components of the program*. The average measure of significance of their group on the five-point Lickert scale was 4.1.[11] Thus, for 76.5 percent of respondents it was very or extremely significant—see table 3. Various aspects are considered.

Not at all significant	Slightly significant	Moderately significant	Very significant	Extremely significant
0%	3.9% (5)	19.5% (25)	35.9% (46)	40.6% (52)

Table 3. Significance of My Group

Clean Slate[12] Phenomenon

The groups that participants are allocated to in Stage 1 are made up of people who do not know one another. So, they present to one another in their

7. Zirschky, "Beyond the Screen," 13.
8. Zirschky, "Beyond the Screen," 52.
9. Zirschky, "Beyond the Screen," 69.
10. Beyond Blue, "Ways to Look After."
11. Applying the five-point Lickert scale, as explained in part I.
12. Coming from participants, the *clean slate* phenomenon is adopted as an *in vivo* code.

group as a *clean slate*, something several interviewees recognized. The clean slate phenomenon was recognized during interviews as a positive thing: "without judgement; helps with openness" (2019); the "clean slate made it easier" (2017). The group facilitator has access to limited data—name, where they are from, medical information, and a brief report from a local group leader that may include family and personal information. But fellow group members only have available a group list, containing basic biographical information—name and where they are from. Apart from this, the group only know what a member reveals, consciously or unconsciously. Temperament, personality, and certain behaviours become apparent in the group, and more so as they relax and gain confidence. A person's family composition, academic grades, sporting interests and achievements, future ambitions, and other information known to one's regular group of friends is unknown in the group. This, and often much more, only becomes known as the individual chooses to share it; to trust their group with their personal information. As within their group they know and become known, they sometimes learn more about one another than is known to their regular group of friends, local group leaders, or even parents.

Discussion in focus groups confirmed the value, uniqueness, and even critical importance of the clean slate principle:

> For me one of the most unique things is the clean slate thing. You go to other things, youth camps, church camps, school camp. They're all with friends, with people you know. You're all in those groups, but at Leadership especially, with people you don't know. Stage 1 you start opening up to them and by the time you're in Stage 3, you've created an environment where you're able to share and each stage gets deeper and deeper. That's definitely something unique.

> Every year, in the last days of Leadership, my group always mentions how they barely knew each other and how awkward they were around each other, and now marvelling at how well they know each other. "It feels like I've known you guys for ages."

Describing Their Group

To explore how respondents viewed their group, they were asked what adjectives they would use to describe it. One hundred and seventy different adjectives (and sometimes more detailed descriptions) were identified by respondents to describe their group. Some were one-off; others are grouped and categorized into the following emerging themes:

- Accepting
- Open
- Fun
- Diverse
- Authentic
- Non-static
- Joining
- Caring
- Unique
- Motivational.

The most common descriptors were those related to the acceptance and care they experienced. Amongst a series of other similar descriptive words, supportive, caring, encouraging, accepting, friendly, kind, loving, welcoming, and understanding were mentioned a total of 120 times. Acceptance emerged as a defining group experience for a high number of respondents. Linked to and possibly even a contributing factor for feelings of acceptance and care, was the high level of comfort and openness they identified in describing their group, including open-mindedness (related to diversity) and openness in sharing, which is a factor linked to the development of *communitas*. A significant number identified their group as being diverse, meaning it was made up of a collection of boys who were very different from one another in experience and temperament. This positive factual statement was illustrated by the observation of one respondent:

> I remember a strong sense of camaraderie between the group. Everyone embraced each other's diversity, which was a particularly refreshing thing to experience at that adolescent age. (2014)

This was confirmed in the responses of interviewees, for example:

> For me it was a lesson in people that I thought were rag tag and would just [want to] play games, but they had a lot going on.

The recognition of diversity sits in creative paradoxical tension with comments made by respondents that one thing they discover through sharing is that they are all the same and have the same issues; that they are normal and okay. Two described their group experience illustrating the willingness of participants to put aside their own interests and differences for the sake of others and caring for them.

> A diverse, competitive, truth-seeking group of personalities that were challenged to forego our differences for the benefit of group unity. (2006)

> A group of individuals that joined together to embrace their differences and to help each other succeed. (2006)

Authenticity, including the descriptors real, genuine, and honest, emerged as a minor theme. Any hint of a negative depiction of their group was generally related to what the group was like in the beginning. Respondents frequently compared the beginning with the end and the change that had taken place in their group during the week. A "band of misfits" or an "odd bunch" became a functioning group.

> We were an odd bunch at the start and changed dramatically at the end of the camp, not just individually but as a team. At the start we were unorthodox, misunderstood each other, uncooperative, and divided. In the end, however, we were kind, encouraging, understanding, cooperative, united, and friendly. (2019)

It is not uncommon for a group to develop and celebrate its unique identity, even adopting a group name or identity such as wearing something in common. This can be a way of masking—sweeping group members along, often by a dominant member—living up to an image which may get in the way of individuals being able to deal with sensitive issues that do not match the group identity (e.g., in a group that presented a tough image, one member needing to deal with suicidal thoughts and acknowledge these in the group). However, respondents do describe their group in unique terms that invoke a distinctively masculine camaraderie and togetherness, for example, crazy, fearless, wild, and tough.

Stages of Group Development

Respondents were asked to describe the stages their group went through during the week. Generally, respondents described how their group began and how it finished off the week—from a "chunky awkwardness" to a group of brothers, sad to leave one another. Some were able to identify stages between beginning and ending and others described an ebb and flow, including tensions arising and needing to be dealt with during their journey. A small group of participants adopted the standard forming–storming–norming–performing terminology, with three identifying their sadness on leaving: "sad but on a high note"; "sadness as they realise they may not see each other again" (2016) (a mourning stage).

By far, the majority of the 121 respondents described a positive forward momentum of group stages and a very positive ending. For example:

> After identifying initial awkwardness, not knowing each other and being uncomfortable, this was followed by: "then, things got abrasive with strong personalities clashing." But "we progressed to forming a strong friendship, brothers really. We were all completely comfortable with one another. (2014)

It is acknowledged that stages of group life theories are well documented and are often presented in a simple format, as is done to participants at *Leadership*. Respondents' recognition of these stages indicates their understanding, though with limited recognition of the need for re-norming after a storming experience. It also indicates at times a desire of young men to ignore the intermediate stages, hastening towards the final stage. No group, including adolescent boys, wants to appear unsuccessful. Thus, it was expected (but also borne out from observation and facilitator reports) that respondents would express a view that their group had reached a functioning, comfortable stage. This was almost universally the case, with only a few reservations. The overwhelmingly positive descriptions of their final group stage outweigh any reservations from a small minority, though those views are also important.

A cluster of respondents expressed their final group stage (performing) as one of:

- Acceptance of each other; unity; supportive; encouraging (24)
- Friendship (19)
- Being like brothers (16)
- Trust (12)
- Having bonded (10)
- Closeness and comradery (10)

- Connection (5)
- Family (5)
- Understanding (3)
- Sense of community (2)
- Belonging (1)
- Mateship (1).

Their explanations of those identified descriptors included:

- "A family of loving brothers in Christ"
- "Special friends"
- "Like we had been friends for ever"
- "Doing things together as if we had known each other our whole lives"
- "As if we'd known each other for years"
- "Reaching a stage of 'group think'" (i.e., *communitas*).

A key theme of acceptance continued to emerge and linked to this, the cluster of trust, connection, and belonging. Friendship/brothers/family/mateship were also common descriptors used. During interviews two referred to the brotherhood formed as, "the brother I never had."

Friends and Brothers

Kaster notes something also seen in *Leadership*, particularly in the small group experience, that "a great many of the youth who attend HSTPs want to stay a little longer"[13]—similar to Peter on the Mount of Transfiguration. A Stage 1 *Leadership* participant commented:

> By the end of the week we were more than just a group; we were family; we were brothers, and it was sad when leadership came to an end because some of us felt like we weren't ready to leave yet. (2013)

The frequent reference to becoming brothers is further highlighted. This is part of the essence of the group and the overall community. It continues across stages and into the staff community and it continues into the

---

13. Kaster, "Fuel My Faith," 172.

long term, even beyond and separate from any regular annual *Leadership* involvement. An observation made by a focus group participant, referring to the strength of the "brotherhood of *Leadership*" (or "the tribe or whatever we want to call it") is that it is not pushed, and "because we don't have to push it, means it's the real thing . . . when you start pushing those things, [like an] alumni, you just don't get it." As with *communitas*, brotherhood *happens*, almost spontaneously as one becomes involved in the *Leadership* program, suggesting this as a factor contributing to its apparent success.

Zirschky contrasts transitory relationships with his concept of communion and *koinonia*. In his view, those who experience communion through membership in a small group where they become "sharers in Christ," find spontaneously given "acceptance and love," and regard one another as "brothers and sisters."[14] The characteristics of a group experiencing communion are "being present with, for, and within one another"; "share of themselves deeply" as in (1 Cor 2:26); "not merely to hear . . . but to listen with the intention of understanding"; actively giving of oneself for the other."[15] This is the character of an effective small group and a lead-in to examining the concept of *communitas* and its application to *Leadership* (see chapter 5).

Stimulus to a Well-Functioning Group

Respondents were asked what the key event was that became the stimulus in their group becoming a well-functioning and caring team or, if this did not occur, what got in the way. Many stated that their group had become a well-functioning and caring team, without specifying the stimulus. Some did suggest it was the whole experience—not a specific event. The three events that were identified most commonly were:

- Overnight Expedition (31%)—including the reflection and honesty in discussions after the event (even the choices of worship as the stimulus event related to worship the night after the overnight expedition).
- My Group (24%)—including the first night, opening up to one another, and taking the risk of sharing.
- Music Workshop (10%).

14. Zirschky, "Beyond the Screen," 68–69.
15. Zirschky, "Beyond the Screen," 95, 97.

PART I: PROGRAM ELEMENTS AND KEY CONCEPTS

This indicates a consistency in the most significant events in the Stage 1 program. Several other specific events were identified as the stimulus event for individuals, indicating the importance of every event for some participants. The six most significant events are listed in table 4.

ACTIVITY	NUMBER	%
Overnight Expedition	39	31
My Group	30	24
Music Workshop	13	10
Group problem-solving/team building activities	11	9
Handball[16]	6	5
Worship	3 (2 the night after expedition)	2

Table 4. Stimulus to Group Becoming a Well-Functioning Team

Group Facilitators

Each *Leadership* group has one or two allocated facilitator(s). This role is critical, so respondents were asked to identify characteristics demonstrated by their group facilitators that stood out most for them. Of the twenty-eight possibilities (all of which were selected at least once), the seven most significant characteristics are set out in table 5.

CHARACTERISTIC	%
They shared their stories	33.1
They embraced openness and transparency	29.3
They accepted me as I was	27.8
They did not put others down or act as though they were better than others	27.1
They earnt and extended trust	26.0
They encouraged a sense of belonging	24.1
They modeled a sense of God's presence	18.8

Table 5. Most Significant Characteristics Identified in Group Facilitators

---

16. A sport that is new to many, involving learning and teaching new skills, coaching, strategy, and teamwork in the context of their group, tested in competition with other groups.

That facilitators shared their stories was identified as the most highly demonstrated characteristic (33.1%). Linked to this is the second most highly selected characteristic of openness and transparency (29.3%), in turn linked to trust (26.0%), and to the earlier noted and valued characteristic of authenticity (see part I). Reinforcing a previously noted emerging theme was the cluster of characteristics: openness, transparency, acceptance, trust, belonging, connection, and feeling loved.

Sharing Story

Zirschky's identified characteristics of a small group experiencing communion are: "being present with, for, and within one another"; "share of themselves deeply"; "not merely to hear . . . but to listen with the intention of understanding"; "actively giving of oneself for the other."[17] These characteristics describe a *Leadership* small group—My Group—where sharing of a personal story was the characteristic most highly recognized by group members in their facilitators and was something they then engaged in themselves within their groups. The impact, identified in the survey data, is confirmed and interpreted by a focus group member:

> When you do share those stories of your own struggles, they immediately trust you more. Immediately. It is quite impressive how much even in the discussions that night, it suddenly becomes way much more serious, and the trust is there and one by one they share.

Another focus group member commented that sharing your personal story demonstrated "that you are human, and they can connect with you." He also thought it was important to use the story to show a "progression"—that they can look to staff, older men who are "in Christ" and see there is a "progression" they can strive towards, though it will be different for them. Sharing of one's personal story is further developed in chapter 5, as a significant stimulus to the experience of *communitas*.

Identity

In discussing *community*, reference is made to the importance of naming and renaming and its link to returning home ready for engagement in

---

17. Zirschky, "Beyond the Screen," 95, 97.

mission.[18] Further, Douglass relates this emerging identity experience with self-naming, which sometimes at *Leadership* takes place in the small group when participants are encouraged by, and sometimes surprised with, what others see in them and realize this may be part of their identity. Douglass places value in participants naming their emerging identities themselves, naming opening "vocational possibilities," fostering "healing and reconciliation," raising "awareness of one's relationship with God," and strengthening young people's relationships with their pastors and churches.[19]

Some *Leadership* activities provide opportunity to recognize roles and skills in others and self. Considering some of the dynamics that occur in a small group, Proffitt and Young offer insights on the link between other-awareness and self-awareness. In becoming more aware of others, one becomes more aware of self, quoting a male HSTP student, "You've got to stop thinking of self. And you've got to start thinking of others, and I feel as if now I've become more aware of others, and that's actually helped me become more aware of myself."[20]

Incarnational Community

Proffitt and Young highlight another important consideration, one that has not been much articulated at *Leadership*, that in such an incarnational community, youth are able to "'try-out' the person God has already made them to be." Sustained contact is significant, as are "common catalytic structures," "small covenant groups," "collegial learning cohorts," and "peer and adult mentoring." Small covenant groups allow participants to "engage in deep conversations and get to know a few people well," "talking about their experiences of the day, debriefing concerns, and telling stories of their lives," developing "high levels of trust," "explor[ing] hopes and dreams, questions about faith and God's action in the world, and vexing problems about the human condition." In this, bringing the incarnational nature of the community again into focus, participants are enabled to "look for Christ in each other."[21] While all these characteristics are noted in *Leadership* groups, the challenge may be to overtly identify and articulate a deeper understanding of the incarnational nature of the group experience.

18. Douglass. "Holy Noticing," 101–10.
19. Douglass, "Holy Noticing," 112–16.
20. Proffitt and Young, "Catalyzing Community," 68.
21. Proffitt and Young, "Catalyzing Community," 69–71.

My Group Summary

The My Group experience, especially in Stage 1 is part of the valued *Leadership* experience and its effectiveness. That participants come to their group not knowing anyone—the *clean slate* phenomenon—was recognized as a positive experience that gave them freedom to share. Many program activities, including those to be dealt with separately in the following sections, are often linked by participants to My Group and are key vehicles towards their group becoming a well-functioning team; the development of *communitas*.

Characteristics that participants used to describe their group were condensed and identified, the theme of acceptance being the most common. Authenticity and uniqueness also featured. A further important characteristic added was diversity. Stages of group development were identified. All groups described a forward momentum towards becoming a *performing* team.

Participants are more ready to overlook any negative thought attached to their group, than be seen to be critical of their group—the group they belong to (My Group). Those interviewed generally agreed that one is less likely to be critical of their own group; the positive is more likely to linger; it's the people they have spent a week together with and got to know and accept as brothers. Those who later served on staff and then observed or facilitated other groups are more ready to adopt a critical stance. A comment from an experienced staff member reveals how any potential negative group experience is mitigated: "I think Leadership does a great job in this area and something we've continued to work on. Holding out hope for the group that if they show some courage, they will see significant growth and progress."

Key to effective and transformational group functioning was the role of facilitators, participants noting their openness, and being prepared to share their personal stories.

Self-naming and affirming positives in others became an element of group dynamics, contributing to identity formation. Seeing *Leadership* and one's group as an incarnational community—"look[ing] for Christ in each other"—is noted as a challenge for more open understanding and articulation.

Overnight Expedition—Putting Learning into Practice, Freedom to Make Own Decisions

> I had never ever been on an overnight expedition before, let alone go bush bashing so for me it was a new, unique, and significant

> experience of having to carry all your gear and having to bash your way through all the lantana. It was also an extremely tough experience, and I was very exhausted by the end of it. (2018)

For this respondent, it was a new, difficult, and unique experience. For others it was team building, experiencing being able to be a leader, and enjoying the freedom to make their own decisions.

Survey respondents were asked how significant the Overnight Expedition was for them *in comparison with other components of the program*. Their average rating was 4.1, between very and extremely significant; for 80 percent it was very or extremely significant—see table 6.

Not at all significant	Slightly significant	Moderately significant	Very significant	Extremely significant
2.2% (3)	4.4% (6)	13.3% (18)	45.9% (62)	34.1% (46)

Table 6. Significance of Overnight Expedition

They were then invited to respond to a further question: If it was significant, what was it that made the Overnight Expedition so significant for them? All responses were positive and can be classified into several topics on what was significant. These are detailed with examples drawn from participant comments.

The Impact on Teamwork

This was the most common theme. There were twenty-seven responses related to the opportunity for practical outworking of teamwork learning, accepting their imperfection, and dealing with the struggles they faced.

> It was the overnight expedition where we started to see each other as part of a team. It gave us an opportunity to come together and work on the problem together. After completing the expedition, we saw ourselves as more of community which gave us the strength to come together to talk about and deal with the problems we were each facing in our own lives. (2013)

> It showed that we weren't all perfect and had similar struggles and goals. This meant that celebrating with a team made the experience even more amazing. It was a very difficult first day but by the end

of it we were all relating to something as one and had the energy to help others even though we were struggling ourselves. (2016)

Accepting and Dealing with Problems

There was a realization that "problems happen," that acceptance and tolerance are useful attitudes, that neither I nor others are perfect, and that this brings the challenge of reaching a solution.

> I think the overnight hike helped us realise that it's possible for multiple people to screw up (not just me) and that led us to be more accepting/tolerant of each other and our faults. (Despite having a map we got lost, we forgot tent poles, we left some food behind at the campsite, we left a group member at the campsite, and left to get into cars to go to the drop off point without him). (2007)

Putting Learning into Practice

The Overnight Expedition provided opportunity for putting their learning into practice; trying themselves out; exercising leadership *now*.

> Having a common goal that was planned and organised by the group was a new and worthwhile experience. We were a bit surprised when we were told that everything from planning the hike, to navigation and campsite selection was all up to our collective decision . . . Being trusted to plan together as a team formulated a collective responsibility and enabled us to set our own bar for success. This all concluded with a real sense of achievement when the overnight expedition was completed. (2009)

> The complete handing-over of the reins to a group of boys to navigate. We decided the route to take. We decided to turn left or right. We interpreted the map. We decided when to stop for breaks. That level of responsibility made the experience significant. Otherwise, it would be just like any other BB hike. (2016)

> It was the first time I had gone out into the world and been in charge of sorting everything out without input from someone in charge. (2017)

PART I: PROGRAM ELEMENTS AND KEY CONCEPTS

Time for Reflection

There were unhurried times—times for reflection—personally and in their group. These occurred at their campsite and around the fire; also, during a mini-Solo where some said they experienced God (there were fifteen responses on this activity alone).

> Around the fire that night. I remember sharing a story of a time where I felt like I messed up badly and damaged someone else, and our facilitator empathised with me, and then said that he thought I'd done really well in that situation, and the rest of the group agreed. And I remember feeling a real peace and comfort. (2014)

> On the hour I had alone on the expedition I felt like I was really connected to God and in my life. I have never felt closer to God and that really was an amazing experience. (2019)

Fun, Physical, and Free

Away from the highly programmed course, the Overnight Expedition, though physically difficult for some, responded to the desires of young men for physical activity, enjoying mates, and freedom.

> It was a fun physical activity. Living wild for a night! (2012)

Overnight Expedition Summary

The Overnight Expedition is not highly programmed, allowing for informality, group decision-making, and spontaneity. It was important for teamwork development (a pivotal team development experience for some groups); it provided opportunity away from the main camp headquarters and only with My Group for more than twenty-four hours to discuss deep issues. Findings are very clear—that for many, having to plot their own course and camp out overnight was a new and challenging experience. Making decisions, accepting and adjusting to the consequences, and dealing with them communicated that staff regarded them as trustworthy and capable. Having a wide variation of experience in group members was considered during interviews and was regarded by interviewees as a positive opportunity to allocate tasks to match skills and a chance to develop further skills in teaching, caring for, or mentoring others—a chance to serve; to lead. The time spent in reflection on a mini-Solo was where the spiritual and God entered.

Thus, Overnight Expedition, described by one interviewee as "something quite profound" (2014), is another extension of the My Group experience; it is significant for group development (for *communitas* formation); it provides opportunity for personal spiritual reflection; and it communicates a worthiness to lead.

Music Workshop—Personal Spiritual Challenge

> I think it not only provided me with an opportunity to reflect on my life and struggles but also realise that others were struggling too (2013 and similar from seven others).
>
> Music workshop took away my guilt and made me feel loved. (2014)

Respondents were asked how significant Music Workshop was for them *in comparison with other components of the program*. Their responses are set out in table 7.

Not at all significant	Slightly significant	Moderately significant	Very significant	Extremely significant
8.3% (11)	13.5% (18)	24.8% (33)	29.3% (39)	24.1% (32)

Table 7. Significance of Music Workshop

Respondents average rating was 3.5, between moderately and very significant, with 53.4 percent very or extremely significant. They were then invited to respond to a further question: If it was significant, what was it that made Music Workshop so significant for them? Several clear themes emerged, which are now detailed.

Dealing with Issues

Twenty saw it as an opportunity to deal with issues they couldn't talk about elsewhere; finding out, sometimes for the first time, that they weren't alone

PART I: PROGRAM ELEMENTS AND KEY CONCEPTS

and that others had the same struggles. Sharing "struggles" and "not alone" were the key words used, for example:

> I think the other powerful aspect was the fact that I wasn't alone in my struggles. Knowing young men around me were experiencing similar issues was so comforting and gave me a deeper sense of truly "knowing" someone. (2009)

> It was a safe place to talk about issues with others that are experiencing the same problems (2016, 2018, and two others).

> It was a very real conversation, and it was the first time I have had that kind of conversation (2018).

> Knowing I'm not the only one. (2018)

Douglass makes a HSTP observation that is very similar to the small group experience at *Leadership*:

> The safety of intentional Christian community seems to give teenagers permission to share dimensions of their lives they have not shared elsewhere. In the holding environment of a safe social space away from home, teenagers feel free to take risks with their emerging identities, even entrusting these communities with information they had formerly held in private.[22]

The *Leadership* experience is highlighted in these additional comments:

> It was great to see some people be candid and open about life; it is a unique and rare opportunity. (2013)

> It was an honest discussion that I have never been a part of before. A real conversation. (2014)

Opening Up[23]

Sixteen reported that it gave them opportunity to *open up*:

> It was what really opened me up and brought home where I was with God. (2017)

---

22. Douglass, *Holy Noticing*, 113.

23. *Opening up* refers to sharing and talking about one's personal thoughts and feelings.

PROGRAM ELEMENTS AND KEY CONCEPTS—STAGE 1

Spiritual Issues

Sixteen made comments that suggested that the session raised the bar for them on spiritual issues and called for a personal response, not necessarily perfection, but a striving towards this:

> Began to understand the true presence of God for the first time in my life. (2014)

Teamwork Enhanced

Ten commented that Music Workshop enhanced teamwork and impacted their group in some way; it was team building; it showed that all were equal; they connected at a deeper level, knowing each other:

> Connecting at a deeper level with the guys in my group and spiritual as well. (2006)

Mystery

Six made comments related to the mystery surrounding Music Workshop—they were surprised; it was unexpected; it was full-on; it was intense.

> It was the most unexpected workshop ever. That surprise in itself was enough for me to be "shocked" into action. That night I shared more about myself in group time than all previous nights. (2018)

Singing

Five commented about the experience of "blokes singing together."[24]

> A big bunch of blokes singing together. (2013)

> It was very empowering to have that many boys singing as one. (2017)

---

24. One of the final parts of the session is the group giving a presentation of their interpretation of the meaning of the song they have analyzed individually and as a group—linking it also to the struggles they have dealt with. The most common presentation is a drama; not many groups sing, so these comments about "blokes" singing indicates its powerfulness.

PART I: PROGRAM ELEMENTS AND KEY CONCEPTS

Music Workshop Summary

Music Workshop enhanced teamwork. It was an opportunity to *open up* and to share, often for the first time, personal feelings about topics that are taboo in other settings, leading to a sense of relief that others, even others trying to live as a Christian, had the same struggles and issues; that they weren't facing these struggles alone. It was a safe place to do this—a similar observation to that noted in the HSTP. The overt spiritual content, challenging where participants are with God, called them into reflection, required a response and helped them to connect with others on a spiritual level. Music Workshop is an extension of the My Group experience and is an indication of the readiness of young men to engage with spiritual issues and personal spiritual reflection in a space that is safe, nonjudgmental, and supportive. They also responded well to the surprise element, and this may have heightened their attention through an experience of liminality and dissonance, even if not articulated as such. The spiritual content continues when they surprised themselves as a group of boys engaging in worship (through singing) together in a meaningful way—not always a thing *blokes* do.

Other Stage 1 Activities

Survey respondents were asked if there was something else in Stage 1 that was significant for them. They were asked to select up to five activities that were the most significant for them from a list of twenty-eight Stage 1 activities.

One question is whether these activities were more significant than those already specifically dealt with. Based on comments of respondents to the questions on group formation and functioning, this is unlikely. Nevertheless, a wide range of other activities are regarded as significant by individual participants. Each of the twenty-four activities listed from the Stage 1 program is important for someone. The seven most selected are presented in table 8.

ACTIVITY	RESPONDENTS (%)
Worship	52.6
Formal dinner	45.1
Handball	40.6

ACTIVITY	RESPONDENTS (%)
Anonymous letter to father[25]	26.3
Morning devotions	25.6
Practical problem-solving	24.8
White shirts[26]	24.1

Table 8. Other Stage 1 Activities Nominated as Significant

Worship was rated highest by respondents (52.6%)—more commonly than morning devotions (25.6%), the other activity with a frank spiritual component. The second highest selection (45.1% of respondents) was the formal dinner. As will be seen, the formal dinner, remained important across stages. One observes the beginning of a trend across stages of the importance of worship and the formal dinner.

Handball was next in significance. Handball is a Stage 1 activity only and outside Overnight Expedition is the major physical activity. Its significance is possibly related to the fact that it is a physical activity (important for many young men), it is competitive, and contributes substantially to teamwork development in their groups.

There is a significant 14 percent gap between these top three choices and other choices, though this is not interpreted as indicating that other activities were not important for some participants. Writing the anonymous letter to their fathers, morning devotions, practical problem-solving, and white shirts completed the top seven selections, all chosen by more than 20 percent of respondents. They participate in their groups in worship and sit together at their group table at the formal dinner, but more expressly, apart from the personal task of writing a letter to their fathers, all other top eight choices are to do with their group, reinforcing an understanding of its critical role and significance in the effectiveness of the program.

---

25. A letter written in private saying whatever they want to their fathers. The letters are anonymous and are used to see if any themes arise that chaplains or others need to input on. The letters are not sent but a participant may ask for a copy. For a further example of content from 2014, see chapter 1.

26. White shirts are part of the Stage 1 introductory session where all (staff and participants) come in a white Tshirt—indicating that all existing and previous rank/importance is left behind and all are equal. It also becomes a statement of group identity as they are encouraged to do whatever they wish with the shirt and at the end of the program each group presents their group story through what they have depicted on their shirts.

The anonymous letter to fathers was commented on to a considerable extent during semi-structured interviews and in focus groups, heightening the survey data on its significance—illustrating the importance of family for young men, even if, for some, it is a longing for the family and fathering they do not have. As well as the significance and uniqueness of a letter and that it was written words, further insights shared in interviews were:

> It's a sort of therapeutic exercise and can help in defining the relationship even if you never communicate to the other person, because you yourself become more self-aware. (2014)
>
> Writing a letter forces us to look deeply on how our parents view us and how we want them to view us. (2017)
>
> I don't write much to my father and so for a lot of people, including me, it was an opportunity to actually be honest and be real and for some blokes, they may not have spoken to their father for quite a while and so it was an opportunity for them to possibly get to know them again. (2018)

A staff member with three years' facilitation experience commented during a focus group that he has observed boys in his group writing the letter to their father and has seen "how emotionally challenging and hard that is for them. And afterwards expressing how meaningful it was to do it."

The letter serves different purposes for different people, including a cathartic benefit and clarification towards the future and possible action. This is reinforced in their group if they decide to share it and may feature in a post-*Leadership* action plan.

Differences between Participant Respondents and Staff Respondents (Stage 1)

There were more similarities than differences, but differences were noted between the responses of those who joined the staff of *Leadership* after completing the three stages (referred to as "staff respondents") and responses of participants who did not join the staff (referred to as "participant respondents"). Key differences between these two groups of respondents in relation to the Stage 1 program are now discussed.

Activities that were key to their group becoming a well-functioning team—My Group, Overnight Expedition, and Music Workshop—while highly significant to all, were placed in a different order of comparative significance. Participant respondents valued their group more highly; staff respondents rated Overnight Expedition and Music Workshop more highly. Participant respondents were less willing to be critical of their group. There was a striking difference in the higher value placed on the writing of an anonymous letter to their fathers (32.6% of participants compared with 9.1% of staff).

An explanation from staff that carries some weight is that staff, and this is progressive with experience (i.e., experienced staff more than new staff), see the progression across activities within and across stages.

Additional Comments

To complete the examination of Stage 1, in an open-ended question, respondents were invited to add anything about Stage 1 that would assist with the research. Forty-eight took the opportunity (fifty-five different comments). Where comments related to individual program components, they have been incorporated into the findings and discussion. Many took this opportunity to make a reflective statement on the value of the program for their lives, affirming the effectiveness and apparent success of the *Leadership* program. The comments were categorized, as detailed in table 9.

CATEGORY	NUMBER	DETAILS
Positive general comments and impact on their lives	27	These cover a range of different areas—see below for further detail and examples
Positive comments about a specific component	10	Sexual integrity session; escape the room; group (2, with some aspect of group being mentioned 13 times), NASA, worship; handball, DADA (2); overnight expedition
Positive comments about staff	5	Their quality; long-term value of feedback and affirmation; openness and being prepared to listen and answer questions; godly men to look up to and emulate; "give our cabin leader a raise"—see below for further detail and examples
Positive comments about the food	2	Porridge[27] and the food generally

27. Porridge is referred to several times and is recognized as having become a *Leadership* symbol or tradition that is passed onto succeeding cohorts—that is, that we all eat porridge for breakfast (something they do not do at home, so something unique).

PART I: PROGRAM ELEMENTS AND KEY CONCEPTS

CATEGORY	NUMBER	DETAILS
Suggestions offered	7	More free time (3); activities with facilitators; more one-on-one with chaplains; earlier nights; alternative to camping
Negative comments about the program	3	About others in his group; not liking camping; some encouragements to share was invasive

Table 9. Additional General Comments from Participants about Stage 1

Two categories are further exampled, through providing comments from respondents. Others are adequately summarized in table 9.

Positive General Comments and Impact on Their Lives

The overall experience of leadership stage 1, was exceptionally positive for me. I recall being very hesitant at first prior to attending, however, once I completed it, I was really excited to return. One of the best experiences in my childhood. (2007)

For me leadership was all about the community, the genuine love and being allowed and encouraged to be me. I went through stage 1 at a time when I was really struggling to work out who I was. I was stuck between trying to fit in and be liked and live life in a way that fit with my morals and who I wanted to become. Leadership allowed me to let my guard down for long enough to process what was going on in my life and deal with it. I didn't feel like I had to pretend to have it all together anymore. It was one of the first times that I felt like my peers accepted me for who I was. (2007)

The devotions and worship have always been a standout experience from Stage 1 onwards. They are clearly different to my current church worship experience, so they are really uplifting and encouraging and help me connect with God. (2011)

I think this stage did begin my thinking about manhood—started putting those categories in my head. (2013)

Just that I look back at Stage 1 as being absolutely crucial to who I am today. That first time at Leadership, being in the environment, that deep self-reflection and the intensity sent me on a path that I can be proud of. (2014)

> Leadership was the most amazing week of my life. The course was the changing point in my life. (2019)

Positive Comments about Staff

Respondents also took opportunity to record positive comments about the staff they met at *Leadership*. The following participant comments illustrate the impact of staff on the lives of participants and their contribution to the apparent success of *Leadership*.

> I think the most important part of "buying" into the leadership culture was the men who were already a part of it and ran it wholeheartedly. From group facilitators, stage leaders and even the kitchen staff, I felt we all developed a respect for the program because of the quality of the people running it. That's what I remember most about my leadership stage 1 experience (2011).

Negative Cases

Though small in number, the negative cases need to be recognized. The three situations so characterized are listed in table 9: one about others in his group; one not liking camping; one concerned that some encouragement to share was invasive. The third of these needs to be taken note of and attention given to making it easy for a participant to raise such concerns at the time; the other two are matters of personal preference.

Summary of Chapter

The findings and discussion suggest factors which lead to the apparent success of *Leadership* and summarize participant views on the experiences the program provides. These include experiencing acceptance and becoming relaxed with who one is and with others, to the point of gaining self-confidence and being willing and able to engage openly in self-reflection, worship, story sharing, and change; an experience of community, leading to *communitas*.

The discussion also reinforces the significance of staff, particularly group facilitators in delivering *Leadership* as a program that is effective in the development of young men. The respondent-identified characteristics demonstrated by group facilitators were presented—characteristics such as sharing personal life stories, being open and transparent, and acceptance. Respondents rate staff higher than staff rate themselves, suggesting an essence of humility among staff, to the extent of having incorporated the example of servant leadership within their practice and persona. Respondents extend their positive views of staff to include the whole *Leadership* staff community. The effectiveness of the program is its uniqueness, and its apparent success is in the offering of a lasting community, populated by respected men (of all ages and experience) who are regarded as worthy role models, and into which community each individual participant in a new cohort is personally invited and experiences acceptance and a sense of belonging.

Thus, the themes of uniqueness, acceptance, freedom, and spiritual aspects (culminating in worship) have emerged, together with a hint of recognizing in a non-negative way a theme of imperfection of self and others. The positive impact of the Stage 1 experience on the lives of participants is clear from the data and reinforces the various elements that together in a unique combination provide knowledge as to why the program is apparently successful.

3

Program Elements and Key Concepts—Stage 2

> Stage 2 was a huge part of my journey to manhood, hearing from God for the first time in solo was a pillar for me to build my life on. The leadership felt more like my spiritual home than my local church because it was better at accepting me, loving me and I met God there more easily. (2008[1])

IN STAGE 2, PARTICIPANTS are placed in small groups with a facilitator. The central focus of Stage 2 is the three-night Solo.[2] Prior to this, much time is spent on various aspects of preparation (physical, social, emotional, and spiritual), commencing with a pre-course journal. Post-Solo is given over to celebration and affirmation of manhood (the rites of passage focus). Other program elements include a multiage, mixed gender panel where participants can ask any questions they wish about relationships and sexual issues.

The four most significant Stage 2 program elements are Solo, the time immediately post Solo, the Solo celebration,[3] and the Panel (relationships

---

1. In this chapter, when participant quotes are included, the year is the year they completed Stage 2.

2. Solo is an experience alone in a bush location for three nights. It allows for silence, solitude, and reflection to be experienced. It follows extensive preparation across physical, social, emotional, and spiritual domains, with safety considerations built in.

3. This event involves a journey of some distance together, with instructions that lead them on a journey where at different posts, significant staff members offer teaching on the fruit of the Spirit.

session).[4] In this chapter, these elements are dealt with in detail, followed by reference to other program elements.

As well as the identified program components, the overall *Leadership* community and My Group identified and discussed in Stage 1 continue to be significant in Stage 2—as is confirmed when discussing post-Solo experiences. They are the contextual groups for identity and celebration, heightened on the completion of something big.

Solo (Silence, Solitude, Reflection)

> Solo was literally one of the best experiences of my life, and I have had a lot of crazy experiences! (2013)

Participants were asked how significant Solo was for them *in comparison with other components of the program*. Solo was rated 4.7—between very and extremely significant, with 94.6 percent nominating very or extremely significant (see table 10).

Not at all significant	Slightly significant	Moderately significant	Very significant	Extremely significant
0.0%	1.8%	3.6%	19.1%	75.5%
0	2	4	21	83

Table 10. Significance of Solo

Solo was the most highly rated component of *Leadership* across all three stages, confirming an earlier study where this component was recognized as the central phenomenon in *Leadership*, creating an anticipation from Stage 1, providing a transformational experience in Stage 2, and creating a motivational forward momentum towards Stage 3.[5]

From a list of eighteen possibilities, respondents were then asked to select up to three Solo experiences that were most significant to them. Their selections are set out in table 11.

---

4. The Panel is a session conducted pre-Solo where Stage 2 participants are able to anonymously, though respectfully, ask any questions they wish about relationships and sexuality issues (including dating and the female perspective). Membership of the panel is: an older married man, a youngish married couple, and a young single man.

5. Smith, "Leadership Development Program."

PROGRAM ELEMENTS AND KEY CONCEPTS—STAGE 2

EXPERIENCES	RESPONDENTS (%)
Letter from parents[6]	55.9
Being by myself	40.6
Sense of God's presence	38.7
Reading the Bible	36.9
Letter from BB captain or youth leader	30.6
Being in nature	27.9
Writing in my journal	25.2
Praying	24.3
Fasting	16.2
Being independent	14.4
Getting away from technology	13.5
Being creative	8.1
Sense of danger	7.2
Sleeping under the stars	7.2
Thoughts of home	6.3
Being away from my parents	5.4
No one telling me what to do all the time	5.4
Not having to worry about a girlfriend	1.8

Table 11. Most Significant Solo Experiences

Clearly the letter they receive from their parents and read while alone on Solo was the most commonly selected significant experience (55.9% of respondents), fifteen percentage points higher than the next most significant experience, confirming the significance of family for young men[7] even though it may be wanting in some respects. Responses to parental letters included surprise (e.g., that their dads would write them a letter, maybe the only letter he has ever written; about what their parents said; love and aspirations never shared before; other very personal stories and memories). An additional consideration is when the letters contain material and expression of feelings that are in conflict with how participants perceive their family relationships.

---

6. Obtained confidentially pre-course from parents who are encouraged to affirm, not criticize, and handed to participants in a blank envelope as they are placed at their Solo sites, together with a letter from BB Captain or youth leader.

7. White et al., *Youth and Society*; Tiller et al., *Youth Survey Report*.

The full significance of Solo is declared strongly in comments about the post-Solo celebration experience. Being by themselves was significant (40.6%), as were the spiritual experiences—sensing God's presence (38.7%), reading the Bible (36.9%), and prayer (24.3%). Concerning location, 27.9 percent considered being in nature in their top three significant experiences. Writing in their journal was placed in their top three activities of significance by 25.2 percent. Ford makes an interesting observation of similarities between Henri Nouwen and Vincent Van Gough, describing a link between loneliness and positive solitude, that "writing, creativity, and prayer are not always ways out of the wilderness but a way to make the wilderness blossom, to turn the ache of feeling lonely and turn loneliness into a fulfilling solitude."[8] It can be assumed that this was the experience of *Leadership* participants on Solo who identified journaling, praying, and creativity as significant.

Of interest also are the experiences that were not significant: being independent (14.4%) and getting away from technology (13.5%), and even more so, they were not distracted by thoughts of home (6.3%), parents (5.4%), or girlfriends (1.8%).

One interviewee illustrated both the change in attitude that occurs and the spiritual nature of the experience for some participants:

> I thought it was just like a camping exercise—prove that you're a man. It's not that at all. I didn't realise how much of a spiritual experience it was—especially being just you and God. (2018)

In 2013, two years after completing Stage 2, a participant wrote a personal and full reflection of his Stage 2 experience (repeated in more detail in Appendix I):

> Solo pushed me to my limits in every way possible and was an experience that I will never forget. I was physically challenged and spiritually challenged in my search for God's voice and answers. The only way I can describe how I was feeling by the last day, is that I felt very raw and bare. It was just . . . me, without any layers or masks to hide behind. I discovered a lot about myself, and I also had an amazing encounter with God that left me feeling giddy with joy. That same night, we had a Solo celebration that affirmed us on our completion of Solo. For me, this night was a rite of passage from boyhood into manhood. Stage 2 has left a lasting impact

---

8. Ford, *Lonely Mystic*, 126.

on my life in the way that I relate with others and in my relationship with God.

Solo Summary

Solo, the most highly rated activity in the whole three-stage *Leadership* program, sits as the centrepiece of *Leadership*. It is the pinnacle event in Stage 2, looked forward to from Stage 1, and spurring participants on towards Stage 3. It makes a large contribution to the uniqueness of the program and is recognized by participants as a significant achievement, a spiritual highlight in their walk with God, and a challenge overcome: something others their age have never done. Solo features prominently in findings, has been discussed throughout the report, and its significance is thoroughly established as a key element in the uniqueness and apparent success of *Leadership*.

Solo Celebration

Respondents were asked how significant the Solo Celebration was for them *in comparison with other components of the program*. Solo Celebration, held on the night of their completion of Solo, is a ceremonial event with actual and symbolic components, related to rites of passage and becoming a man. Averaged across all respondents, it was rated 4.0 (very significant)—see table 12.

Not at all significant	Slightly significant	Moderately significant	Very significant	Extremely significant
0.0% (0)	8.1% (9)	20.9% (21)	35.5% (39)	35.5% (9)

Table 12. Significance of Solo Celebration

They were then given the invitation, if it was important, to share what it was that made the Solo Celebration so significant for them. At least 25 percent of respondents interpreted this question as referring to the immediate post-Solo experience that is also very significant, arguably for some of greater significance than the evening event. In some responses, however, they did not particularize which event they were describing. To an extent, their comments merge and could refer to either event or even are conceptually combined into the key experience of that day. In interviews and focus groups, the two events were discussed separately, and the responses were that both are highly valued, with most not wanting to identify which was more important. Each of the two identified celebratory events is considered separately.

The Immediate Post-Solo Experience

> One of the really positive memories I've got is just after solo. Just debriefing and chatting with your group and facilitator. That was the biggest moment. (2015)

The immediate reentry into community occurs one at a time (the moment of first contact with someone), then with other participants and their facilitator. This event, or series of linked events begins the moment they emerge from Solo and meet up together with their group and facilitator to share breakfast together.

> Enjoyed the fire and the breakfast we had together in our groups after solo was the best meal I think I've ever had in my entire life. (2014)

They then meet with the whole Stage 2 cohort. It includes the initial excitement and relief that Solo is completed, their eagerness to tell at least their superficial stories in their own group, then coming together, ceremonially blowing their emergency whistles, and sharing more food. They then separate back into their own groups and begin a serious and unhurried debrief[9] at their own pace and in their own place during most of the morning, including sharing stories of transformation and learning, before returning to the main campsite for lunch to be hailed as *heroes* by participants from Stages 1 and 3 and staff—"a victory thing" (2019). That special recognition of those completing Solo is justified because of the overall significance of the event, as earlier identified—the most significantly regarded event of the whole course, including across the three stages.

9. The debriefing model used throughout *Leadership* is based on a reverse application of Critical Incident Stress Debriefing (CISD) (Leadership Queensland, *Staff Development Learning Guide*). It is used in all stages following all major experiences as a strategy for drawing out the learning and, if appropriate, dealing with disappointment as well as success. The post-Solo situation puts debriefing into critical focus and is arguably the most challenging debriefing exercise in *Leadership*. It is important that staff follow best practice guidelines, principles, and practices across the whole *Leadership* program, and this is particularly stressed in debriefing.

PROGRAM ELEMENTS AND KEY CONCEPTS—STAGE 2

This event or series of events is specifically responded to in the research data. Respondents talk about sharing (they haven't spoken with anyone for three days), the community coming back together, something having been completed, telling their stories, a sense of accomplishment, and seeing their mates. Key dimensions of this celebration identified by respondents were that they were celebrating an experience, something real, tangible, and personal. They express feelings of accomplishment, achievement, and pride. "I felt I had accomplished something bigger than myself that not every boy has accomplished" (2019). The community coming back together was significant—friends with whom to share their "independent experience" (2008); celebrating together their own and others' experiences "was amazing" (2009); being back with their group was regarded as the best experience as they all really wanted to see each other again. Twelve years after the experience, one participant put it this way:

> I have a distinct memory . . . sharing experiences and being grateful for seeing my group members again and hearing their progressions and sharing my own. This was such a pivotal moment—we'd all been through the Solo experience—but all done it separately. So profound to have been separated along the path (out of eyesight) but also so close that we were close. Each of us had a slightly different experience of the same experience—and it was such a unique thing to be back with them in their presence after going through the few days of Solo. (2008)

They celebrated sharing "what God had revealed to them" (2017); "how we connected with God" (2017); "being with the Lord and only the Lord for three days" (2019). There was a sense of having completed something that was a real challenge: "To [now] show what happened in our hearts and minds during Solo" (2012). As one put it, "discuss[ing] our experience in solemn humility" (2015). We were able to "talk openly about experiences with those that you had completed the journey with" (2009). One respondent captured the fullness of the whole morning (initial meeting up, debriefing, and reflecting):

> The sense of accomplishment was incredible. Being able to blow that whistle with my small group till our ears nearly bled was painfully fun. The time we spent debriefing was also a large part of my stage 2 experience. Reflecting on shared solo experiences and reflecting on my letters was very rewarding. (2011)

Others added comments about the significance of group, yet also having a sense of personal achievement and independence:

> After struggling with the loneliness and quiet and hunger (fasting[10]), it was a very emotional and amazing experience to be back with my mates and be able to tell the stories of our "survival." (2011)

> The morning when solo finished was such a sense of accomplishment. Solo felt like a mammoth task I would never be able to complete but then there I was with the other end joining my group around a morning fire for breakfast and chocolate (we had saved the chocolate bars you each get given to eat together at the end as kind of a group loyalty pact). (2012)

> That we made it. It was like having proof that we could all be independent and that if we took away all these luxuries we would still be us and we would still be fine. (2012)

Focus groups confirmed the significance of the initial coming together after Solo, though at the same time, they acknowledged the evening celebration. A key area of importance in the initial meeting up was sharing (food and stories) with their group—specifically, sharing with mates:

> You're welcomed back by friends. For me, that was one of my favourite parts of Stage 2. The first time you see people for three or four days.

> I think what was most significant, gave me the most satisfaction, and is most remembered, was sharing with my group after Solo, sharing bread and cheese and bacon rolls. And it was so simple. It was this incredible feeling of satisfaction and achievement and that we were back together.

One, now himself a facilitator, offered these insights on the importance of space, leading to them developing personal insight into themselves and their potential before they are formally told this:

> What I've found significant from a facilitator's point of view is allowing space. They were all coming up and started sharing straight away; then quiet; then sharing again. The day allowed them to get all that stuff out first, and then they are told they've got what it takes; they already know what it takes.

---

10. Fasting is an individual choice, not a requirement. Part of their pre-event briefing is on the significance and value of fasting, plus the dangers. They are provided with basic food for the duration of the experience.

A key insight was that they were able to share their experiences "with those you had completed the journey with" (2009). This is an important insight: that sometimes the only ones with whom one can fully share such an experience are those who have shared the journey. The noises they heard, the rain, the whatever, is uniquely their experience.

> I can tell people about it, but they don't get it, whereas everyone else had this unique solo experience where it was my own, but it could be shared.

But they do share more widely. The next group of people they want to share with are those at *Leadership* in other stages from their home BB company or local group, and sometimes other people at the course with whom they have a significant relationship—those they know have done the same journey and who are a link beyond *Leadership*. Only then can they share more widely and only then are they ready for the serious debrief in their groups that follows. They may join others in later, though at another time.

Evening Celebration Event

> It genuinely felt like I was transitioning from this scared teenager to a man of God. It also helped solidify that Solo was actually something significant and important in my life and should be something that I am proud of.

The actual evening event continues the theme of a journey, ending on the top of a steep hill, where Stage 2 staff welcome them with a warm fire and nourishment and they are presented with an individualized certificate, acknowledging particular fruits of the Spirit seen as emerging in them, and their readiness to be godly men. Participants link into this event other *ceremonial traditions* such as wearing their Solo markers and, though in winter, having already jumped into the freezing swimming pool together. The focus on the evening Solo celebration event adds a further dimension. One survey respondent compared the two events in this way:

> Is it the solo celebration where we walked out at night and towards the top of the hill? If so, it wasn't that significant to me. I understand that it was a formal ceremony of us becoming a man, but I feel like the meet up on the stage[11] directly after the solo experience was

---

11. The stage is a cement structure built by the campsite in the bush for large

> more significant where we got to see everyone in the daylight, and we got to see everyone looking dirty, tired, and sore. You felt more rawness on the stage than the solo celebration night. (2019)

That comment articulates an important insight into the reality of the initial coming together. However, the responses of others are highly positive on both events, as demonstrated by this respondent:

> All that I expected from what the program gave was a stage-wide debrief of experiences. Instead, being validated by leaders I respect . . . atop a mountain was a special experience. Since then I've definitely fallen back on my time during solo as a moment of transition and acceptance into manhood. (2017)

The key themes emerging from responses, some with an illustrative comment added, include affirmation and validation—"Affirmation of 'you've got what it takes'"; affirmation by facilitators and experienced staff.

> The affirmation of respected older men was huge. Being told that "I have what it takes." (2011)

> Experiencing older men who I respected a lot affirming specific qualities in me and encouraging me to continue to grow and live out those qualities. (2012)

> Nice to be validated/affirmed in a group. (2008)

> Getting affirmed by men has a profound effect. It makes you feel acknowledged and empowered. (2014)

> It was the capstone in what had been an intense experience. Finally, it settles in. I've done something hard and worthwhile—something worthy of celebration, being endorsed not superficially and generically, but truly and deeply was an experience and feeling that has stayed with me. (2015)

The nature of the event was a surprise and was accompanied by secrecy, suspense, and delayed gratifications. Symbols, including the fire, the journey, and a special mug presented to them were significant.

> It was really nice to get physical things that remind us of the journey (on top of the yellow triangle markers).[12] I still have the mug/cup and certificate I was given. (2018)

---

gatherings of tent campers.

12. The yellow triangle marker is what marks the entry to each Solo site, which they

Another recurring theme was that they were sharing the event with others who've done it.

> It was an amazing feeling knowing that I had just completed a very difficult task and sharing the experience with people who had gone through it too. (2018)

Participants refer to the importance they felt in receiving unique individualized personal affirmation in certificates presented; not all the same; linking to the fruit of the Spirit.

> The idea that we achieved something and that we each had different fruits of the spirit. (2019)

> The fact that leaders recognised fruits of the spirit I displayed in my life and took the opportunity to share it with me encouraged me a great deal. (2014)

> The Solo celebration helped to identify that the past few nights was a significant change. It also reassured me that the facilitators had identified aspects of my character that I didn't know were there. (2017)

> I thought the evening was very personalised. Like the Fruit of the Spirit. It wasn't just like one script. The leaders actually got to know you . . . just for you. And that's what I really liked about it. It shows that the leaders really have a relationship with us and they knew us on a people level—not just, they're our leader.

For some, the event took on the form of a rite of passage or marking a period of transition in their lives.

> At the time I wasn't sure about someone external telling me I was a man. I didn't think that someone who barely knew me could tell me I was a man, yet looking back, I think what perhaps you were trying to do was encourage people to think as if they were men—and I think that worked for me. (2014)

> It felt like a rite of passage. (2017)

---

take with them and often wear around their neck. During the ceremony, words are addressed to each person individually, affirming them and presenting them with a certificate (includes their Solo photo) and a mug, endorsed with "You've got what it takes."

PART I: PROGRAM ELEMENTS AND KEY CONCEPTS

Solo Celebration Summary

Post-Solo celebration (in both identified forms) is highly important. It provides a sense of finishing or completing something that has been a real challenge. And it confirms the affirmation of young men as having capacity now (not later), as advocated by experienced youth ministry workers[13]; of already demonstrating positive character traits and having what it takes to become godly men. As with Solo, Solo celebration is a factor that contributes to the apparent success of *Leadership*.

Becoming a Man Theme

> The recognition that although I've had struggles in my life, I had the ability to be a true Christian man. (2014)

The Stage 2 Solo celebration recognition that participants *have what it takes* to become godly men is linked into the becoming a man theme in the survey and the rites of passage lens. Survey respondents were asked how significant the becoming a man theme was for them *in comparison with other components* of the Stage 2 program. A small number indicated that it was not significant at all to them (five, or 4.6%). A further five or 4.6 percent indicated that it was slightly significant. Seventy-one (or 64.7%) of respondents indicated that the theme was very or extremely significant—see table 13. Averaged across respondents, the significance score was 4.0 (i.e., very significant).

Not at all significant	Slightly significant	Moderately significant	Very significant	Extremely significant
4.6%	4.6%	26.4%	31.8%	32.7%
5	5	29	35	36

Table 13. Significance of Becoming a Man Theme

They were then asked if it was significant, what was it that made the becoming a man (rites of passage) theme so significant to them. Seventy-six responded to this invitation.

---

13. E.g., Dean, "Fessing Up"; Rahn, "Focusing Youth Ministry"; Dever, "9 Ways."

Only two of the seventy-six comments made can be construed as being negative. One was ambivalent about his own masculinity (2010) and the other argued against "stereotypical masculinity" (2016). One who considered the theme to be only somewhat significant acknowledged that it could be valuable to some but was "a little cumbersome—or unnecessary in some way" if one comes from "a fairly healthy community/family where there are healthy expressions of becoming a man" (2008)—a comment somewhat in contrast with others cited later who considered the confirmation and affirmation of others to be an important role now for them. Some at the lower end of the significance scale were generally commenting on the timing. One said he didn't feel like a man as he knew he had so much more growing to do (2018). As another said twelve years later, "In the moment it wasn't so significant." He added:

> But in the weeks/months/years afterwards it was supremely significant for me to return to that photo and the affirmation written and signed on the back of the card—to remind myself that I'd been through the process and how I'd emerged the other side as a man of God. (2008)

Another raised doubts about "imposing rites of passage on a culture that doesn't have many of its own, not having a noetic frame of reference for such a thing." His reservations continued as "my supposed manhood was not recognised outside the boundaries of leadership . . . I'm not convinced I could have considered myself a man until a few years later, after a fairly major crisis" (2011). Still on timing, one simply said, it "seemed to be at the right time in our lives" (2008). Another said, "I think most boys are at the perfect age for a turning point" (2010). One positively linked the experience to his final (graduating) year of high school (2012) and another commented, "It was the question already on my mind when I came to Stage 2" (2019). One thus concludes that the timing and placing of this theme in the Stage 2 program is appropriate and contributes to the apparent success of *Leadership*.

The range of points of significance placed on the theme by others included that it was something they had not seriously thought of previously; provided valuable information and a stimulus to thinking about becoming a man; provided a challenge to think about the kind of man they wanted to be; was a significant transformational experience; gave a sense of belonging—the confirmation and affirmation of others was important; and was something that has continued to impact them, some completing the survey many years after their experience.

> It helped give me an understanding of what becoming a man means to me. (2015)

> I didn't know how to be a man of God before. (2014)

> I felt quite lost in relation to this stuff before we talked about it at Leadership. This gave me more of a sense of understanding. (2019)

> It provided grounding (2011); it was powerful. (2014, 2017)

> It was an "epic journey" (2007); a pivotal moment/point (2009)—something not offered outside of Leadership (2014); a transition (2014); it clicked (2018); "a very significant realisation" (2018); a turning point (2019); "the call to action and the call to responsibility" to solve problems for others. (2019)

> Affirmation and acceptance (2010, 2013, 2017); really gave me a sense of belonging (2013); now belonging to a bigger group. (2018)

> No longer... viewed as children but rather as men... and now it was my job to help others to achieve the same. (2017)

There is some difference of opinion and experience of becoming a man and being recognized as making this transition. As will be discussed later when considering the lens of rites of passage (chapter 7), becoming a man is more likely to be spread over a series of events, yet completing Solo and the affirmation that follows is at least a key event (and is *the* rite of passage event for some). Thus, the inclusion of the becoming a man theme, linked to these specific events is appropriate and is an element contributing to the apparent success of *Leadership*. The becoming a man theme during Stage 2 is seen by fatherless boys as particularly helpful. Three who identified themselves as being in this category shared:

> The themes helped shape my ethics and values and leading me into the man I am today. (2009)

> It helped me adjust into becoming a responsible adult. (2011)

> It helped give me an understanding of what becoming a man means to me. And I really felt as if I was being welcomed in with no judgement or reservation from the leaders' team. (2015)

Becoming a Man Theme Summary

This theme, which is presented throughout the Stage 2 program and is a significant component of the formal Solo celebration, is explored further in considering the rites of passage lens (chapter 7). While different views are considered, those from a world or peer group perspective and those from an historical Christian perspective, no attempt is made to define the term, and, that it has different meanings for different people, is confirmed in the findings. That this focus was selected most highly as a significant event outside of Solo, Solo celebration and the Panel, confirms its importance. There is a sense of appreciation from participants that they are considered worthy of big challenges and have what it takes to be godly men. This element of *Leadership* is recognized as a contribution to the program's apparent success, with particular relevance for fatherless boys.

A critical consideration in programs such as *Leadership* is the timing of when to introduce themes and activities. Responses to the invitation in the question on how significant the theme was and their comments on the theme, indicate that the theme, included in Stage 2 of *Leadership*, is appropriately placed as it is the time when the majority of boys are considering this phase of their development.

The Panel—Relationships and Sexual Issues

> An honest discussion I have never been part of before, a real conversation (2014).

Respondents were asked how significant the Panel was for them *in comparison with other components of the program*. The Panel was rated at 3.2, between moderately and very significant, as illustrated in table 14.

Not at all significant	Slightly significant	Moderately significant	Very significant	Extremely significant
9.2% (10)	14.7% (16)	29.4% (32)	37.6% (41)	9.2% (10)

Table 14. Significance of the Panel

Some respondents did not remember this session, or at least did not remember it being called by this title.[14] Those who did respond with

---

14. The title of this session has changed over recent years and the content emphasis

knowledge made comments including that it was helpful to be able to ask questions of each of the category of people represented. They particularly mentioned the value of being able to hear a young woman's point of view, appreciating others saying they had made mistakes too, and the honesty and openness. A sample of their responses follows:[15]

> Normalising sexuality and seeing older men talk about it freely and truthfully. (2011)

> Learning about different perspectives of relationships; taught me to respect women in a completely different way from just respecting them as another person, but as someone I would one day potentially want to build a life with. (2012)

> It was great to see some people be candid and open about life; it is a unique and rare opportunity. (2013)

> I couldn't believe how open they were. Incredibly so. And it gave me hope. That young and old, in all stages of growth and in this, struggle against life and sin together. (2015)

> I was/am unsure how I navigate many aspects of romantic relationships—when to get married, how to know who to date, what to do/not do during dating. Hearing the discussion from a variety of ages and genders helped me realize that being unsure is okay— as long as you have a considered approach that caters for that prospective partner, the specifics can vary between couples. (2017)

Having not understood what the *Panel* was, in responding to an invitation to nominate other significant Stage 2 experiences, respondents identified the relationships session as dealing with that content—sexual integrity—and commented favourably on the makeup of the panel. They added: "the subject of relationships is very relatable for a young bloke— girls are on the mind with great frequency" (2017); "real-life solutions to real-life problems with real-life examples and real-life people" (2019).

---

changed as some of the original session scope is now dealt with in a different session.

15. Here, and in other places, the year that a quoted respondent completed Stage 2 is included, if appropriate, to emphasize the recency of the comment or the range of dates across the target years or the memory of the event/activity many years later.

Panel Summary

The opportunity of engaging with a panel of different persons—older and younger, male and female—is valued as a unique one. As with the other pressing personal topics for young men, relationship and sexual issues are acknowledged by participants as being frequently in mind. *Leadership* provides an opportunity to engage in discussions and ask the questions they cannot ask anywhere else. The Panel builds on a sexual integrity session in Stage 1 and invites frank questions to an older man, a young man, and a married couple, those who have made mistakes and those who wish they could have had someone to direct the questions to when they were aged sixteen. It is part of a cross-stage theme, dealing with sexual issues at different levels in different stages, matching their levels of inquiry and maturity. If this session is appreciated, and it is by participants, then it contributes to the apparent success, uniqueness, and effectiveness of *Leadership*.

Other Stage 2 Experiences

Respondents were asked whether there was something else in Stage 2 that was significant for them and were invited to select up to five such activities from a list of twenty-one, then to explain how those activities were significant for them.

Expanding on the becoming a man theme, *becoming a man of God* was the most commonly selected activity when all responses were collated. Responses selected by 20 percent or more respondents are set out in table 15.

ACTIVITY	RESPONDENTS (%)	PARTICIPANT RESPONDENTS (%)	STAFF RESPONDENTS (%)
Becoming a man of God	37.0	33.8	48.4
Letter to self[16]	34.3	35.1	35.5
Formal dinner	32.4	39.2	19.4
Worship	31.5	28.4	41.9
Being back with my group	30.6	28.4	35.5

16. In Stage 2, after Solo, participants write a letter to themselves, knowing it will be posted to them six months later. They tend to include reference to decisions made and future goals set, asking themselves how they are going with their plans and goals.

ACTIVITY	RESPONDENTS (%)	PARTICIPANT RESPONDENTS (%)	STAFF RESPONDENTS (%)
Journal keeping	30.6	33.8	25.8
Solo preparation—social/emotional	25.0	18.9	38.7
Solo preparation—spiritual	21.3	16.2	35.5
Relationships sessions	20.7	21.6	16.1
The tough bits	19.4	20.3	16.1
Valiant man	16.7	14.9	22.6
Solo preparation—physical	15.7	12.2	22.6
Morning devotions	15.7	14.9	19.4
Solo preparation—acclimatization	14.8	17.6	9.7
How to spend a day in prayer	13.9	20.3	0.
Graduation ceremony	13.9	17.6	6.5
Problem-solving	13.00	13.5	12.9
Black shirts	11.1	13.5	6.5
Growth agreements	10.2	9.5	12.9
Celebration service	10.2	4.1	25.8
Four faces of man	6.5	8.1	3.2
Opening service	0.9	0.0	3.2

Table 15. Other Stage 2 Experiences of Significance

Given that all options were chosen by someone, and except for one option, by multiple respondents, their explanations of why their choices were significant were individual and personal. Even though Solo (and activities already specifically dealt with) was excluded through the *something else* phrase in the question, and Solo was not an option in the list of activities presented, 50 percent of the fifty-eight respondents found a way of including it in the explanation of their choices—the only activity mentioned by any significant number in their explanations—confirming again its paramount significance. Comments on Solo and the other activities already dealt with have been linked back to those discussions. What is dealt with here are those additional activities where respondents have offered important insights.

Respondents were also invited to add anything else about Stage 2 that would assist with the research. As with the previous question, in the second invitation, Solo again appeared as the prominent commonly mentioned activity, even though here also, it was excluded by an *anything else* phrase. Responses to the two questions covered similar territory, including:

Becoming a Man of God

This is something . . . [I] find quite daunting and I've been afraid of not knowing what the "right way" of being a man of God is. This helped me how to do it. (2019)

I was able to find who I am in God. (2007)

Letter to Self

I'd forgotten about it completely. When I read it, I remembered all that I had done on leadership and realized that while I'd followed through on some of my goals, I had abandoned most of them with stage 2 a distant memory. It was the kick start I needed to get back on my journey as a man. (2017)

I received the letter when I was going through a bit of a tough time, and I am so glad we got the opportunity to write these when we were in a good place. (2019)

Formal Dinner

Though it is no longer a novel experience, the formal dinner does not lose its appeal across stages:

[Solo] was celebrated at the formal dinner with friends who had gone through something powerful too. (2009)

Worship

Worship is chosen because it is seen as exciting and different at *Leadership* from what they are used to.

Being Back with My Group

The significance of this experience has been well documented previously in the immediate post-Solo celebration experience.

Journal Keeping

This is a new experience for many. They report on it being helpful to look back on later and reflect on. King articulates an understanding of the value of journaling and suggests that youth workers should "Encourage young people to try journaling and help them learn the process. Use these journals to share life with each other. Engaging one other in this way is sacramental and binds us together in the presence of the divine."[17] Post-Solo, in particular, participants use their journals to share life and continue sharing their story. It is interesting that King adds the dimensions of a journal being sacramental, that it binds people together and is in the presence of God. At *Leadership*, the journals are theirs to decide who they share it with or choose not to share it with, including their parents.

Solo Preparation

The various aspects of Solo preparation (social/emotional, spiritual, physical, and acclimatization) were commented on, for example, "the preparation of solo in all its aspects was one of the most significant things we did as a lot of us were still playing and mucking about and weren't really thinking about how tough solo was going to be" (2019); spiritual preparation helped plan what to read in the Bible and this brought fruit and was appreciated. Acclimatization received special mention for its usefulness.

---

17. King, *Presence-Centered*, 149.

Anything Else to Add

Specifically, on the question of whether they would like to add anything else on Stage 2 that would assist with the research, four simply said "no" or "nope." One offered a negative comment about not being comfortable with his group. One offered a suggestion for the future about additional preparation sessions for Solo. Most commented positively about specific activities (as above) or about the program generally, demonstrating consistency across the last eight or more years: "can't think of anything to add at this time, very much enjoyed it" (2012); "It was pretty awesome" (2012); "would run it exactly as it was run for me" (2014); "Was a great time in my life and I wouldn't change anything" (2018); "not much to say, stage two was amazing" (2018); "Again, perfect" (2019).

Differences between Participant Respondents and Staff Respondents

While there are differences between participant respondents and staff respondents, often they are a difference in degree or interpretation and definition (e.g., Was something very significant or extremely significant?), rather than whether or not they were significant. Another factor is that they were making a comparative statement, not suggesting because it was not in their top three or five, that a particular activity or experience was not significant. There were some differences in relation to particular activities. Examples include that staff respondents recognize the overtly spiritual more frankly. Participant respondents who have not served on staff give a higher priority to the informal, especially with their group, but, in contrast, the formal dinner was selected by 39.2 percent but much less selected by staff respondents (19.4%). Worship and two areas of Solo preparation were regarded as more significant by staff respondents (41.9%; 38.7% and 35.5% compared with 28.4%; 18.9% and 16.2%). "How to spend a day in prayer" was selected as a significant session by 20.3 percent of participant respondents, yet, strangely, by no staff respondents. The celebration service was selected by 25.8 percent of staff respondents and only by 4.1 percent of participant respondents—similar to other results where the formal celebration events were more highly valued by staff respondents, while participant respondents looked to the more informal and spontaneous events. Yet, there was something different about the graduation ceremony, selected

PART I: PROGRAM ELEMENTS AND KEY CONCEPTS

by 17.6 percent of participant respondents and only 6.5 percent of staff respondents.

Summary of Chapter

Survey questions covering the Stage 2 *Leadership* program canvassed the major components of Solo, Solo celebration, becoming a man, and the panel (or relationships as some understood this component). There was scope also for respondents to identify other significant components.

Solo emerged as the most significant event in the whole of the *Leadership* program—across all three stages. Two aspects of celebrating Solo emerged, first the immediate excitement of completion and joining up to share experiences with their mates, their group, and progressively with the wider *Leadership* community. The second aspect was the formal Solo celebration ceremony which takes place the same evening and takes on the nature of a recognition of manhood, viewed also as a rite of passage. Becoming a man and having *what it takes* are key terms of affirmation shared individually with each participant, along with identification of fruits of the Spirit they are observed to already be displaying.

The multi-age panel, including a young (married) woman, is appreciated as an honest and real discussion on relationships and anything of a sexual nature. Respondents say they have never been part of such a discussion before and they appreciate the frankness, openness, and honesty shared in this unique opportunity. Those comments and themes continue throughout the whole program: providing new experiences and real conversations with other men—young and old—on issues of relevant, pressing, and immediate concern for young men. They cannot do this or do not have this opportunity at home, or in the local BB or youth groups, or churches. It's only at *Leadership*, as expressed in the words of one respondent: "*Leadership* just did it." *Leadership* is a safe place, including to express oneself and try out new ideas or behaviours. Worship is different at *Leadership* (more involved and enthusiastic); they have not written a journal before but find this useful.

Apart from the major components, there are many and varied activities and experiences that are highly valued by Stage 2 participants—usually something individual. Several that emerge as important for a significant number of participants include worship, getting a letter from their parents on Solo, the formal dinner, and a resource on how to spend a day in prayer.

The significance of Solo, something difficult successfully completed as a young man, along with mates doing it at the same time, cannot be overemphasized. The question is raised whether it is Solo that is the real rite of passage.

Finally, it should be noted that the responses are overwhelmingly positive. The very few with negative content are explained as one-off experiences of one or two individuals or a matter of timing or readiness. Stage 2 is an intense, but balanced, program, summed up by this participant, in the context of the Solo celebration, but invoking other themes of support, change, new confidence, and blessing:

> It was our own private space on top of the hill. It was incredible to feel supported by everyone around me and the staff. You could also see how everybody had changed and had a new confidence in their step as they received their blessing. (2019)

The Stage 2 experience continues to provide opportunity to ask difficult questions. It picks up the value of silence, solitude, and reflection tasted briefly in Stage 1, but now a key experience over a four-day/three-night Solo in wilderness. It also contributes to developing themes: transformation, uniqueness, spiritual dimension, and freedom/empowerment—leading into a further examination of *Leadership* through the various lenses applied in part II and the emerging substantiative theory in part IV.

4

Program Elements and Key Concepts—Stage 3

A DIFFERENCE IN STAGE 3 is that participants come as *already men* and operate as a whole-stage community cohort, not in small groups. There are two central foci: writing and declaration of a personal mission statement[1] and preparing and carrying out a Duo[2] experience—in the bush for three nights with one other person. A third key program component is studying the Covey *7 Habits*[3] program—dated now but made relevant through presentation strategies. Each of these program elements will be examined in detail, with other experiences also identified.

As acknowledged in introducing the discussion of Stage 2, the components identified in Stage 1, overall *Leadership* community and My Group continue to be significant—My Group in Stage 3 being the whole cohort, and the overall *Leadership* community being the context within which Stage 3 and therefore the whole *Leadership* experience is completed, acknowledged, and celebrated.

---

1. Participants are given guidance, time, and opportunity to write their own personal mission statement which they deliver in front of their cohort and senior staff at the end of the week.

2. Stage 3 participants are paired with one other (occasionally a group of three if there is an odd number in the cohort), spending three nights together in a bush location. They can move around but not communicate with other Duos. They are encouraged to share their current issues and future dreams with their partner.

3. Based on the *7 Habits of Highly Effective People* program (see Covey, *7 Habits*), each habit is presented by stage facilitators with a contemporary application.

PROGRAM ELEMENTS AND KEY CONCEPTS—STAGE 3

Mission Statement

> This statement portrays the man that I will endeavor to become. During the graduation ceremony at the end of Leadership 12, I was given the opportunity to state publicly my Mission Statement in front of my family and peers. This was another moment I will never forget. (2012[4])

Survey respondents were asked how significant writing their mission statement had been for them *compared with the other components of the program*. The averaged significance score was 4.0—very significant, with 40 percent saying it was extremely significant—see table 16.

Not at all significant	Slightly significant	Moderately significant	Very significant	Extremely significant
4.0%	1.3%	21.3%	33.3%	40.0%
3	1	16	25	30

Table 16. Significance of Mission Statement

Respondents were then asked if it had been significant, what it was that made writing their mission statement significant for them. Fifty-six responded to this invitation. The themes of their comments were:

- Opportunity and time—that there was this opportunity and adequate time was appreciated. It was "a chance to stop and think"—about "the man I wanted to be"; "my priorities"; "my goals."
- Written document—the fact that it was written seems to have increased its significance

> I have revisited my mission statement multiple times over the years as it has been ever evolving, but the opportunity to put pen to paper to begin writing was the culmination of the three-year journey. (2010)

> While in Stage 2 was about becoming a man, the mission statement and Stage 3 really made me think about what kind of man I wanted to be. And by writing it down on paper it really helped to formulate those thoughts and to put them into action. (2018)

---

4. Where dates are included in participant quotes in this chapter, it is the year the participant completed Stage 3.

- Speaking it/declaring it—in front of mates (*brothers*)

    I wrote the mission statement as a promise to myself of the man I am and the man I am going to become and reading it out loud in front of my brothers made me feel proud and made me feel like I wasn't alone. (2015)

- Continuing to refer to it.

    My mission statement is something I carry with me to this day. I got an abbreviated version tattooed on my arm, so I do my best to live every day by its words. (2011)

    I still use my mission statement and still have it on my wall. It is something I have encouraged others to do, and it is also something that best describes my time at Leadership. In my opinion, it is the penultimate piece of Leadership—what the 3 stages build up to. (2013)

    The thought and focus that I put into my mission statement was significant. And the desire to live out that statement and even add to it has persevered in the years since. I make a point to read my mission statement at least once a year to see how I am tracking and how I can improve my walk to becoming a Godly man and leader in the different areas of my life. (2012)

With permission, this participant's mission statement (as posted by him on Facebook) is shared:

> ### *My Mission Statement*
>
> I am [name in full]. I am a man, a man of integrity—a man who values his friends, family, and all relationships in his life. A man that has realized that old habits must be removed and replaced.
>
> I value respect for myself and respect for others' values and opinions. I value a strong relationship with God in my life. I value strength and courage in my life so I may better serve and obey God and others. I value humor but also recognize that there is a time and place for seriousness.
>
> Throughout the remainder of my life, I will endeavor to strengthen my relationship with God by loving him, honoring him, obeying him, and putting him first in all aspects of my life. I will spend time searching God's word and seeking his voice to strengthen my knowledge of him. I will work towards becoming a man who is proactive not reactive. I will put first things first, spending more time on things of importance rather than unimportant things so that the relationships in my life will strengthen. I will be a man that will be available to listen to anybody and put away any judgments or opinions by seeking first to understand and then be understood. I will commit to approaching life situations with a win-win attitude no matter how difficult, so that others will be benefited instead of only trying to benefit myself. I will think before I act and be humble, gracious, generous, and patient in my dealings with others. When the time comes that I have my own wife and children, I will strive to care, love, protect, and take time to serve them. I will spend time praying for others, close ones, and fellow Christians. I will seek to serve others by always carrying a servant attitude with me. I will endeavor to be a witness of my faith to others and look for ways to increase their knowledge of God. I will lead effectively, without hesitation, and with great strength and courage in any areas of leadership given to me.
>
> This is the man I will work toward becoming—a man who will be strong and courageous and a man that lives to serve God and others.

Figure 1. Sample Mission Statement

Writing their mission statement was something many found difficult and took seriously.

> I found it extremely difficult to write a mission statement, something that was true to me and true to what I had prayed into, what God wanted for me . . . (2019)

> I found it pretty hard because I didn't want to write things that I knew I wasn't going to commit to . . . I wanted to write something that would impact my life. (2019)

One interviewee's comment is shared in detail to explain the challenge further:

> I felt like I started and restarted it about five or six times and I didn't really get anything going . . . then after that first line it became a lot easier to keep going. For me, I still remember at the time I kept drawing towards this imagery that I thought sounded cool and then stopping myself feeling like it's not about sounding cool or creating these great images. It's meant to be reflecting the kind of man I want to be . . . and what I would say is that before you started it, wrestling with the intention to make this real or make it valuable, more than just a school essay.

Delivering their mission statement in front of their mates with whom they had shared the three stages of *Leadership* was important to them. In fact, this took away a possible sense of nervousness or it being a liminal experience (see chapter 6); it was a real and meaningful experience in the here and now. Holding the sword as they delivered their statement was important and symbolic. The following comment illustrates one focus group participant's view of the uniqueness of the mission statement, including into the future, and also the long-term contact they have, in this case three years after completing Stage 3.

> Something unique is the Mission Statement. You might get it on other camps like writing who you want to be, but no other camp I've been to has put such importance on the Mission Statement, such emphasis, like this is who you want to be; this is who you are going to be. In the next 50 years you can look back on it and ask, am I that man yet. That's something so unique, and then also on our Stage 3 chat, Michael . . . posted the other day, just randomly, "I just checked my mission statement. You guys should have a look." There's no other camp I've been on where you can get encouraged to look back at the thing you wrote and see are you living the way you said you would.

Mission Statement Summary

Participants acknowledge that they found writing their mission statement very difficult, but a serious enterprise, particularly comments such as that they wanted it to be true to themselves and to what they had prayed into, and wanting to write something that would impact their life. The significance of the mission statement was that they were provided with the opportunity; that it became a written document (tattooed on his arm in one case); they declared it publicly in front of mates; put it on social media or on their bedroom wall; and they continue to refer to it many years later. It has impacted and continues to impact their lives, underlying the apparent success of *Leadership*—recognizing that the mission statement is an important contributing element.

Duo (Sharing with Another)

> Joe's[5] the only person in my life who has totally accepted me. On Duo, we told each other stuff we had done, terrible stuff in our younger years. It was stuff we've never told anybody else before and once we told each other, it was then in the past.

Survey respondents were asked how significant Duo was for them *relative to other parts of the program*. The averaged significance score was 3.8, between moderately and very significant, leaning more towards very significant—69.3 percent saying it was very or extremely significant—see table 17.

Not at all significant	Slightly significant	Moderately significant	Very significant	Extremely significant
4.0%	10.7%	16.0%	36.0%	33.3%
3	8	12	27	25

Table 17. Significance of Duo

Respondents were then asked if it had been significant, what it was that made Duo significant for them. Sixty responded to this invitation. The themes of their comments were:

- The benefit of sharing a friendship with someone who had shared the same journey; finding creative solutions to personal problems by bouncing ideas off each other
- Getting to know someone more deeply, more intimately; "journeying deeply with another man" (2015); developing trust sufficient to tell "my deepest and darkest secrets" (2016)
- Making life-long friendships with Duo partners (six say their friendship is still strong, some after six years (2014, 2014, 2015, 2015, 2018, 2019)

---

5. Not his real name.

- Being able to share with someone on a different journey without it affecting their friendship
- Being in nature
- It was sometimes hard work
- It was the completion of their *Leadership* journey; "it solidified leadership." (2013)

Three respondents (4%) indicated that Duo was "not at all significant" and eight (10.7%) that this activity was "slightly significant." Though in a significant minority compared with other responses, these responses are noted and comments later in response to general questions about Stage 3 shed some light on this—that in the difficult challenge of placing people in Duos, some do not work out. The majority, however, seem to enjoy the time (as in the above comments) and/or commit to learning and making something positive of the experience.

Having said that, most Duos complete the experience positively and their Duo partner is the one they will most likely maintain contact with post-*Leadership*. One Duo experience, including exceptional circumstances and a recent event, is shared, using observation and the words of Al (real names not used), recorded, and checked with him.

> ## JOE AND AL—DUO PARTNERS IN 2016
>
> Al did Stage 3 in 2016. In 2021, he was in Queensland on uni holidays during the Victorian COVID-19 crisis. He asked their still functioning 2016 Stage 3 private chat group, "Does anybody know where Joe's memorial is?" and one of them contacted me. Joe died three years earlier from a medical condition.
>
> The big thing Al wanted to do in Queensland was visit Joe's memorial, though he did not know where it was or what form it took. They did all stages of *Leadership* together and what I didn't realize at the time is that Joe was Al's Duo partner. When Joe died, Al was in Europe on a gap year and didn't know about it until sometime later. He would have come up from Melbourne at the time if he was here.
>
> In fact, there is a memorial set up. Joe's parents' home backs onto a golf course. Just over the fence, on the edge of the golf course is Joe's memorial; it's not at the crematorium or the cemetery; it's there in a garden, with a few other things that Joe's parents have placed there. I accompanied Al and he spent some time at the memorial. We could hear noises from the house so we went in and Joe's parents were both at home. They knew Al immediately because still sitting on their cupboard is the Duo photo of their son, Joe, and his Duo partner, Al. It was the one *Leadership* photo that their son had wanted them to put in a frame and display. Though they had never met him before, they knew Al immediately just looking at him, so it was very meaningful all around. Al said that the big thing about Joe was his acceptance. He said something like, "Joe's the only person in my life who has totally accepted me. On Duo, we told each other stuff we had done, terrible stuff in our younger years. It was stuff we've never told anybody else before and once we told each other, it was then in the past."
>
> January 2021

Figure 2. Joe and Al—Duo Partners

Duo Summary

A participant's reflection on Stage 3 Duo, written a year later, is offered as a summary:

> [Duo] was also very challenging, as Solo was, but in a very different way. There weren't the problems like loneliness or shelter. The big challenge was opening up to someone else about personal issues and sharing on deeper topics than just your average chat about the footy. Some of the things that came up were confronting and challenging to talk about but were very beneficial to the both of us as we could relate on certain things and help each other. . . . It

was also during my time on Duo that I wrote my Mission Statement. (2012)

7 Habits (Personal Effectiveness)

> Some of them have just stuck in my mind as I tell people about them because I use them in my day-to-day life. (2016)

Survey respondents were asked how significant the *7 Habits* had been for them *compared with the other components of the program*. The significance score was 3.4, midway between moderately and very significant—see table 18.

Not at all significant	Slightly significant	Moderately significant	Very significant	Extremely significant
2.70% (2)	24.3% (18)	27.0% (29)	20.3% (15)	25.7% (19)

Table 18. Significance of *7 Habits*

- The *7 Habits* are able to be related to spiritual principles.

  > It is a great tool . . . I enjoyed the spiritual application the most. (2010)

- The *7 Habits* were useful and remain useful. They were helpful as a foundation for writing their mission statement.

  > The 7 Habits has given me great tools to use in my approach to life and improve my relationships with others. I should reflect on them and consider them more frequently in my life. Beginning with the End in Mind and Put First Things First have both been very helpful in my approach to uni, managing workloads, volunteering, and generally organising my time. (2013)

  > I still use many of those habits. (2015)

- They remember particular habits up to ten years later; the habit most remembered is "Be Proactive."

> It was quite significant, particularly the habit of being proactive. This is one in particular I continue to remind myself of, as well as Win-Win. (2010)
>
> The foundations of how to live proactively rather than reactively have remained pillars of my life. (2018)

- Some also remembered and articulated the overall Dependence—Independence—Interdependence framework of the *7 Habits*.

> [It] has become embedded in my thinking. I naturally gravitate towards Independent, and in recent years have been wrestling to become Interdependent. (2015)

While the Stephen Covey *7 Habits* material has been around a long time, and this is a potential criticism, the data indicated that it still resonates with seventeen-to-nineteen-year-old young men, uses catchy titles they remember, and provides them with some anchor points. Focus group responses confirm this, stating that they look beyond old videos to the updated and contemporary presentations and applications of their facilitators, which makes the program still highly relevant to young adults today.

> What [facilitators named] do is apply it to us, specifically to us, young Christian men. It might get a bit old, but they continuously upgrade it and continuously make it relevant to the people they're saying it to, which I think is really good of them.
>
> The content is 100% not out of date. The videos are old, but by Stage 3, they get over that pretty easy and that should not be a stumbling block.

7 Habits Summary

Comments of participants support a view that they regard this component as significant and of contemporary application for young adults (now, and into their futures).

Other Stage 3 Experiences

Survey respondents were asked whether there was something else in Stage 3 that was significant for them and were invited to select up to five activities from a list of eighteen that were the most significant for them. It is noted that worship was most selected—by 45.8 percent of respondents—see table 19.

ACTIVITY	RESPONDENTS (%)	PARTICIPANT RESPONDENTS (%)	STAFF RESPONDENTS (%)
Worship	45.8	47.6	44.8
Be Proactive	38.1	38.1	31.0
Holding the sword	37.5	35.7	41.4
Being back with my mates	34.7	40.5	24.1
Seek First to Understand, then Be Understood	34.7	33.3	34.5
Formal dinner	34.7	40.5	27.6
Begin with the End in Mind	33.3	26.2	44.4
Morning devotions	31.9	26.2	41.4
Put First Things First	26.4	23.8	27.6
Think Win-Win	25.0	28.6	20.7
Graduation ceremony	19.4	28.6	6.9
Elective sessions	18.1	19.0	17.2
Celebration service	15.3	14.3	17.2
Action planning	13.9	7.1	24.1
Sharpen the Saw	12.5	11.9	13.8
Synergize	11.1	2.4	24.1
Growth agreements	9.7	9.5	10.3
Opening service	2.8	2.4	3.5

Table 19. Other Stage 3 Activities in Order of Significance

Respondents were then invited to explain how those activities they selected were significant for them. What this question did was include each of the "7 Habits", thus refreshing respondents' memories and this is reflected in their choices. The explanations they gave, and the additional comments made include that:

- It was emotional.

    There were a mix of emotions, including sadness.

- There was sadness, yet hope.

    It was the final stage of the course. The final graduation ceremony was . . . interesting. Sad. The final skit we gave for what our week was like was nostalgic and sad but there was a good hope that we were better prepared for the future.

- It signified endings.

    Coming back for stage 3 was a big thing as it was the last participant stage of the course and would probably be the last time you got to see some of my leadership cohort. This made certain events quite special. Holding the sword in front of the guys you spent the last two stages with felt pretty special along with sitting next to them at the formal dinner as I knew we were coming to the end of something special. (2015)

Significance of the Sword

This was mentioned several times, as these examples illustrate:

> Holding the sword while reading my mission statement is also significant as it's a rite of passage that speaks to the masculine psyche (the warrior's heart). (2018)

> Holding the sword made the mission statement more significant as I was declaring who I will become in front of the rest of stage 3. (2018)

> It shows strength, loyalty, and companionship between all the participants because knights held their swords for the King before battle, which is what was being symbolised. (2018)

> The mission statement and holding the sword were definitely the most powerful moments of the entire leadership course for me. Rather than being told the hows and whys, we were actually making a huge step that would affect our lives and those around us. (2019)

Morning Devotions

For some, getting up early to join voluntary morning devotions was a challenge and provided rewards:

> Morning devotions were one of the big things for me. Forcing myself to wake up and walk up the hill in the cold every day just to sit there and listen was very impactful and also a bit of a challenge to continue to do, no matter what, every morning. (2017)

Formal Dinner

This topic continues to be identified as significant (as it is for all stages):

> The formal dinner was an occasion that in past years was mostly just yah!!! You did it, but in stage 3 it also acted as a sort of farewell to the course that had in three weeks helped to shape me into a man and decide what kind of man to be. (2018)

> I really found the last formal dinner and graduation service to be extremely important as they were the closing acts of my leadership journey. I liked the feeling of being with the course as a whole for the last time and to hear people regale their stories even though they happened only a few days ago. There's just something about those two days that feels different because you know it's about to end but there is still much to happen. (2018)

Celebration

As indicated in some of the comments above, there was a heightened sense of celebration (for the final time) with mates.

Electives

The flexibility of choosing other topics of immediate interest and hearing some wisdom shared was appreciated.

Anything Else?

A further invitation was given to add anything else about Stage 3 that would assist with the research. Themes from what was shared were that they appreciated being treated as men and being offered a great deal of self-management, attributed to the approach of their facilitators. They refer to themselves as *men* in Stage 3 and feel that's how they are treated; they feel they were given tools to live their lives by; and it was more of a personal journey than a community journey. Three responses are alerts for the future. One participant felt that some others were not serious; a similar point was raised as earlier, that some Duos did not work; and a concern expressed was that some of what was taught was "secular psychology."

Sense of Completion—Excitement, Yet Sadness

Presenting one's mission statement is one of the culminating activities of the *Leadership* program. Its significance highlights that they feel they are treated as men, it is shared with peers (now best and lifelong mates), and they appreciate the acknowledgment of their readiness to chart their future as men. As they raise the sword, there is a symbolism that they have left boyhood behind and are going forward as men. It is the completion of *Leadership*. Together with other final experiences at the end of Stage 3 (their last formal dinner; their last graduation ceremony; their last *Leadership*-style worship time), they experience a sense of having completed something—and it is highly significant that it has been done with a group of mates with whom they have shared the journey, now men together. They have done this in an atmosphere of acceptance for who they are and are becoming, celebrating the whole journey and its completion is an act of worship.

The formal dinner was ranked highly significant by participant respondents (consistent with other stages). The graduation ceremony was more highly ranked by participants in Stage 3 than in other stages. The excitement accompanying the sense of completion at the end of Stage 3 is tempered with a touch of sadness that they have completed the program and do not have the next stage to look forward to next year. Thus, taking staff a little by surprise, the formal celebratory parts have increased markedly in significance in Stage 3, as have the competing emotions—understandings that need to be recognized in planning, a point made during a focus group with experienced staff:

> Something that I haven't really appreciated, and it hit me reading it, is the sense of sadness that they have leaving the leadership community and I think it's primarily because of the culture of leadership, of kindness and mateship and things like that and that they realize that they're leaving that culture without a guarantee that they'll be back again. It explains why the formal dinner and the graduation is particularly significant for Stage 3 because I think they're processing this kind of sense of loss. They're beginning to feel sad about leaving.

Differences Between Participant Respondents and Staff Respondents

As in the Stage 1 and 2 programs, in Stage 3 there are certain differences between responses from participant respondents and staff respondents, but only in relation to one of the three key program components. Some differences emerged in relation to other Stage 3 activities or experiences. These are outlined here. As well as the activities and experiences, 40.5 percent of participant respondents ranked equal second, being back with their mates, whereas only 24.1 percent of staff respondents chose this as a top five significant experience.

As noted with Stage 2 activities and experiences, differences are often in degree or interpretation and definition (e.g., Was something very significant or extremely significant?), rather than whether or not they were significant. Another factor is that they were making a comparative statement, not suggesting that a particular activity or experience was not significant. This applies particularly in relation to the major program components, where a difference in degree of significance of the *7 Habits* was noted (more highly rated by staff respondents). While the spiritual aspect, worship, was now selected most highly by both participants and staff, another spiritual aspect, morning devotions, was selected more by staff respondents. Change from earlier stages was noted in Stage 3 participants, for whom formal activities had now increased in significance, in particular the graduation ceremony—their last such event. Interestingly, being back with mates (for the last time) was highly significant for participant respondents (40.5%), but not greatly recognized by staff respondents (24.1%).

Summary of Chapter

Three primary elements were dealt with in the Stage 3 review—writing/presenting a personal mission statement, Duo, and *7 Habits*. Other components were also identified as significant, including, most prominently, worship, the formal dinner, being back with mates, the graduation ceremony, and holding up a sword while delivering their mission statements. They were given choices and were treated as men working towards a mission.

There were feelings of sadness related to this being the end of their *Leadership* journey and this also heightened the importance of celebration in the formal dinner, worship, and the graduation ceremony, more so than attached to Stages 1 and 2. Doing all this with their mates of three courses was also significant. A participant comment is offered as summation of the Stage 3 experience:

> Stage three was probably the most emotional stage, you just know that there is a good chance that you would not see a lot of the people there ever again. [Sharing] an isolated camp with like-minded Christians is something that can't be explained. I just want to thank whoever is reading this for their contribution to the course. (2019)

The full significance of Stage 3 being a completion, with the accompanying emotions has been demonstrated, possibly providing a fresh and more in-depth understanding for staff as they walk the Stage 3 journey with participants.

Part II

Lenses

IN PART II, THE findings and discussion on the six lenses through which *Leadership* has been examined are presented.

Each of the chapters follows the pattern of dealing with the pre-research theory review and then presenting the research findings. The two coalescence chapters bring the findings together with discussion and theological reflection. The first coalescence of lenses (chapters 5–8: Communitas, Liminality, Rites of Passage, and Wilderness) is termed the lenses of infilling[1] (chapter 9); and the second coalescence of lenses (chapters 10 and 11: Servant Leadership and Masculine Spirituality) is termed the lenses of outpouring[2] (chapter 12). In chapters 9 and 12, the interaction of theology and social sciences is explored.

---

1. Infilling: the lenses that are the context for individual or group experience and transformation that equip people for doing leadership, serving others, and delivering effective ministry.

2. Outpouring: having been prepared through personal/group experience, the exercise of leadership and service towards others.

5

Communitas

THE CONCEPT OF *COMMUNITAS* has drawn much attention in recent times. *Leadership* incorporates elements necessary for *communitas* to emerge. The Oxford Dictionary defines *communitas* as: "a community; a body of people acting collectively"; or, in "cultural anthropology as a strong sense of solidarity and bonding that develops among people experiencing a ritual, rite of passage, or other transitional state together." These two definitions of *communitas* are clearly describing different levels of group engagement and functioning. The first may be a precursor to the greater depth embodied in the second, and it is the second that more closely describes the approach taken here, as further developed by Edith Turner[1]:

> Communitas is inspired fellowship; a group's pleasure in sharing common experiences; being "in the zone"—as in music, sport, and work; the sense felt by a group when their life together takes on full meaning. The experience of communitas, almost beyond strict definition and with almost endless variations, often appears unexpectedly.

Review of Theory

Based on his understanding of Victor Turner's work on rites of passage experiences of African tribes, and then writing in the context of missional church, or missional *communitas*, Alan Hirsch considers that *communitas*

---

1. Turner, *Communitas*.

and liminality (see chapter 6) are always linked; and that *communitas* involves a "unique experience of *togetherness*."[2] Interest within the US summer camp phenomenon supplements this work[3] and retreat literature is helpful in drawing some of the identified themes together. A study by Timothy Nagy of a retreat for young adult college students[4] draws together much of the essence of *Leadership*. This includes placement in a small group, a reserved demographic, sharing personally and deeply, the emergence of a spontaneous *communitas*, the existence of unique leadership rituals, symbols and philosophies, and the establishment of a leadership environment/community, as well as liminality and rites of passage (explored in chapter 7)—particularly relevant in the Solo experience in Stage 2 of *Leadership*, where status and identity are stripped away in a liminal space experience for three days alone in the bush. Sacred spaces are identified, and silence and solitude are practiced, all related to the emergence of *communitas*.

The major application of *communitas* to *Leadership* is the small group, particularly in Stage 1, continuing into Stage 2, but of less significance in Stage 3 where the whole-stage group is the general focus. The significance of what becomes My Group in Stage 1 has been acknowledged. Because participants relate experiences that are similar to the elements described as an experience of *communitas*, this concept, applied to the My Group phenomenon and other aspects of the program, is a useful lens through which the program is examined.

Communitas may be referred to as a "pivotal moment"[5] or "turning point."[6] Experiencing *communitas* is also similar to the description of "experiencing epic":[7]

> The Epic is not something you plan, really.
> It's something you find yourself swept up into—often in spite of all your plans.
> And the thing is, typically it starts out so unassumingly, so very un-epic, you have no idea what you are actually headed for. Or what it will cost you.

2. Hirsch, *Forgotten Ways*, 221.

3. Sorenson, "Summer Camp"; Bialeschki et al., "Camp Experiences"; Kendellen et al., "Facilitators and Barriers."

4. Nagy, "Lens of Liminality."

5. Corvig, "Lessons in Leadership," 15.

6. Dawes and Larson, "How Youth Get Engaged," 265.

7. Eldredge (Padre), "Momentum."

This quote resonates with the current discussion and extends the idea in this analysis of the *Leadership* program and *communitas*. The concept of epic[8] or *communitas* adopted here is to do with a personal story in the context of God's story, sharing exciting events and adventures in spiritual and personal realms. It leads to a transformational experience and has application to young men. Sharing of a personal story, by group facilitators and by participants, has already been recognized as a key to the development of *communitas*. The theological aspects are further explored in chapter 9.

Categories of Communitas

Victor Turner considers the relationship between *communitas* and structure.[9] He suggests that "the spontaneity and immediacy of communitas . . . can seldom be maintained for very long. Communitas itself soon develops as structure." He proposes three categories of *communitas*: "existential or spontaneous communitas," "normative communitas" (where "existential communitas is organised into a . . . social system"), and "ideological communitas" ("models of societies based on existential communitas"). Turner is applying *communitas* to an organizational setting over time—not within a temporary community such as *Leadership*, where structure seems to be the antithesis of *communitas*. The category adopted in this study is spontaneous *communitas*, applied in a short-term community. It is acknowledged that "spontaneous communitas is a phase, a moment, not a permanent condition,"[10] and requires renewal to be sustained.

Process of Communitas

Turner adopts the concept of "instant mutuality when each person fully experiences the being of another."[11] He then draws on Martin Buber for

---

8. The traditional definition of "epic" relates to poetry—an epic poem, with legendary or traditional heroes (see Free Dictionary, "epic"); a brave story, a story about exciting events or adventures (see Merriam-Webster, "epic"). Other definitions include: imposing, impressive, surpassing the ordinary, and the internet slang, "extremely awesome" (see Internet Slang, "epic"). It is also acknowledged that John Eldredge has written "Epic: The Story God is Telling" and, through him and his son, Sam, there is a link with their "And Sons Magazine."

9. Turner, *Ritual Process*, 132.
10. Turner, *Ritual Process*, 140.
11. Turner, *Ritual Process*, 136.

further development of this thought: "only men who are capable of truly saying *Thou to* one another can truly say *We with* one another."[12] *We* cannot arise if someone in the group is using greed, power, or self-importance. This was demonstrated in the researcher's observation of two contrasting *Leadership* Stage 1 groups. In one group, a participant so dominated the group with his own voice and needs that neither *we* nor *communitas* could emerge. In the other, *communitas* was almost immediate. The group adopted norms for functioning where all were able to have a say and there was affirmation and acknowledgment of every member. The older, more mature, more physical members of the group did not dominate as they may have been able to but took the lead often in ensuring all were listened to and valued.

Hirsch identifies other beneficial ingredients that enhance the development of *communitas*. In considering "missional leadership," he suggests this "involves facilitating the emergence of novelty by building and nurturing networks of communications, creating a learning culture where questioning is encouraged and innovation is rewarded, creating a climate of trust and mutual support, and recognizing viable novelty when it emerges, while affirming the freedom to make mistakes."[13] These are desired ingredients of *Leadership communitas*: encouraging novelty and questioning, rewarding innovation, building a climate of trust and support, allowing freedom to be oneself, providing challenge, encouraging the development of goals, moving out of one's comfort zone, risk-taking, adventure, embarking on a common mission of discovery, and finding each other. If these characteristics are present, this may be why *communitas* occurs so spontaneously and may contribute to understanding the apparent success of *Leadership*.

Examples of Communitas

Referring again to the work of Victor Turner, Hirsch comments: "*Communitas* in his [Turner's] view now *happens* in situations where individuals are driven to find each other through common experiences of ordeal, humbling, transition, and marginalization. It involves intense feelings of social togetherness and belonging brought about by having to rely on each other in order to survive." He continues that in *communitas*, "in the context of a shared ordeal, the boys [undertaking the rites of passage together] 'find'

---

12. Buber, *Between Man and Man*, 213–14.
13. Hirsch, *Forgotten Ways*, 233.

each other in new ways. They experience newfound comradery," involving "adventure and movement and it describes that unique experience of *togetherness*."[14]

The young adult retreat study by Nagy referenced above proposes that "this retreat inspires faith sharing due to its establishment of cultural forms, including rituals, Ignatian Spirituality,[15] and symbols, in a sacred space which, upon participation, creates a quasi-spontaneous *communitas*, that is conducive to faith sharing" or, "sharing personal story with a group."[16] In investigating certain aspects of *Leadership*, Smith noted: "Sacred spaces are identified; silence and solitude are practiced. Two *Leadership* participants when interviewed referred to the silence of Solo, likening this to the Elijah (1 Kgs 19:11–13) story of experiencing the presence of God, not in the wind, earthquake, or fire, but in the silence ('the gentle whisper')."[17] In part I, sharing of one's personal story is identified as a key factor, even a critical stimulus, in the development of *communitas* at *Leadership*. This is consistent with a conclusion of Nagy that retreats intentionally structured to build effective *communitas* "can be channels for helping young adults to open up, address fears and issues, and plan for the future."[18] Much of the essence of the discussion of Nagy describes *Leadership* and leads into a brief consideration of the link with liminality.

Communitas and Liminality

Though the choice in this research study is to deal with *communitas* and liminality as separate concepts, it is acknowledged that often these two concepts are linked.[19] Hirsch articulates a theology of *communitas*, using as his evidence the liminal experience of Abraham in moving towards the promised land, "the profoundly liminal exodus experience," the themes of liminality and *communitas* from the "lives and ministries of Samuel, Elijah,

---

14. Hirsch, *Forgotten Ways*, 221.

15. Ignatian spirituality is a spirituality for everyday life. It insists that God is present in our world and active in our lives. It is a pathway to deeper prayer, good decisions guided by keen discernment, and an active life of service to others. See IgnatianSpirituality.com, "What Is?"

16. Nagy, "Lens of Liminality," 41.

17. Smith, "Leadership Development Program," 84.

18. Nagy, "Lens of Liminality," 58–59.

19. Lee and Cowan, "Priority Concerns"; Hirsch, *Forgotten Ways*, 223.

PART II: LENSES

Samson, and David," "the book of Acts ... so brimful with *communitas* and liminality," and concludes that "liminality and *communitas* are normative for pilgrim people of God in the Bible."[20] Turner suggests that spontaneous *communitas* "appears to flourish best in spontaneous liminal situations—phases betwixt and between states where social-structural role-playing is dominant, and especially between status equals."[21] "Creating a vigorous transformative vision can also create liminality along with the resultant *communitas*."[22]

The Research Findings

Zirschky, cited in chapter 2, describes the characteristics of a group experiencing communion as "being present with, for, and within one another"; "sharing of themselves deeply" as in (1 Cor 2:26); "not merely to hear ... but to listen with the intention of understanding"; "actively giving of oneself for the other."[23] These characteristics of an effective small group lead into an examination of *communitas* in the *Leadership* context.

In preparation towards applying the lens of *communitas*, research survey respondents were asked what the key stimulus event was when their Stage 1 group became a well-functioning and caring team. A variety of different events were identified as significant to individuals—see table 4 in chapter 2. Two key events were My Group, including *opening up* to one another, and taking the risk of sharing; and the Overnight Expedition, including the reflection and honesty in discussions after the event. These were followed by Music Workshop. It is noted that the Overnight Expedition and Music Workshop were frequently regarded as being critical positive group experiences.

Drawing on Buber,[24] Turner,[25] Hirsch,[26] and Nagy,[27] a series of characteristics identified with *communitas* was put to survey respondents, along with other options to see what factors were of similar or different

20. Hirsch, *Forgotten Ways*, 223.
21. Turner, *Ritual Process*, 138.
22. Hirsch, *Forgotten Ways*, 232.
23. Zirschky, *Beyond the Screen*, 95, 97.
24. Buber, *Between Man and Man*.
25. Turner, *Ritual Process*.
26. Hirsch, *Forgotten Ways*.
27. Nagy, "Lens of Liminality."

importance. Survey respondents were invited to select up to five possibilities from a given list.

One hundred and twenty-four responded to this invitation. Overall, fourteen different *pivotal moments* were nominated in their top five, each by more than 20 percent of respondents. The full list is outlined in table 20 indicating which pivotal moments were most highly chosen as well as which moments were not often chosen.

PIVOTAL MOMENT	RESPONDENTS (%)
Sharing stories—personally and deeply	54.3
A climate of trust and mutual support	38.8
Our facilitator	29.5
People listening for understanding	28.7
The experience of comradery and togetherness	27.9
Freedom to make mistakes	27.1
A sense of adventure experienced together	27.1
Freedom to be ourselves	24.0
The *Leadership* environment	24.0
The safe environment	23.3
Discovering each other in a real way	23.3
A mix of different people together	21.7
We had a challenge to work on	21.7
Having goals to achieve	20.2
Freedom to ask questions	18.6
Having a common mission	17.8
A non-usual environment	13.2
People giving of themselves for others	13.2
Risk-taking was OK	12.4
Innovation and experimentation supported	7.8
We were in an established culture	7.8
We experienced instant mutuality—fully experiencing the being of others	7.0
A ritual, symbol or tradition	7.0
Sacred spaces	5.4
Freedom to set our own agenda	4.7
Liminal space	3.9

PART II: LENSES

PIVOTAL MOMENT	RESPONDENTS (%)
Silence; solitude	3.1
The novelty	2.3

Table 20. Pivotal Moments in Achieving *Communitas*

Sharing of one's personal story—personally and deeply—within the group was rated highest in contributing to *communitas*, confirming the findings in part I. That moment, pivotal to their group arriving at *communitas*, was identified by 54.3 percent of respondents, far more highly than any other possibility, the next highest being *a climate of trust and mutual support* at 38.8 percent, reflecting the themes of acceptance and support that mark participants' view of *Leadership* at every point. Next was *our facilitator* at 29.5 percent, pointing to the role of staff, and then a wide selection of other moments that were pivotal to between 28.7 percent and 20.2 percent of respondents. The other key pivotal moments, chosen by 20 percent or more as indicators of *communitas*, are the *experience of comradery and togetherness* (27.9%), *freedom to make mistakes* (27.1%), *a sense of adventure experienced together* (27.1%), *freedom to be ourselves* (24.0%), *discovering each other in a real way* (23.3%), *having a challenge to work on* (21.7%), and *having goals to achieve* (20.2%).

Except for *novelty* and *innovation*,[28] responses were similar to those identified by Buber[29] and Hirsch[30] as indicators. However, there were some other moments chosen in the top five by at least 20 percent of respondents that are not specifically indicators of *communitas* identified in the literature, including *our facilitator* (29.5%), *people listening for understanding* (28.7%), *the Leadership environment* (24.0%), *the safe environment* (23.3%), and *a mix of different people together* (21.7%).

Thus, it is noted that participants identified some characteristics connected to *communitas*, that other research has not identified, in particular, the two moments that refer to the established environment.

The *culture, ritual, sacred spaces, liminal space,* and *silence/solitude* were not rated highly—possibly an unexplored or unarticulated area for fifteen-year-old young men. The understanding of these elements appears

28. Hirsch, *Forgotten Ways*, 233.
29. Buber, *Between Man and Man*.
30. Hirsch, *Forgotten Ways*.

to grow across stages, as in Stage 2, where the silence/solitude of Solo and the symbolism of rocks and ceremony is highly regarded, and in Stage 3, with the symbolism of a sword and the regard in which ceremony is held. In being limited to five choices, characteristics regarded as the most highly significant emerged, which does not mean that other lesser-selected characteristics were unimportant.

Participant respondents rated the role of their *facilitator* (33.3% or the third highest) and the *experience of comradery and togetherness* (30.1% or fourth highest) more highly as pivotal moments than did staff respondents (both at 19.4%); staff respondents regarded that they *had a challenge to work on* and the non-usual *environment* more highly than did participant respondents (29.0% compared with 17.2%). These differences may be accounted for by the normal adolescent regard for their mentors and teachers (facilitators) and that staff respondents are more attuned to seeing the significance of challenge and environment. Staff generally are highly significant to the development of *communitas* and the delivery of the program.

Summary of Chapter

Communitas is not merely community, though it occurs within community. It usually emerges in a small group that may be part of a larger community or *societas*. Ideally, the group does not have a strict structure or expectation imposed on it. It may have a loose agenda or list of work to be done, but also the freedom to manage its own agenda, timing, and the like.

The most common elements that are conducive to the emergence of *communitas* are that the group has a challenge to work on; some hard work to do; an adventure to experience together. It will be in a non-usual environment, have a sense of novelty, freedom to be oneself, with disparate participants forming the group so they have opportunity to discover one another, leading to sharing something deep inside each member. Questioning, risk-taking, and experimentation are encouraged and making mistakes is acceptable. Innovation is rewarded. A climate of essential and ultimate trust is established. These elements add to the observation that the *Leadership* program does incorporate elements necessary for *communitas*.

Communitas is present during rites of passage or other ritual experiences or ceremonies; it occurs in situations of liminality such as during a retreat. This may be accompanied by an established culture, including rituals and symbols. *Communitas* can be transformative for a group and an individual member. Participants may experience a newfound "comradery"[31] and togetherness.[32] The emergence of *communitas* is usually spontaneous and its timing unpredictable. It may be described as the arrival of "instant mutuality when each person fully experiences the being of another"[33]—a sense of *We*.[34] The research findings were that participants report experiencing characteristics of *communitas*.

Communitas needs to be refueled, or it may retreat into satisfaction with what has been achieved, or into mere formality or structure. New challenges, to go further, need to be introduced and this itself be mutually accepted as a continuing ingredient of *communitas* within the group. The link *communitas* has with liminality and rites of passage has been acknowledged and will be considered in chapter 9, linking theological reflection with social science insights through mutual critical correlation.

The findings have indicated that characteristics of the theoretical lens of *communitas* are evident in the *Leadership* program, particularly in the small group experience in Stage 1. *Leadership* matches the adopted Edith Turner definition of *communitas* with its elements of inspired fellowship, pleasure in sharing common experiences, being in *the zone*, and a sense felt when life together takes on full meaning.[35] This examination of the program through the lens of *communitas* does assist in establishing the apparent success of the program and acknowledges the unique role of staff, particularly group facilitators. *Communitas* is the essence of the unique *Leadership* group experience. Other emerging themes of *Leadership* that are confirmed through the lens of *communitas* are acceptance (the importance of the climate of trust and support) and freedom (to make mistakes and be ourselves). Theological reflection on *communitas* is continued in chapter 9 as this lens and others are linked in coalescence.

---

31. Turner, *Ritual Process*, 134.
32. Hirsch, *Forgotten Ways*, 240.
33. Turner, *Ritual Process*.
34. Buber, *Between Man and Man*, 62.
35. Turner, *Communitas*.

6

Liminality

WHILE IT IS PROGRESSIVE across the three *Leadership* course stages, change and transformation is most marked in Stage 1. This is most likely because when first encountering the experience, the concepts presented are dramatically different to their experience in their world. That impact continues in later stages, where it is more targeted in activities such as Solo. In theoretical terms, this may be understood as creating situations of *cognitive dissonance*,[1] that lead to entry into *liminal space* that is accommodated often through transformational change.

Review of Theory

As noted, *communitas* and liminality are frequently linked and claimed to be interdependent. Liminality is dealt with here as a separate concept, commencing with reference to the work of Victor Turner, who describes liminality as "the transition process accompanying a fundamental change of state or social position."[2] One moves from a context of security (safety, nurture, security, protection) into a context of liminality (ordeal, danger,

---

1. Cognitive dissonance occurs when new ideas or experiences are encountered that challenge one's existing views. It may create discomfort or challenge one's equilibrium or lead to feelings of vulnerability and an experience of being in liminal space, requiring accommodation of the new ideas or experiences. Introduced carefully, it is a useful strategy to challenge a person towards new thinking and transformation.

2. Turner, *Ritual Process*, 220, 221.

marginality, adventure). The *Leadership* group provides the potential ordeal and adventure, but also the opportunity, safety, and freedom to explore, suggesting that liminality may be a factor related to the apparent success of *Leadership*.

Richard Rohr offers helpful descriptions of liminal space (sometimes referred to as *threshold space*) in making the major point that "all transformation takes place in liminal space." The characteristics he lists include, being "betwixt and between," having "left one room but not yet entered the next room," being "between stages of life [or] . . . faith," being in a "teachable space." He adds that liminal space does not occur in a "once-a-week church service" but that it needs "something longer, different, and daring."[3]

Hirsch offers some summary statements that are helpful: "*Liminality* therefore applies to that situation where people find themselves in an in-between, marginal state in relation to the surrounding society, a place that could involve significant danger and disorientation, but not necessarily so."[4] The links between *communitas*, liminality, and rites of passage are important in reviewing the apparent success of *Leadership*, with the rites of passage experience emerging from an individual's liminality. In the context of *Leadership*, liminality theory has a positive connotation, encouraging participants to look forward towards new understandings, new experiences, and new statuses. There is currently expanding literature on liminality, including in Christian literature, popular writing, and scholarship. This will be further examined in chapter 9, including reference to Baker,[5] and to Best,[6] who introduces an application of liminality to the COVID-19 pandemic. At *Leadership*, even encountering the new experience of servant leadership, a lens to be considered later, may have a liminal aspect.

The Research Findings

Survey respondents were asked if they remembered staff talking about being in liminal space, and if so, to select up to three possible occasions during *Leadership* that they most felt they were in liminal space. Responses are set out in table 21. What is most nominated and what is least commonly nominated are important.

3. Rohr, *Adam's Return*, 135–36.
4. Hirsch, *Forgotten Ways*, 221.
5. Baker, "Welcome to the Bubble."
6. Best, "Liminality, Communitas, and Hope."

OCCASION	PARTICIPANT RESPONDENTS (%)	STAFF RESPONDENTS (%)	EXPERIENCED STAFF (12) (%)
During Solo	55.0	87.5	75.0
The whole of Stage 1	30.0	50.0	25.0
Arriving for Stage 1	20.0	25.0	16.7
During Duo	25.0	12.5	0.0
Arriving for Stage 3	20.0	12.5	0.0
During Music Workshop	15.0	25.0	41.7
Arriving for Stage 2	15.0	12.5	0.0
Delivering my mission statement in public	10.0	25.0	33.3
My first group session in Stage 1	15.0	12.5	16.7
On Overnight Expedition	10.0	0.0	25.0
Black Shirts session in Stage 2	5.0	12.5	8.3
My first opening service	5.0	12.5	0.0
The introductory session for Stage 1 (White Shirt session)	5.0	0.0	33.3
The "Tough Bits" session	0.0	0.0	0.0

Table 21. Occasions Most Felt in Liminal Space

This question was only responded to by twenty-eight participants, indicating a low level of understanding of the concept of liminality (a number had not yet completed Stage 2 where the concept of liminality is specifically introduced)—something confirmed during interviews, though in the case of a participant who completed Stage 3 in 2019 and surprisingly another who completed Stage 1 in 2019, detailed understandings were expressed:

> Ah. Yes. I remember liminal space quite well. Liminal space is a place of being between places. It's a place of uncertainty, in a holding pattern. But liminal space always had somewhere to go and it's always comes from somewhere so it is an area where you're stepping into something new. Solo is an example of liminal space. The whole idea is being in a holding pattern that was solo—day, night, day, night, day, night, day. (Stage 3, 2019)

PART II: LENSES

> It's a new concept in exercising it and using the terminology. But the overall idea's not; the meaning is not new. But I think Leadership makes a conscious effort to promote the value of liminal space and its development in the design of the course. (It is) space for self-reflection. The relative isolation of Camp Somerset and spaces throughout the course. The idea of separation and site to slowly remove yourself and then bring yourself back to God. (Stage 1, 2019)

There are some differences between participant respondents and staff respondents which throw some light on participants' responses. Participant respondents were the only group to acknowledge the Stage 3 experiences (during Duo and arriving for Stage 3) as liminal experiences of any note, indicting, as noted elsewhere, that Stage 3 is a highly emotional experience for those participating in it at the end of their *Leadership* journey. To them, that is liminal, rather than delivering their mission statement in the presence of their mates. Staff respondents felt Music Workshop (Stage 1) and delivering one's mission statement in public (Stage 3) to be more a liminal experience than did participant respondents. The most striking differences are the 33.3 percent of experienced staff who nominated as liminal the introductory session for Stage 1 (as compared with 5% of participant respondents) and 25 percent who nominated the Overnight Expedition (as compared with 10% of participant respondents), indicating that they expected there to be a liminal experience when there was not. Either participants did not recognize this or were comfortable in those spaces. The latter understanding is consistent with other findings. What participants see as more stressful and liminal are activities done alone or before they are in their groups—arriving for each stage, during Solo and, during Duo. Only Solo has a common understanding across participant and staff groups as being the most liminal experience—an experience that quickly dissipates as they enter a post-Solo celebration with their mates in their group. Experiences in their groups are less likely to be stressful, and less likely to be seen as liminal than other experiences, or participants embrace liminal space in group activities as a vehicle towards achieving desired and shared outcomes.

The experience of entering, being in, and exiting liminal space is presented to participants in each stage as a series of roller-coaster experiences represented in figures 4, 5, and 6.

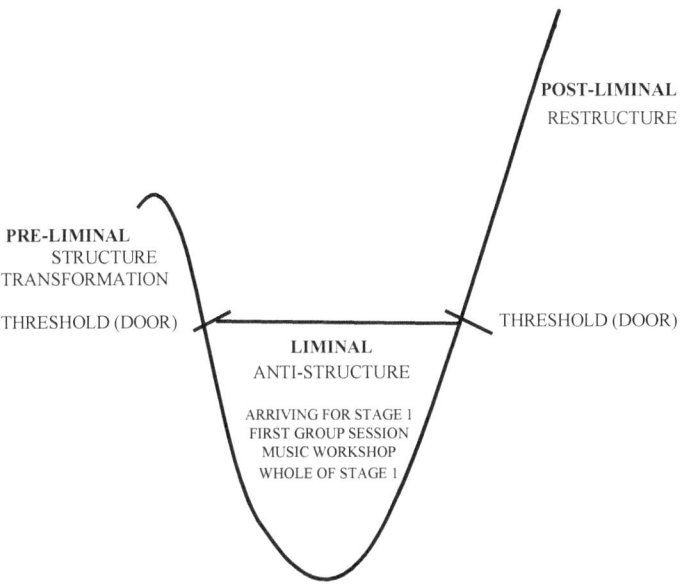

Figure 3. Movement through Liminal Space in Stage 1

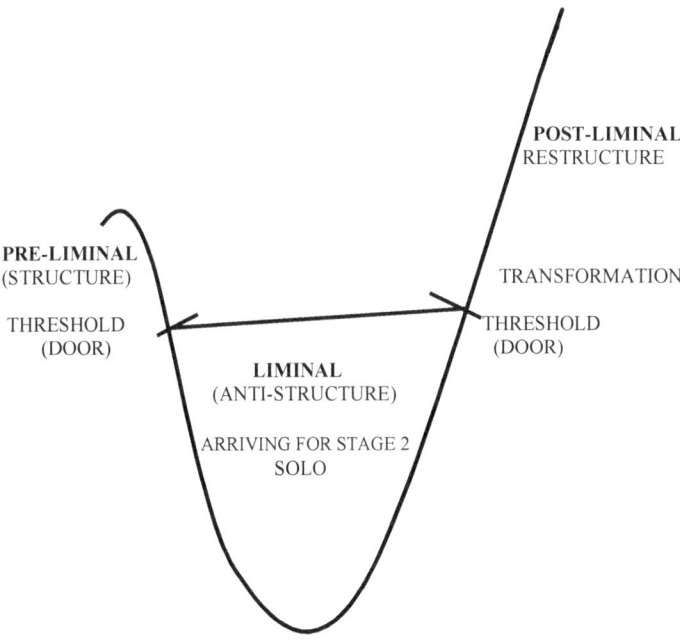

Figure 4. Movement through Liminal Space in Stage 1

PART II: LENSES

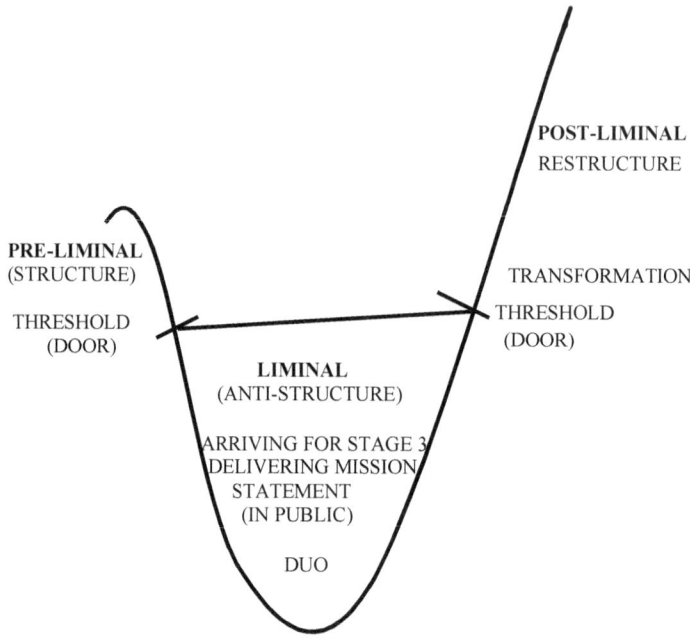

Figure 5. Movement through Liminal Space in Stage 3

In *Leadership* Stage 1, the concepts presented include servanthood, equality, relationships (rather than rules or responsibilities), experienced in a small group and a course community that is unique—different to anything previously experienced. This creates situations that have the potential for experiencing cognitive dissonance, liminal space, and transformational change. Stage 2 participants, pre-Solo, are presented with paradoxes to challenge their equilibrium or *normal* thinking related to male initiation and as they prepare to commence Solo are presented with the concept of liminal space, named and explained in these terms:

- You are leaving the trappings of your ordinary life behind.
- Again, coming back to *Leadership*, you have exited one door, but have not yet entered the next door.
- You experienced liminal space in coming to Stage 1.
- Solo will be a new liminal experience.

The twenty-eight who responded to the survey question as to whether they remembered staff talking about liminal space, identified sixty-nine statements explaining their liminal space experience (they were each able to choose up to three)—93 percent of responses coming from those who had done the Stage 2 course. Their responses are collated in table 22.

STATEMENT	PARTICIPANT RESPONDENTS (%)	STAFF RESPONDENTS (%)	EXPERIENCED STAFF (%)
It started me off on some new thinking	45.0	12.5	23.1
Being between stages of life	40.0	37.5	23.1
Being in transition	30.0	37.5	53.9
Leaving behind situations of security, protection, safety	20.0	50.0	30.8
Having left one room but not yet entered the next room	20.0	12.5	53.9
I made a permanent change	20.0	0.0	7.7
Being in a teachable space (a learning space)	15.0	12.5	30.8
A feeling or disorientation	15.0	12.5	15.4
Doing something different and daring	10.0	25.0	0.0
It provided learning moments	10.0	12.5	15.4
Being in a space of ordeal, danger, marginality, adventure	10.0	0.0	0.0
It made me feel uncomfortable	10.0	12.5	7.7
Being between stages of faith	5.0	25.0	0.0
It was transformational	5.0	12.5	7.7
Being betwixt and between	5.0	12.5	15.4
I adopted a different way of understanding or explaining something	5.0	0.0	7.7

PART II: LENSES

STATEMENT	PARTICIPANT RESPONDENTS (%)	STAFF RESPONDENTS (%)	EXPERIENCED STAFF (%)
Having left my ordinary life behind	0.0	12.5	7.7
Being expected to adopt a stance of servant leadership	0.0	0.0	0.0

Table 22. Statements Explaining Experience of Liminal Space

Participant respondents explain their experiences as: that it *started me off on some new thinking*, *being between stages of life*, and *being in transition*. Staff respondents explain it as: *leaving behind situations of security, protection, safety*, then *being between stages of life* or *being in transition*. Experienced staff offered different responses: *being in transition* and *having left one room but not yet entered the next room* (this being a standard explanation of liminal space which staff use). However, the apparent differences between groups are not that great in reality, as one focus group respondent explained:

> When I was looking at liminal space and you see there's a big disparity between what the participants say and what the staff say, I think that is purely an understanding of the concept and that once the staff start understanding the concept and they're not 17 anymore, they start seeing it. Rather than recognizing oh I'm in liminal space, they're re-evaluating their whole from within as they understand things, which I think is what that big gap is. I don't think it's a disparity in actuality. I think it's just understanding.

Participants and staff saw liminal space as something in between—between stages of life, between situations of security or between rooms, with a hope that there was something new to come. It is noteworthy that participant respondents chose new thinking and making a permanent change when staff respondents did not.

A final word on liminality and linking it to the life of Jesus, in the moving from one place to another, comes from another focus group member:

> What I liked about that was it's true, and we would see this in the life of Jesus that spirituality is an opportunity in all aspects and not just those that are primarily designed to attack a problem or create a solution but seen as you're walking from one place to another. There's an opportunity there and we would hope, that's the case.

While theorists link the concepts of liminality and *communitas*,[7] this is not what survey respondents did. This may simply be because *communitas* was explained in detail in the survey, but liminality was not. Although liminality is a common ingredient both for individual transformation and the group experience of *communitas*, it is not necessary to articulate it, label it, or even to understand it.

Summary of Chapter

Liminality is linked with *communitas* and rites of passage events. It is described in different ways: in transition, threshold space, being "betwixt and between," between stages, leaving something behind to name a few. Liminality or liminal space is not frequently articulated by *Leadership* participants. However, it is recognized as an element of the program at several points. Passing through liminal space frequently leads to transformation. Three phases are recognized: pre-liminal, liminal, and post-liminal. In *Leadership*, liminality is present when arriving for each new stage (the unknown). It is experienced for the whole of Stage 1, specifically so at the first group session and Music Workshop. In Stage 2, Solo is the most obvious liminal experience. In Stage 3, it is Duo and for some, delivering their mission statement in public. However, it is less a factor in activities that are within the safety of their group: the Overnight Expedition in Stage 1, and for many, the mission statement declared with their mates in Stage 3.

---

7. Lee and Cowan, "Priority Concerns"; Hirsch, *Forgotten Ways*.

7

Rites of Passage

Everyone really becomes a man at their own time.

RITES OF PASSAGE IS a developing area of interest in meeting the needs of men, with many revisiting tribal and early church initiation ceremonies.[1] The concept and practice of rites of passage for young men—the end of the transition phase between boy and man—has been incorporated into the *Leadership* program. A specific example in Stage 2 Solo preparation sessions is drawn from the work of Richard Rohr—his five essential messages of male initiation,[2] which participants are invited to reflect on as they consider their own journey towards becoming men:

1. Life is hard.
2. You are not important.
3. Your life is not about you.
4. You are not in control.
5. You are going to die.

Rites of passage is a useful lens through which to understand the program and how it is valued by participants and staff. The findings include

---

1. Eldredge, *Wild at Heart*; *Fathered by God*; Rohr, *Adam's Return*; "Masculine Spirituality."
2. Rohr, *Adam's Return*.

reference to the concept, becoming a man. This is important in response to the perceived needs of boys, such as the need for fathering, and is a program element positively highlighted by participants, including fatherless boys (see chapter 3).

Review of Theory

The term *rites of passage* was coined and described by Van Gennep.[3] His seminal work is acknowledged, even today. The three phases he outlined: separation (pre-liminal rites), transition (liminal rites), and incorporation (post-liminal rites) still mark contemporary practices. A further important point made by Van Gennep is "that the passage from one social position to another is identified with a *territorial passage*, such as the entrance into a village or a house, the movement from one room to another, or the crossing of streets or squares." Wilson paraphrases Van Gennep's description of rites of passage as "rituals performed at major transition points in a person's life and are designed to facilitate these transitions, both for the individual and for the society recognizing the person's change of status."[4] The interest for the research on *Leadership* is the rites of passage from boyhood to manhood. Emphasizing its importance, Wilson refers to this "change from childhood to adulthood [as] one of the most significant social and psychological transitions in a man's life." Importantly, he also acknowledges that in rites of passage, there are considerable cultural differences in age/stage, cultural recognition, ritual, myths, and stories.[5] Consideration of rites of passage as an informing theory brings together the historical and the contemporary and exposes gaps in the modern literature at a time of renewed interest in this concept. It explores whether this is an element contributing to the apparent success of the *Leadership* program.

In the 1990s, in Western society, concerns were emerging for boys and men. It was noted that boys were failing at school and were lacking fathering.[6] There was a desire to unlock the key to how boys become fine men[7]

---

3. Van Gennep, *Rites of Passage*, 192.
4. Wilson, *Making Men*, 8–9.
5. Wilson, *Making Men*, 1.
6. The Australian Government, Department of Education, Science and Training commissioned a report "prompted by contemporary concerns about boys' schooling." Lingard et al., "Educational Needs."
7. For example, a "Boys to Fine Men" Conference in 2003 (University of Newcastle).

PART II: LENSES

and rites of passage became a topic of interest, including in Christian communities.[8] This interest persisted into the first decade of the twenty-first century and was often popularized by Christian writers.[9] Tribal initiation ceremonies were revisited, most notable that of the Massai people and their practice of requiring a boy to kill a lion as a pre-requirement to initiation, which became symbolic of male initiation,[10] and the practices of Indigenous Australians were included in the discussion, as Van Gennep had done earlier and later by Rohr.[11] Early church ceremonies were also revisited, in particular, confirmation and baptism.[12]

Further contextualizing the situation, Karianjahi reflects that with industrialization and modernization, and in some cases economic pressure and urbanization, "transition markers," "anchorage points," and rites of passage for youth to adulthood have been lost, along with the "loss of identity and clarity of roles." This has come with "the manifestation of risky behaviour as youth experiment with perceived adult privileges," while "older generations have unwittingly abandoned their responsibilities of passing on community values and mores to younger generations, alienating youth from mainstream culture."[13]

What were the initiating events of modern Western society? It is unclear how Australian boys transitioned to manhood over the years. For some it was through apprenticeships such as working with their fathers on their farms or in their trades. For other boys, during the First and Second World Wars it was enlistment, which may account for the incidence of underage enlistment of boys searching for a masculine identity. Though that was often in the name of patriotism, to serve "God, King and Country," the recruitment posters left no doubt that it was a call to stand up as a man and a call into a different status. In considering the coming to adulthood in America, Hine observed that "compared with most other societies, ours [American] is short on ritual that meaningfully recognise young people's

---

8. Lee and Clark, *Boys to Men*; Lewis, *Modern-Day Knight*.

9. Davis, *Extreme Pursuit*; Eldredge, *Wild at Heart*; *Way of the Wild*; Farrar, *King Me*; Molitor, *Boy's Passage*; Moore, *Rite of Passage*; Rohr, *Adam's Return*.

10. Molitor, *Boys' Passage*.

11. Van Gennup, *Rites of Passage*, xvii, 79, 84; Rohr, *Adam's Return*, 14–15; "Masculine Spirituality."

12. Rohr, *Adam's Return*; "Masculine Spirituality."

13. Karianjahi, "Church as Village," 10.

arrival at maturity."[14] In identifying the senior prom as "one of the few" examples, he then dismisses this event, noting that there is a "more recent tendency by young people to use the event [the senior prom] as an aggressive assertion of maturity," rather than a rite of passage.

In today's complex world, with changes to social structures, the pathway to manhood has become unclear, if it ever *was* clear. Before the industrial revolution, boys did not experience adolescence; they became men and took adult responsibilities when they went to work. Jesus had no need for adolescence. He moved from boy to man through a rite of passage experience in Jerusalem when aged twelve years (Luke 2:41–52). Moore[15] highlights the negatives of the cultural invention of adolescence for delaying attainment of adulthood (manhood for boys), a phase that is extending its age spread in both directions (beginning earlier and ending later).

In Australia and elsewhere, factors such as an increase in fatherless families, the failure of boys at school, an increase in male gangs, and substance abuse and violence led to a renewed interest in rites of passage, or the apparent lack of them, to manhood.[16] There was concern that in the absence of clear and legitimate rites of passage, boys would and do find other rites as they seek to experiment with what it is to be a man and achieve that status. They will look to other uninitiated boys to initiate them and they will look to girls to affirm their manhood, creating "pseudo rites of passage."[17] Attempts at self-initiation or peer-to-peer initiation such as dangerous physical risk-taking, alcohol or other substance abuse, driving recklessly, and youth-to-youth physical violence in the name of proving one's manhood, have led to serious physical injury or death. These and other activities, such as engaging in sexual exploits to prove one's manhood, may have serious legal or psychological consequences. Moore noted that "boys are engaging in higher levels of extreme behaviour than ever before" (from as young as nine) and even if not directly involved, they "are influenced by peers and the media that suggest that these behaviors [for example, pornography and substance abuse] define masculinity."[18] Historically, there are biblical examples of transitions from boy to man. A selection of these is considered, and then some contemporary examples.

14. Hine, *Rise and Fall*, 13, 14.
15. Moore, *Rite of Passage*.
16. Karianjahi, "Church as Village," 10.
17. Grof, "Rites of Passage."
18. Moore, *Rite of Passage*, 17.

PART II: LENSES

Biblical and Traditional Examples of Fathering, Mentoring, and Rites of Passage

Five approaches with a biblical or traditional significance and basis are referred to as examples. Firstly, Wilson examines the male coming-of-age theme in the Hebrew Bible.[19] McVann examines the life of Jesus and his rite of passage from "prophesised child to adult prophet."[20] New Testament relationships between older and younger men, producing strong young leaders are considered. Marcus examines the Jewish bar mitzvah[21] and an unlikely parallel is drawn by Zahniser between a Buddhist approach and Christian discipleship.[22]

The concept of coming of age or rites of passage was well established in Hebrew culture. Wilson points to the "lacuna in biblical scholarship" in "a study of biblical depictions of maturation from boyhood to manhood" and of "rites of passage" considered with "coming of age."[23] He examines masculinity in the Hebrew Bible and the exegetical application of the rites-of-passage schema to biblical narrative. Wilson[24] referenced Van Gennep[25] in referring to boys who are "not yet considered men, but who are also no longer viewed as boys." This liminal stage in some societies is related to ordeal and imparting of knowledge—removed from their society. It is hoped that this study contributes to filling the *lacuna* in scholarship generally, based on the informing theories and the characteristics they identify.

When Jesus was aged twelve, he accompanied his parents to Jerusalem for the Passover and did not join them immediately for the return journey, being found three days later sitting and communicating on an understanding level with the teachers (Luke 2:40–47). Some regard this as an early step in his rites of passage. The life of Jesus is analyzed by McVann[26] as an example of rites of passage based on the critical moments of his baptism, fasting and wilderness testing, and transition into ministry as a prophet. This is not a rite of passage from boy to man, though that may have been

19. Wilson, *Making Men*.
20. McVann, "One of the Prophets."
21. Marcus, *Jewish Life-Cycle*.
22. Zahniser, "Ritual Process."
23. Wilson, *Making Men*, 2.
24. Wilson, *Making Men*, 9.
25. Van Gennep, *Rites of Passage*.
26. McVann, "One of the Prophets."

part of it, but from a man in preparation to a prophet man. A further phase of Jesus's rite of passage, an aggregation or post-liminal phase, included preaching repentance (Matt 4:12–17), calling his disciples (Matt 4:18–22), and exercising healing miracles (Matt 4:23–25), followed soon afterwards in apparent quick succession with serious teaching (the Sermon on the Mount) (Matt 3–12).

As young men, Mark and Timothy, who became notable Christian leaders in the early church, made many mistakes and lived out their weaknesses. Before they could take their places as significant leaders (important enough to write or contribute to a book included in the Bible or have letters written to them included in the Bible and to be mentioned in other biblical writings), they needed to be mentored by older, more experienced men. In Mark's case, this was Barnabas and Peter (and even Paul in a second attempt); in Timothy's case, it was Paul. Interestingly, while their mothers are mentioned in the biblical narrative, their fathers are not mentioned in any serious way. The coming to maturity of Mark and Timothy had much to do with the element of good mentoring by older men, a characteristic of rites of passage that is repeated in other examples.

Based on an extensive examination of the cultural origins of Jewish rites and ceremonies, most developed as innovations over many years, Marcus makes the point that rites change over time and place and undergo cultural adaptation. The rite of bar mitzvah for Jewish boys is identified as one constituting a passage from boyhood to manhood. It traditionally occurs when a boy is aged thirteen years and one day. While there are differences from place to place on what religious practices a boy can engage in, if he can at all before his bar mitzvah, that ceremony is clearly described as "the age of majority for religious obligations."[27]

Having reviewed the work of Van Gennep on rites of passage, Zahniser draws from a Buddhist approach to rites of passage to propose a process for Christian discipleship, formation or "bonding to meaning" (that is, "bonding to a new identity and . . . to the community in a new way [and] . . . to the beliefs and values of that community").[28] He refers to "transmitting spiritual values or enabling bonding to meaning [as] discipleship." Adopting the theme of "identification with Christ," Zahniser[29] proposes a four-phase Christian rite of initiation and formation (or "bonding to meaning") based

27. Marcus, *Jewish Life-Cycle*, 12.
28. Zahniser, "Ritual Process," 8.
29. Zahniser, "Ritual Process," 13–14.

on early events in Jesus's life: "(1) Separation from parents; (2) Baptism; (3) Solitary ordeal; and (4) Return and proclamation in the power of the Spirit."

Christian, Jewish, and Buddhist traditions provide cultural, sometimes still developing, examples of rites of passage. Mark and Timothy were initiated into responsible manhood through being seriously mentored or discipled—as far as is known, not by their fathers but by others who adopted a father-son role with them. These examples of leaders mentoring/fathering other men's sons should be an encouragement and challenge to those today who are called to such a role, as is sometimes evident at *Leadership*—not in any way denying the primary role of fathers.[30]

Contemporary Examples of Rites of Passage

Karinjahi refers to "the rapid multiplication of rites of passage in churches and other organizations—both faith based and secular—in Kenya" in the last two decades.[31] This may reflect the African culture and be a response to the comparatively recent loss of rites of passage ceremonies and changing cultural circumstances.[32] No longer can a boy kill a lion—so, the need for an alternative is recognized. The growth in the West is much slower, although commercial and not-for-profit organizations and schools (e.g., in Australia, The Rite Journey,[33] "Time and Space,"[34] and the Rites of Passage Institute[35]) have responded to the growth of interest in rites of passage programs for boys, often at significant financial costs to participants, in two cases gaining an international clientele as well, but only reaching a small proportion of the population.

The following statement indicates the strength of Moore's view about the essential nature of a rite of passage:

---

30. In fact, within the *Leadership* program, following completion of Stage 2, with its rites of passage content, a weekend rites of passage event is offered for fathers and sons to emphasize and recognize the role of fathers.

31. Karianjahi, "Church as Village," 21.

32. Some initiation rites became illegal or inconsistent with community living or conflicted with a developing recognition of human rights.

33. Immanuel Lutheran College, "Rite Journey." See Lines and Gallasch, "Right Journey."

34. In Australian Catholic Schools—see Jennings, "I Feel Older."

35. Rites of Passage Institute, "Home."

> If you don't get a grip on Rite of Passage Parenting, your children will struggle with deep questions (When do I grow up? Who am I going to be?) for the rest of their lives. . . . Rites of passage are integral to their purpose, their identity, their reason for being on this earth. If you don't give them the key, they will not be able to unlock the door to capable, responsible, self-reliant adulthood and step into fulfilling, meaningful lives.[36]

Moore likens the rite of passage event to a lunar slingshot that "uses the gravitational pull of the moon to accelerate a spacecraft's momentum and recast its trajectory."[37] The other three essential experiences to equip boys for life that Moore identifies are: "significant tasks, logical consequences, and grace deposits."[38] Each of these occurs both before and after the rite of passage event, as preparation and later in the form of adult consequences and responsibilities in the lives of emerging adults. These additional concepts, including the essential experiences, are Moore's response to cultural shifts that he believes have been taken away from children today.

While it has been only slowly understood and adopted, there have been responses in the community generally and in the church, in America, Australia, and elsewhere, to understand and provide clear and positive rites of passage to manhood. The basis of many of these rites is that it is the boy's father who is the key figure in initiating his son to manhood and that in the absence of a father, there is a need for some other man or men to stand in the role of the boy's father. And, in all cases, the involvement of a group of men is critical for a boy to be affirmed and successfully introduced to the world of men.

Since African rites of passage ceremonies are often referred to in a review of rites of passage for boys, it is interesting to refer to a contemporary African example from Kenyan churches.[39] Claims of the ROPES (Rites of Passage Experiences) programs are that they lead to "transition into the next stages of life with more clarity about their spiritual and relational identities, strong connections with significant others, and the skills to make positive contributions in their communities, while resisting risky and negative behaviour."[40] Karinjahi cited Van Gennep and his three-phase model of a

---

36. Moore, *Rite of Passage*, 69.
37. Moore, *Rite of Passage*, 51.
38. Moore, *Rite of Passage*, 73–232.
39. Karianjahi, "Church as Village."
40. Karianjahi, "Church as Village," 5.

PART II: LENSES

rite of passage and describes each stage: "residential camp" is an example of the separation stage; the liminal period is a "time for forging strong, ordered peer and intergenerational bonds," including with "instructors, mentors and sponsors." "The connection forged between one initiate and another during the rituals is intense . . . their common liminal experience. The bond often lasts a lifetime."[41] The shift towards peers (the initiation age-set) is consistent with my findings[42] that the primary influence to continue with *Leadership* becomes the peer (age-set) group from earlier course stages. Finally, in the third stage, "re-entry into the community [occurs] with new, often more elevated statuses." "In all stages of the rite of passage then, participation from a facilitating community ['the village'] is crucial."[43]

In the diversification of rites of passage programs, though of limited reach, Karinjahi's view of the need for contextualization and cultural analysis is recognized.[44] Further research is indicated, in response to Karinjahi's observation of the "paucity . . . of empirical research on contemporary rites of passage."[45] Though he places that comment in an African context, his concern may be applied more generally.

After examining contemporary developments in rites of passage for boys, Hage suggests that often they are incomplete because they do not include "the central component of transcendental death acknowledgment[46] (Momento Mori[47])" or "an understanding of death and one's mortality." Hage[48] acknowledges the work of Rohr[49] and others (e.g., Lines and Gallasch[50]) in discussing the need for young men to learn how to deal with their pain and power, which is often abused. As others have done, Hage[51] acknowledges Van Gennep's three "patterns of events in the transition of boys to adulthood." He then cites Campbell,[52] who breaks the stages

41. Karianjahi, "Church as Village," 6–7.
42. Smith, "Leadership Development Program."
43. Karianjahi, "Church as Village," 8.
44. Karianjahi, "Church as Village," 22.
45. Karianjahi, "Church as Village," 13.
46. Hage, "Modern Boy's Rite."
47. Meaning "remember death" or "remember that you will die."
48. Hage, "Modern Boy's Rite," 215.
49. Rohr, "Masculine Spirituality."
50. Lines and Gallasch, "Rite Journey."
51. Hage, "Modern Boy's Rite," 216–19, 223.
52. Campbell, *Hero*.

into substages and includes the concept of "the hero's journey." Campbell's substages include, on separation, "the call to adventure," receiving assistance from others, entering "an area of danger," initiation into "true heroic stature through trials and rites," learning to "attend to his emotions," "atonement with his father" (or father figure), and "coming to terms with death and mortality" including "death to self." These substages may throw further light on the rites of passage experience.

The Research Findings

The three phase rites of passage framework of Van Gennep[53]—separation, transition, and incorporation—which has remained largely unchallenged in the work of contemporary scholars[54] was adopted as an indication of *Leadership* being a rites of passage event. This is consistent with biblical examples and almost invariably involves a liminal experience.

Consideration of a *becoming a man* theme leads into examination of the specific lens of rites of passage. Rites of passage follows a clear cross-stage continuum that is recognized by *Leadership* participants. It is introduced in Stage 1, embedded into the Stage 2 program (incorporating Solo and Solo Celebration, which is referred to as a rite of passage event), and continued into Stage 3. However, as one participant respondent clearly put it, one could regard the whole of *Leadership* as a rites of passage experience, or a series of such experiences, culminating in the delivery of their mission statements to conclude Stage 3. This is what he said:

> I think the Leadership course is revered as a rite of passage itself among brigade companies. I think this greater rite of passage also comes back to the course rite of passage, with the choice to leave as a man. I think society paints too broad and weak a picture of what a man should be. Giving me new direction on what a man actually looks like, I was able to choose for myself to become one. No one could make the choice for me and publicly declaring it in stage 3 was a large part of my path to manhood. (Stage 3, 2010)

A further relevant comment came in the invitation to comment on the becoming a man theme:

---

53. Van Gennup, *Rites of Passage*.
54. Campbell, *Hero*; Rohr, "Masculine Spirituality"; Hage, "Modern Boy's Rite"; Karianjahi, "Church as Village."

> I don't remember it being referred to as a rite of passage. Which I really like. I think "Rites of Passage" has become a bit of a buzz phrase, particularly with Christian youth. Leadership instead just did it. The feeling you get, the feeling of becoming a man doesn't deserve to be cheapened with a label. (Stage 2, 2015)

After acknowledging that different experiences are meaningful to different people in "Rites of Passage" from boy to man, in the context of Stage 2 where it is a part of the program, respondents were asked to select up to three *Leadership* experiences from a given list of sixteen possibilities that were the most significant for them towards being recognized as becoming a man. The results, in order of significance of the ten most selected, are set out in table 23.

EXPERIENCE	RESPONDENTS (%)
Solo	48.2
The desire to enter a new phase of life	37.3
Leadership was a safe place (a platform) for practicing new ways of being a man	27.3
A sense of the presence of God	24.6
Solo celebration and ceremony	24.6
The certificate and affirmation	24.6
The fire	21.8
Doing it with mates	21.8
Relationships with older men	21.8
Feeling of entering into a new status in my life	18.2

Table 23. Experiences Contributing to Rites of Passage in Order of Significance

Clearly identified as the most significant experience by respondents in being recognized as becoming a man was *Solo* (48.2%)—again reinforcing the critical importance of this program component. Next in order of significance were *the desire to enter a new phase of life* (37.3%) and that *Leadership was a safe place (a platform) for practicing new ways of being a man* (27.3%), an interesting observation, aligning with comments that *Leadership* is a safe place, and at times the only place, where they have the freedom to ask the questions they cannot ask anywhere else and talk about any topic that concerns them. It is a safe place to say they are men, in an intergenerational community of men, still accepted and not challenged for acting as non-men—as they would be at home, church, and so on. Next selected was *a sense of the presence of God* (24.6%), highlighting the spiritual component of rites of passage, followed by formal post Stage 2 Solo events.

In drawing together the data in table 23 with earlier data, particularly when they relate to Solo being a rite of passage, the following is a summary of what respondents say is a rite of passage:

- A time of separation and being alone, in wilderness, that is, Solo; a physical challenge conquered (getting dirty, individually set challenges—for example, fasting, being hungry), plus emotional/spiritual challenges
- The desire to enter a new phase of life
- A safe place to safely practice being a man (particularly in the absence of a tradition expecting or allowing this)
- Followed by a sense of the presence of God, the fire, doing it with mates, and only then
- Affirmation, celebration, and ceremony.

Participant respondents place the fire and doing it with mates ahead of the ceremonial aspects, whereas the sequence is different with staff respondents who put the ceremonial in first place and recognize the importance of involvement with older men as more important than the fire and mates.

Given the confirmation of the significance that participants place on Solo, the question that was asked in chapter 3, whether Solo itself, as celebrated immediately afterwards, is *the* rite of passage, is repeated. If this is a conclusion reached, one needs then to ask: What about those who do not *complete* Solo and how is *completing* Solo defined? Incorporated within the completion of Solo is the recognition that they have become men through conquering physical and emotional hardship, there is a spiritual awakening, and it is in wilderness. Then follows the affirmation.

Comparing these insights with traditional rites of passage, particularly from the work of Van Gennep[55] and Zahniser,[56] an expanded list of components of rites of passage may be:

- Separation (from family and often a time of solitude)
- Physical challenge (in some cultures involving physical wounding)

55. Van Gennup, *Rites of Passage*.
56. Zahniser, "Ritual Process."

- Emotional challenge
- In wilderness (liminal space)
- With mates (a group being initiated together)
- Affirmed by fire
- Involves a village of men (for affirmation)
- Mindset (looking for a new life phase and status—it's the time)
- Safe place (or tradition) to try it out (initially with their group, then with an expanding group)
- Spiritual and/or new status awakening and commitment
- Celebration.

Survey respondents were asked, looking back on their life now, when they thought they really became a man and whether it was in one event or a series of events. One hundred and twenty of the 135 survey respondents answered this question, a high response given that fourteen had only completed Stage 1 the year before, were only sixteen or seventeen years of age, and had not yet been presented with the *becoming a man* theme in Stage 2. The various events identified are summarized in table 24.

EVENT	NUMBER	PARTICIPANT EXAMPLES
Series of events	41	and a series of people
Leadership—generally	23	it definitely began as a result of leadership
		at Leadership when I gave my life to God
		after all three stages; a combination of stuff from all stages
		all of Stage 1 and 2
		all three stages
Leadership—Stage 1	4	with that extremely long connection with God

EVENT	NUMBER	PARTICIPANT EXAMPLES
Leadership—Stage 2	14	not a specific event, the whole week changed who I was for the better
Solo	7	
Solo celebration	2	I stopped asking myself the question after stage 2. A solo 7-month gap year in Europe really helped to solidify my confidence in myself as a man though
		I really became a man on Stage 2. It was a very significant time where I went from a somewhat immature boy to a man of God
		it might have happened earlier but putting the rock down on the pile helped finalize it for me (Stage 2, 2018)
Leadership—Stage 3	10	
Duo	1	
Leadership—serving on staff	2	
Church, youth group, BB, camps	2	
Graduating from high school/ starting uni	5	
Turning 18	2	but that's not as significant as other factors
Getting a job/earning my own income/job role	4	this was the final step; but each year of Leadership were certainly significant steps too (Stage 1, 2014)
		being deployed to Afghanistan
When able to survive for myself at home (do all the chores)	1	
Moving out of home	4	consolidated it
Becoming independent	2	Leadership accelerated it
First relationship	3	and first break up
Emotional growth in my first (second overall) serious relationship	1	
Learning to respect women	1	
Spiritual and physical growth	1	
After getting through some tough life experiences	1	

PART II: LENSES

EVENT	NUMBER	PARTICIPANT EXAMPLES
When I received messages of encouragement and affirmation	2	
Reading *Wild at Heart* (John Eldredge)	1	
When I took responsibility (e.g., for my mistakes and making tough choices)	7	responsibilities at work
When you start acting like a man	1	Maturity and character

Table 24. Events Significant to Becoming a Man

Forty-one indicated that they became a man through a series of events. This example clearly outlines the working together of multiple events:

> I'd certainly say a series of events. A first girlfriend + first breakup. First time directing a youth camp. Moving out of home. Getting written notes of [affirmation] . . . Reading Wild at Heart (John Eldredge) and realising what my calling in life is (as a man) and how to let go of the wounds from my father and others around me. Many things (in addition to my experiences on Leadership) have contributed to my "becoming a man." (Stage 3, 2009)

Those who identified *Leadership*, frequently referred to the contribution of each stage. This interaction and links between stages is demonstrated in these two examples:

> Stage 2 and solo put me in a place to listen to God and discover who I wanted to be. Stage 3 and especially formulating a mission statement were what empowered me to take life into my own hands and pursue the man I wanted to be. I haven't had a turbulent life at all. My personal experiences have made much less of an impact outside of growth opportunities like Leadership. (Stage 3, 2011)

> Leadership was huge. After Stage 1, I committed myself to God. Through staff model of authentic faith, I was also able to start living the way that furthered God and others instead of myself. Spiritually I saw myself as a man by the time I finished Stage 3 in 2018. (Stage 3, 2018)

As might be expected in context, but so significant a number that its relevance is acknowledged, sixty-one (51.8%) respondents specifically identified *Leadership* as one or more event(s) related to their becoming a man. This percentage is confidently assumed to be higher, considering that *Leadership* would have been included in their series by some of twenty-six who simply answered, "a series of events," without being specific. Eleven felt they had not yet become men though they had experienced some steps, some (14) only completed Stage 1 in 2019 and were then aged sixteen, waiting to do the critical Stage 2. Comparing the *Leadership* experience with an incident of life (e.g., turning eighteen), a respondent wrote:

> It was a series of events including being able to open up to other guys and men a similar age to me and being able to converse with adults without feeling talked down to. Another factor perhaps would be turning 18, however I do not think this is as significant as other factors. (Stage 1, 2017)

For some, responses indicate a sense of ambivalence or a uniqueness from person to person:

> I don't know if I'm a man now. I feel like a boy sometimes, but it feels like I've definitely got closer to what my idea of a man is. I'll just continue to grow. (Stage 3, 2019)

The question was further explored in interviews, with some additional thoughts expressed. A common theme is that becoming a man is *at their own time*—also importing a wartime metaphor, comparing underage soldiers becoming men through fighting alongside other men in war. Other responses were that "it's a journey"; there are "multiple ways"; "when you take responsibility for your own life"; "it varies from person to person"; "letting go of childish feelings." After acknowledging that becoming a man is different for everyone, that for some *Leadership* is important and for others it happens outside of *Leadership*, one interviewee referred to the Stage 2 Solo celebration evening where he was told "you've got what it takes to be a man—a man of God." He offered, "For me I know I definitely took on that okay well now I've got what I takes. I can't question whether I'm a man anymore; it's definite."

Participation in *Leadership* provides some participants with the opportunity to consider and clarify the meaning and experience of rites of passage in their world and context. For more than 50 percent, participation in *Leadership* or some specific aspect of the program is a part of their *becoming a man* experience, contributing to the apparent success of the program. One obvious link this lens provides to the emerging themes is that of imperfection, but positive growth. No one rite of passage experience is perfect or complete, but being in an intergenerational group of men speaks of acceptance and support, is empowering, and offers the circumstantial and experiential freedom that comes from sharing the experience with a group of mates.

Summary of Chapter

The loss of traditional rites of passage and the confusion over what were rites of passage for boys in Western society, including Australia, have been linked with a boy's confusion in searching for identity and manhood. Cultural shifts have impacted the world of boys seeking to know how to become men and some have filled in the void with their own rites of passage activities, many detrimental. In response, churches, schools, and other organizations have sought to develop rites of passage experiences for boys. The work of Van Gennep on rites of passage has been acknowledged, involving his three-phased framework: separation, transition, and incorporation, which continue to be acknowledged in contemporary examples.

The work of various scholars has been examined, including coming of age in the Hebrew Bible, the coming to ministry of Jesus, and the Jewish bar mitzvah, through rites of passage lenses, and they demonstrate cultural and time differences. Biblical examples of Mark and Timothy being mentored to responsible manhood and leadership have been cited. Selected contemporary developments have been described and an African, post-tribal, example has been considered in detail to explain the three identified phases of rites of passage—separation, transition or liminality, and reincorporation.

The lack of research on contemporary rites of passage and the need to fill this gap has been noted. Discussion of the loss of a critical component of historical rites of passage, death acknowledgment (Momento Mori), is an example of the contemporary exploration of the content and essential emphasis of rites of passage for boys, which could be further explored.

The research findings illustrate how important this concept is to *Leadership* participants and how *Leadership* and its key components are rites of passage experiences.

8

Wilderness

> There is a certain inherent spirituality about getting outside (Stage 1, 2014)

CERTAIN ACTIVITIES IN EACH stage of *Leadership* take place in the outdoors. These include an Overnight Expedition (Stage 1), Solo and Solo celebration (Stage 2), and Duo (Stage 3). Some participants see the outdoors—wilderness—as a critical element.[1] It does not need to be extreme wilderness, but it does need to be a location that is remote from other things and people. Wilderness is often the location for rites of passage and is recognized as a productive place for spending time in reflection and prayer. Those who work in this area and in masculine spirituality[2] regard wilderness as an essential ingredient.

Review of Theory

Wilderness has a prominent position in Scripture, and in Jesus's life and ministry. His preparation for ministry, referred to in chapter 7, as part of his rites of passage to prophethood in the testing narrative of Matthew 4:1–11,[3] took place in the wilderness—not a lush green wilderness but a

---

1. Smith, "Leadership Development Program," 89.
2. E.g., Rohr, *Adam's Return*; "Masculine Spirituality"; Eldredge, *Wild at Heart*; *Fathered by God*.
3. McVann, "One of the Prophets."

desert wilderness. At the other end of Jesus's earthly life, he again ventured into the wilderness at a particularly sensitive time: "Jesus went out as usual to the Mount of Olives, and his disciples followed him. On reaching the place, he said to them . . . He withdrew about a stone's throw beyond them, knelt down and prayed . . ." (Luke 22:39–43). This location too seems not to have been lush, but sparse and somewhat bare, yet it too was wilderness, somewhere Jesus went *as usual* to *the place*.

Wilderness is recognized as having healing value and as a place of awe.[4] Research is beginning to emerge on the impact of awe (incorporating amazement and wonder) in nature and its potential to heal. Anderson et al. suggest that "the power of nature to both heal and inspire awe has been noted by many great thinkers."[5] They conducted research with different groups and found that "awe mediates the effect of nature experience on well-being." If awe in nature enhances well-being and has the potential to heal in stress-related situations as these authors claim, then a link may be made between awe and God.

Root, however, while linking personal and spiritual aspects, suggests that rather than experiencing God in nature, group experiences in the bush are about experiencing "our longings and brokenness," and in this, God is found.[6] Experiencing the outdoors leads to "deep reflection on why there is something instead of nothing, on my need, on my questions that have no answers." Whatever the dynamics and spiritual dimensions may be, it is accepted that time spent in the wilderness is likely to be positive and stimulate transformation and preparation. It is of interest to discover the wilderness experience of *Leadership* participants.

The Research Findings

Acknowledging that in each stage, all respondents undertake an activity in the outdoors, they were given a list of experiences and asked to select up to three experiences that made the bush most critical for them as the location for the activity. Responses are presented in table 25.

---

4. Rohr, *Adam's Return*; "Masculine Spirituality"; Eldredge, *Wild at Heart*; *Fathered by God*; McVann, *One of the Prophets*; Root, "What Are We Doing"; Anderson et al., "Awe in Nature Heals."

5. Anderson et al., "Awe in Nature Heals," 1, 6, 7.

6. Root, "What Are We Doing," 179–80.

EXPERIENCE	RESPONDENTS (%)
A sense of God's presence	52.8
A chance to do some deep thinking	52.8
Just being in the outdoors	49.6
Freedom to be myself	37.8
Freedom for our group to do things just ourselves	34.7
The healing nature of wilderness	19.7
Learning from nature	15.0
It was awe-inspiring	12.6
I could be creative	10.2
The experience of liminal space	5.5

Table 25. Wilderness Experiences

In response, there was little difference between their top three choices: *a sense of God's presence* (52.8%), *a chance to do some deep thinking* (52.8%), and *just being in the outdoors* (49.6%). Prayer and inspiration are encompassed in the sense of God's presence; *deep thinking* is encompassed in reflection and focus on the future; *just being in the outdoors* links with a sense of *freedom* which was a focus of responses—*freedom to be myself* (37.8%) and *freedom for our group to do things just ourselves* (34.7%). Featuring minimally in responses was *the healing nature of wilderness* (19.7%) and nature being *awe-inspiring* (12.6%).

It is of interest that respondents did not make any strong link between wilderness and liminal space. As found in chapter 6, they did link Solo and Duo to liminal space, though this seems not linked specifically to the wilderness location. The Stage 1 Overnight Expedition was not seen as a liminal experience—most likely because it was done in their group. So, wilderness of itself is not seen as a liminal experience.

An interviewee offered that wilderness "represents separation from everything else and it represents closest to God." "It is easier to connect with God through nature." Exploring the significance of wilderness provided confirmation that nature or the bush provided a sense of God's presence, unhindered by the trappings of their normal world. Several contributions are included in detail as they reinforce the significance of wilderness contexts:

> It's good, I've always loved it in the bush, but I think it's a good place to try and get close to God, because that's the centre of his creation, there's limited man-made stuff, no cars, or big skyscrapers,

no bus stops, no constant traffic, it's just the middle of nowhere essentially, and that in itself it's good because it's quiet and peaceful, and you can just really get an idea of what you're doing and where you need to go with God or life or anything.

I thought I was just going to do manly stuff, whatever that meant, [probably something with a knife and a tent] but it took you to this place where there wasn't distractions where it became freeing and peaceful. Being in nature is incredibly valuable. I didn't understand it at the time but I knew there was something special and then especially on solo you could drop us off all in hotel rooms and it wouldn't be the same. You could make sure those hotel rooms don't have a view and don't have a TV or anything like that. It wouldn't be the same. It was about being in nature with God, the sounds, the smells, the creation of it.

For me the bush represents like a separation from everything else and it represented closest to God like wearing the space that God has kinda moulded. That was pretty significant because we don't do that in today. [It's] easier to connect with God through nature.

I think it is very significant. I can't imagine anywhere other than the bush because that's where you can hear God's voice. There's nothing to take your focus away from his creation, so I think that is very important.

For me, it was extremely critical because it just reminded me of all the times Jesus went off by himself into the wilderness for prayer and often he got tempted but would show his strengths in his relationship with God. That was shown in those times and so for me it was very very important because it just reminded me that even when we get tempted, we can still push through and not fall into it.

Summary of Chapter

Wilderness is a location for an activity in each stage of *Leadership*. The wilderness context as a location for reflection, prayer, inspiration, focusing on future mission, rites of passage, healing, and inspiring awe has been acknowledged. Jesus's experience is the primary example of the wilderness location in preparation for ministry (Matt 4:1–11) and to communicate with the Father in testing times (Luke 22:39–43). Root adds an insight about finding God in the bush through one's longings and brokenness.[7] Wilderness contributes to the apparent success of *Leadership* through unique experiences in each of the three stages and provides a sense of identification with Jesus in his experience of wilderness. This lens is related often to the theme of freedom and the perfection/imperfection contrast between God, and his creation, including us.

---

7. Root, "What Are We Doing."

9

Lenses of Infilling

Communitas, *Liminality*, *Rites of Passage*, *Wilderness*

THE SIX LENSES THROUGH which *Leadership* has been examined coalesce into two major groupings. The first, the lenses of infilling, is considered in this chapter. *Communitas* and liminality, though dealt with separately in chapters 5 and 6, are historically, psychologically and potentially theologically, inseparable. This momentum is fuelled by specific needs of youth, including young men, and is given further impetus by the current state of the world—a world in liminal space, with a hope of coming together in *communitas* for the sake of the future. Given the anthropological roots of *communitas*, liminality, and their application to rites of passage, these lenses are viewed in coalescence, as too is the lens of wilderness, often the context for *communitas*, liminality, and rites of passage. Bringing the lenses together enables a coordinated theological reflection.

In describing a young adult retreat ministry intentionally structured to build effective *communitas*, Nagy concluded that applying the "framework of *communitas* . . . in . . . ways to help achieve [finding Christ's love] . . . is a helpful way of thinking about young adult retreat ministry. It adds depth and lends a practical theological basis for understanding how and why retreats work."[1] *Leadership* too is located in this genre.

Theology informs the insights generated by the lenses of infilling through highlighting liminal space as a place for God's Spirit to work and for reflection on concepts of grace, faith, and hope. The liminal nature of the *Leadership* experience provides a realization of acceptance by God. God

1. Nagy, "Lens of Liminality," 59.

meets people in the margins of life and people imperfectly living on the edge. A theology of solitude, including wilderness, also informs the insights and is reflected in the experience of Jesus and what he shared with the disciples—using solitude as a call to action, transformation, and community.

This chapter highlights various of the four lenses in different combinations and with theological reflection. It then deals with two specific topics and their contributions to *communitas*: solitude—its link to wilderness and its paradoxical contribution to *communitas*; and story sharing—its contribution to stimulating *communitas* and its incarnational link to God and faith formation.

Liminality and *Communitas*

Liminality emerges as an organizing concept, bringing theology and the social sciences into correlation. While the level of articulation or recognition of liminal space by research survey participants was limited, this is not interpreted to mean that liminal experiences are not paramount and a key to the *Leadership* experience. Spontaneous *communitas* is experienced first in a Stage 1 group and is expanded to incorporate the whole *Leadership* community. This is occurring in different layers of liminality. Broadly, it is the liminal experience of coming away from home, family, and friends for eight to nine days and being presented with a *clean slate*. Narrowly, it is the transitional and potentially transformative experiences of entering a small group or embarking on Solo in wilderness in isolation and with the hope of loneliness giving way to solitude, or venturing into the wilderness with one other person, or the liminal and risky experience of writing and declaring a personal mission statement. To a varying extent, for different people, each of these has the potential to be a rite of passage experience, contributing to the journey from boy to man, something specifically acknowledged in the Stage 2 post-Solo celebration and recognition ceremony.

Research findings were that all groups saw liminal space as something in between (see chapter 6). Freelance writer, Mandi Baker,[2] draws attention to the well-accepted description of liminal space as a time and location of being betwixt and between. Liminal space can be a quiet space for taking a breath. It can be a place that provokes new thinking. It can be a place of tension, discomfort, disorientation or uncertainty, but it can also be where we allow God's Spirit to control our thinking—in a place of new experience

---

2. Baker, "Welcome to the Bubble, 26."

and grace. It can be a space for gaining new strength and understanding, from which to step out courageously in a new faith and to dream. All of that is true to the literature and the developing range of situations to which the theology and social science of liminality is applied. To explore the group of coalesced lenses further, two examples of emerging literature that reference contemporary issues associated with the COVID-19 pandemic as a liminal experience for the world are considered, including articulation of insights on thresholds between pre-liminal, liminal, and post-liminal.

Jonathan Best[3] draws on an understanding of liminality, coupled with *communitas*, to encourage hope in the future in a world of concerns and seeming purposelessness or directionlessness; a world concerned about climate change, the COVID-19 pandemic, and much more; a world where people no longer have a "collective trust in religion" or the general progress of society to fuel a "belief that our individual and communal transitions into the future were under control." He acknowledges the early anthropological work of Van Gennep and Turner, adopting Turner's description of *communitas* as "the deep social bonds that develop between members of a community who are experiencing or have experienced liminality from a rite of passage";[4] "our important connection occurs through a shared liminal experience." Liminality and *communitas* go together. *Communitas* involves a shared liminal experience; liminality without *communitas* is meaningless. His position, in summary, is descriptive of the research findings on the unique *Leadership* experience, incorporating concepts of diversity and a *clean slate*, which lead to greater acceptance and understanding of self and others:

> Through a shared liminality experience, each individual acquires a better understanding of the other person. The community becomes communitas by living through the same transition, ambiguity, and betweenness. Each individual has a sense of what it's like to be the other, thus forging an equality not usually found in community.[5]

Quoting Turner,[6] and resonating with the nonhierarchical, equality of person ethos of *Leadership*, *communitas* is "a spontaneously generated relationship between levelled and equal total and individuated human

---

3. Best, "Liminality, Communitas, and Hope."
4. Turner, *Ritual Process*.
5. Best, *Liminality, Communitas, and Hope*.
6. Turner, *Dramas, Fields, and Metaphors*, 202.

beings, stripped of structural attributes, [which] together constitute what one might call anti-structure."[7]

Best describes liminal theology as a continuation of practical theology: "Doing liminal theology means learning from those who live within everyday life, especially those who push against injustice and inequality. Liminal theology orients us toward this excitement, particularly toward those who represent what is transitory in both society, culture, and intellectual thought."[8]

Liminal theology is a theology of transition and a state of in between, which offers "important opportunities for understanding God's work in the world. More importantly, these areas constitute occasions for building upon and continuing the mission of Christ in a world that so desperately needs a renewed sense of hope, purpose, and love."[9] Or, as summed up, "Simply put, liminal theology is a present-minded theology that explores God's work within the transitional and in-between as it unfolds within contemporary life and community."[10]

Best's view is reinforced by the view of Carson et al., that "once we have understood the power of the liminal, we can recognise how it fits with other Christian themes and cooperate more fully with God's transformative work in liminal processes or places."[11] This is enhanced in community relationships—in experiences of *communitas*.

Theological Reflection, Liminality, and Rites of Passage

The view of Carson et al. in describing Turner's work on rites of passage and liminality, in particular the concepts of structure, involving differentiation and hierarchy, and anti-structure—unstructured or a communion of equal individual—is compared with the description of *Leadership* as nonhierarchical and all equal. It is possible to view the whole of *Leadership* as liminal or anti-structure, which invites a repetition of the question of whether *Leadership*, or even specifically Solo, is a rite of passage. Linking with the coalescence of lenses of outpouring, the liminal phase enhances

---

7. Best, *Liminality, Communitas, and Hope*.
8. Best, *Liminality, Communitas, and Hope*.
9. Best, *Liminality, Communitas, and Hope*.
10. Best, *Liminality, Communitas, and Hope*.
11. Carson et al., *Crossing Thresholds*, 7.

PART II: LENSES

humility which is taken into a person's new roles/status,[12] humility being a key characteristic of servant leadership and masculine spirituality.

A liminal hermeneutic approach to biblical narrative interpretation is offered by Carson et al. as a "lens through which we may obtain a new perspective."[13] The lens addresses the categories of position, pattern, and symbol. The liminal genealogical account recorded in Matthew 1 includes Rahab, who "occupied space on the edges, the boundary, the locale of the Spirit's activity," leading to the conclusion that this is a strong "liminal case for God acting at the edge and in the margins."[14] If God is always where we are,[15] then, as with the meek, the humble, the poor in spirit, the mourners, those who hunger for righteousness, and the merciful (Ps 37:11; Zeph 3:12; Matt 5:3–7), and as with characters such as Rahab (Josh 2), when we feel like we are imperfectly living on the edge, in the margin, in liminal space, that's where we find God, and together find a joining with others in the same experience in a *communitas* of the marginalized; those in a symbolic or real *wilderness*.

What is liminal to one may not be to another; people's experience of liminality is different "depending on where their beginning places were"[16] and events are experienced differently. Carson et al. use a U-shaped curve to illustrate a "roller coaster of discipleship." Simplified, and incorporating rites of passage terminology, one moves from the pre-liminal (structure) crossing a threshold or "descent of emptying" into the liminal (anti-structure), with its incarnational identification, and later, crossing a second threshold into the post-liminal (restructure), the ascent of transformation.[17] The "U" curve is presented in *Leadership* to demonstrate the movement through liminal space that occurs in each of the three *Leadership* stages (see figures 3–5 in chapter 6). Carson et al., following Paul's Philippian teaching of Christ's servanthood and humility, offer a path to redemption, following Christ through the liminal experience and taking on a rites of passage experience:

> The path to your redemption is found in a correlation: become a liminal person; strip yourself of external signs of identity; and

12. Carson et al., *Crossing Thresholds*, 17.
13. Carson et al., *Crossing Thresholds*, 68–83.
14. Carson et al., *Crossing Thresholds*, 71–72.
15. Carson et al., *Crossing Thresholds*, 9.
16. Carson et al., *Crossing Thresholds*, 76.
17. Carson et al., *Crossing Thresholds*, 55, 76, 77.

LENSES OF INFILLING

humbly place yourself before God that you might receive a new transformed name and identity. Only by entering this deep pattern of redemption will you experience the spirit of the liminal One who did the same.[18]

Carson et al. adopt a broad approach to liminality, including a poignant example in the emerging literature on the COVID-19 pandemic, yet they also offer specific theological reflection, applying an analysis of thresholds in their practical theology of liminality (and its correlation with a rites of passage pattern) to many biblical narratives, for example, the narrative of returning and rebuilding such as Ezra and Nehemiah, the pre-liminal and liminal phase of exile, the post-liminal era of return and restorations, and the story of Jonah. Summarizing their work on thresholds, they offer: "Out of the ordinary space-time fabric of *chronos*, thresholds are crossed, anomalies appear, and *Kairos* emerges—the fullness of transcendent time. It is the interruption of liminality that makes room for new revelation." And, they add the incarnational passage, a significant example of Jesus (the Word) from John 1: "The Word not only enters into the liminality of finitude, but also dwells with us."[19]

There are layers of liminality—meta-liminality; macro-liminality; micro-liminality. Meta-liminality is the meta-narrative, incorporating *communitas*, rites of passage, and wilderness. Applying this to *Leadership*, the whole of *Leadership* is at the macro level. This is similar of the experience of a particular HSTP, described by Dean and Hearlson as a "liminal rite of passage"[20] and evaluated by Horn.[21] Applying a pedagogy of pilgrimage, HSTP thrusts participants into a liminal experience, "an experience of dangling between the familiar and the unknown, with a community of equals."[22] Horn suggests that the program "is explicitly organized around this spiritual practice of liminal space" and that it therefore "illustrates how the theme of pilgrimage can be translated theologically and pedagogically for youth."[23] Horn implies theological meaning to the *here* and *there* concept by relating it to Jesus with the disciples, the road to Emmaus, the road

---

18. Carson et al., *Crossing Thresholds*, 78–79.
19. Carson et al., *Crossing Thresholds*, 74, 77–78, 82.
20. Dean and Hearlson, *Creative Process*, 50.
21. Horn, "Prepare Me."
22. Horn, "Prepare Me," 194.
23. Horn, "Prepare Me," 194.

to Damascus, and the desert road where Philip engages with the eunuch—a picture of travelling from one place to another,[24] in wilderness.

Wilderness, Liminality, *Communitas*, and Rites of Passage

At the micro level, in *Leadership* Stage 1, the liminal experience of My Group immediately involves scope for *communitas* to emerge and this is further enhanced through other experiences, including a short solo in *wilderness*. Stage 2 develops these experiences and then moves into the obvious and strictly liminal experience of three days of Solo in *wilderness*, emerging from this with a response of renewed spontaneous *communitas*, followed by a celebration likened to indigenous/tribal *rites of passage* experiences. Stage 3 builds further, widening the *communitas* experience to a larger group and presenting the liminal experiences of a duo in *wilderness* and public declaration of their personal life mission.

Reference to the importance of recognizing the role of liminal space is a shared characteristic of HSTP and *Leadership*. Dean and Hearlson suggest that HSTP itself becomes a "liminal rite of passage." Without naming it as a liminal experience, sixteen-year-old Jay reflected on the wilderness portion of Gordon-Conwell's Compass program:[25]

> I definitely feel like [it was important] not being in my room at home with the different distractions . . . Here I go outside and it's just me and God. And so I think that helps me—It makes it a more special time.[26]

"Suspended between two different possibilities—the way of life of home and school, and new vocational possibilities revealed by their experience in a HSTP—teenagers in HSTP find themselves vulnerable and open to new possibilities, to others, and to God."[27]

McVann suggests that Jesus experienced his own rite of passage in his baptism and temptation.[28] Wilderness was where Jesus was tested and

---

24. Horn, "Prepare Me," 194–95.

25. This program of the Gordon-Conwell Theological College runs for a month, in three contexts: (1) wilderness adventure; (2) seminary education; (3) ministry abroad plus three years mentoring by a pastor or church leader. The wilderness adventure is unique to this program.

26. Dean and Hearlson, *Creative Process*, 50.

27. Dean and Hearlson, *Creative Process*, 51–52.

28. McVann, "One of the Prophets."

prepared for ministry (Matt 4:1–11) and was a key component of his example—using solitude and a wilderness space to pray (Matt 14:23; Luke 5:16). Sometimes this was a Solo experience; sometimes it involved his close others. He recognized duos in sending out seventy-two workers in twos (Luke 10:1) with a commission and a plan to return and share their experience, which they did (Luke 10:17), similar to returning Duo partners in *Leadership* Stage 3. However, at that early stage of spiritual development and training, *Leadership* Duos are focused more on sharing, growth, and transformation than on mission, except the mission to each other and their developing personal mission statement or vocation. *Leadership* Solo takes on the nature of at least contributing largely to, if not taking on the full characteristics of a rite of passage, with wilderness and solitude being key components.

Solitude

Solitude is directly linked to and encompassed within liminal and wilderness experiences. Long and Averill distinguish between negative and positive experiences of solitude and suggest that more psychological research has been directed to the negative experiences characterized by loneliness. Psychological research into the positive experiences of solitude has been relatively neglected. From a social perspective, Long and Averill suggest that "solitude's benefits often outweigh its detriments"—such benefits as they recognize in the experiences of philosophers, artists, writers, and spiritual leaders (Moses, Jesus, Mohammed, and the Buddha).[29]

Long and Averill recognize four categories of benefits of solitude, each of which is relevant for *Leadership*: (1) freedom (negative benefits—freedom from constraints; and positive benefits—"freedom to engage in activities . . . because of the presence of necessary resources"); (2) creativity (imagination is stimulated and self-transformation occurs); (3) intimacy (paradoxically speaking—feelings of intimacy while in solitude are common); (4) spirituality (e.g., tribal cultures "solitary quest for a higher level of consciousness into their adolescents' rites of passage").[30] In summary, Long and Averill conclude that the benefits of solitude include "the freedom to engage in intrinsically motivated activities, creativity (including self-transformation), intimacy, and spirituality"—or in psychological terms, "the opportunity . . . for a lessening and subsequent reconstitution

29. Long and Averill, "Solitude," 21, 37.
30. Long and Averill, "Solitude," 24–28.

of cognitive structures."³¹ Other benefits of solitude have been noted. In a study of early adolescents, Larson suggested that solitude "might provide a needed opportunity to relax and step back from the demands of enacting a public self with peers" and "may play a role in the developmental task of negotiating greater autonomy" in family relationships.³²

There are limitations to being able to draw on the benefits of solitude, though achieving this capacity is desirable. In the absence of external supports, some may not have the "inner resources to find meaning" and this could make it difficult for the person to engage in "productive activities."³³ This is relevant for those preparing themselves or others for solitude but is difficult to overcome in a short-term preparation. If the experience of solitude is voluntarily entered into, such as its incorporation into the decision to undertake Stage 2 of *Leadership*, it is likely to be conducive to personality development and creativity.³⁴

Understanding of the impact of having spent Solo in wilderness, and part of it in solitude, is assisted by Hernandez's examination of the spirituality of Henri Nouwen,³⁵ quoting Nouwen that "Solitude always calls us to community."³⁶ "We are led to a mysterious sense of togetherness when solitude comes face to face with solitude and they start to greet each other," and "community is not the place where we are no longer alone but the place where we respect, protect, and reverently greet one another's alones."³⁷ This provides insight to the interplay of aloneness and solitude with togetherness and community, experienced at *Leadership* vicariously during Solo and importantly together in the immediate post-Solo celebrations.

Communitas and Story Sharing

Sharing of one's personal story is frequently recognized as a step towards communitas. It is further considered here.

Findings from the research often linked *communitas* with story sharing and as a way of relaying liminal and rites of passage experiences to

31. Long and Averill, "Solitude," 39.
32. Larson, "Emergence of Solitude," 91.
33. Long and Averill, "Solitude," 40.
34. Galanaki, "Are Children Able," 436.
35. Hernandez, *Soul Care*, 58–59.
36. Nouwen et al., *Spiritual Direction*.
37. Nouwen, *Bread for the Journey*.

others (see chapters 2 and 5). As noted, sharing a personal story—personally and deeply—within the group was rated highest of factors contributing to *communitas*. It is not just personal story sharing; it is sharing the story of God, the normative practical theological task of sharing how God is working in the world—as Jesus did in his frequent mode of telling his own story and his teaching through story. The power of storytelling is recognized by Hernandez in examining the spirituality of Henri Nouwen who he quotes: "[Telling a story] creates space, we can dwell in a story, walk around, find our own place. The story confronts, but does not oppress; the story inspires, but does not manipulate."[38] Further weight is given to the power of story in the experience of HSTP: "Teenagers powerfully encounter new stories"[39] and "shared stories transform and deepen young people's faith."[40]

Continuing to draw on Nouwen, Hernandez[41] further describes the power of storytelling, claiming that it has healing power, requiring the hearer to "receive the story with a compassionate heart, a heart that does not judge or condemn but recognizes how the [other's] story connects with our own."[42] These understandings from Nouwen reflect the *Leadership* experience of acceptance, which contributes to the speedy emergence of spontaneous *communitas*. The story invites us to an encounter, a dialogue, a mutual sharing[43]—a picture of *communitas* sometimes being shared in a liminal moment such as within My Group.

Exploring theological reflection further, Wimberley makes a link between storytelling and faith formation: "Shared stories transform and deepen young people's faith. . . . When spiritual companions tend to these stories, they treat the 'sacred texts' of young people's lives as essential parts of the gift exchange between them;selves and young people."[44] When narrating/interpreting, an identity event occurs as an event is narrated, and as this is repeated, the event moves towards transcendence. A question to consider: Is *Leadership* as a whole the experience that is narrated—reaching for transcendence; or is *Leadership* made up of many different events that are narrated; or both? For example, within a Stage 1 group, sharing a personal

38. Hernandez, *Soul Care*, 55.
39. Steers, "Let Me Try," 218.
40. Wimberly, "Give Me Mentors," 88.
41. Hernandez, *Soul Care*, 55.
42. Nouwen, *Reaching Out*, 96.
43. Nouwen, *Living Reminder*, 65–66.
44. Wimberly, *Give Me Mentors*, 88.

story is often a difficult step to take, but it leads to others having the confidence and desire to do the same, and thus, a story becomes personally affirming for others. After the week, the whole *Leadership* experience is shared as a transformational event.

Root presents a scenario that leads to a dramatic turn in approach to youth ministry's central focus—from the weekly youth group with a focus on providing fun. "Focusing on the Good has become central to our ministry. I'd actually say that youth ministry is for joy, because youth ministry invites young people to focus on the Good, and only God is Good. *Joy is when you find the Good as an end.*"[45] This transformation of approach emerged from the sharing of a personal story, which led to others sharing their story and an intergenerational community emerged. Enlarging on this theme, Root makes the statement that: "Youth ministry should forget about competing in the battle of *things* and instead profoundly concern ourselves with *stories*," recognizing that the church has many stories to share and young people should be exposed to them,[46] which is similar to Stanton's emphasis on Bible engagement.[47] Linking story with identity formation, "to have an identity in Christ, then, is to have the story of the living Christ encountering you (or someone in your community), and in turn to have the story of Jesus' own life, death, and resurrection now be the shape of your story."[48]

Story sharing is an appropriate strategy in working with youth as adolescents are attracted to narrative. "Stories that convey the truth of God at work in creation; of God at work among humanity; and the stories of what God has done through history are more quickly embraced by young people than sterile propositionalism."[49] "Helping your youth tell, listen to and interpret stories will build community among your group and will equip them to engage more fully with Scripture."[50] Nouwen takes it further: "As soon as an embarrassing or exhilarating idea is taken out of its isolation and brought into a relationship, with God or with another person, something new happens. Once we take the risk and experience acceptance, our thoughts themselves receive a new quality and are transformed into prayer."[51]

45. Root, *End of Youth Ministry?*, 111.
46. Root, *End of Youth Ministry?*, 165.
47. Stanton, *Wide Awake*.
48. Root, *End of Youth Ministry?*, 165–66.
49. King, *Presence-Centered*, 142.
50. King, *Presence-Centered*, 145.
51. Nouwen et al., *Spiritual Direction*, 61.

Summary of Chapter

The lenses of *communitas*, liminality, rites of passage, and wilderness (solitude), grouped as the lenses of infilling, are evident in the interactions between Jesus and the disciples. A sense of *communitas* developed among Jesus's followers. The disciples had frequent experiences of being put into liminal space—for example, on the boat in the storm (Mark 4:35–41) and at Jesus's arrest, trial, and crucifixion (Matt 26 and 27). Their whole experience took on the nature of a rite of passage, especially seen in the ups and downs of Peter—the Rock (Matt 16:18), his denial of Jesus (Matt 26:69–75), and his restoration and forthright affirmation (John 21:15–19). Jesus took them into wilderness, both literally (Matt 26:36) and figuratively between his burial and resurrection Matt 27:57—28:10.).

Liminal space has been identified as a place for God's Spirit to work, where God meets imperfect people on the margins; a place to experience the incarnation. It is a place for positive solitude, prayer, and reflection. Liminality and *communitas* provide hope in the future, even in a world of serious concerns which are shared by and concern young people. Liminal space is a place for God's transformation to occur and then be celebrated in *communitas*. Liminality and *communitas* meet in rites of passage, with wilderness often being the context.

The importance of personal story sharing is given special attention because of its stimulus to *communitas* as seen in Stage 1 groups (see chapters 2 and 5). It is linked here with liminality and rites of passage, with wilderness being a rich story context. Story sharing is often where God shows up and this leads to individual and group transformation.

This coalescence of lenses has provided valuable insights in examining *Leadership* and in considering the factors that lead to the apparent success of the program. Findings, informed by theology, reflect the themes that emerged from examination of the program elements. These have been taken into consideration in developing the substantive theory (chapter 14). There is increasing and contemporary interest in each of the lenses in theological and social science literature, spurred on in part by the current state of the world. *Leadership* can respond to this opportunity and be at the forefront of the further development of relevant programs for young men[52] in today's world. Individually, and as a coalescence, the lenses provide an ongoing group of concepts through which the program can be further developed.

52. Also for young women through the corresponding program provided annually for girls.

10

Servant Leadership

> I strive to live out a lot of what is taught, modeled, and discussed at Leadership—being someone who is a servant leader and particularly trying to guide others to live with integrity, deciding what they value most and then letting that guide their actions. (Stage 1, 2013)

IT IS CLAIMED THAT "leadership is one of the most comprehensively researched social influence processes in the behavioural sciences," but that servant leadership (a major focus in this research) "remains understudied."[1]

The concept of servant leadership has been introduced into secular literature and organizational practice[2] and supplemented in popular organizational literature.[3] However, the teaching of Jesus (Matt 20:26–28; Mark 9:35; 10:43; Luke 22:24; and John 13:1–17), as articulated by Paul (Phil 2:1–11), is foundational for examining servant leadership.

In this chapter, historical literature is set against recent and developing literature on servant leadership and attempts made at integration with current models of leadership, for example, the work of Eva et al. who reviewed 285 articles on servant leadership spanning twenty years up to 2018.[4]

Servant leadership is a key concept of *Leadership* and hence is an important lens through which to view the program. It is the leadership

---

1. Parris and Peachey, "Literature Review," 377–78.
2. Greenleaf, *Servant Leadership* (2002); Sendjaya and Sarros, *Servant Leadership*.
3. For example, McGee-Cooper and Trammell, *Essentials*.
4. Eva et al., "Servant Leadership."

style that is articulated and modeled by staff throughout the three stages of *Leadership*. Participants are frequently challenged to reflect the servant leadership of Jesus.

Theological and secular writings are considered before declaring a definitional statement. This assisted in determining what characteristics and measures of servant leadership were used as the elements of this investigatory lens, towards determining whether servant leadership is critical to the apparent success of *Leadership*.

Review of Theory

Introduction

Credit for the introduction of the phrase *servant leadership* is often given to Greenleaf.[5] Greenleaf did introduce the concept of servant leadership into secular literature and organizational practice. He made very few and rather oblique references to Jesus in his text and reduced Jesus to the symbolic. Authors Sendjaya and Sarros challenged the notion that Greenleaf had developed the whole idea of servant leadership in these terms:

> As appealing and refreshing as Greenleaf's conceptualization of servant leadership is, Greenleaf is not the individual who first introduced the notion of servant leadership to everyday human endeavour. It was Christianity's founder, Jesus Christ, who first taught the concept of servant leadership . . . more than two thousand years ago.[6]

Servanthood is a rich biblical concept, based in the Old Testament concept of *servant* and the servanthood of Jesus. Of recent years, there has been increasing recognition in secular literature of the value of servant leadership as organizations, businesses, and the like seek to find leadership models that achieve optimum organizational effectiveness.[7] Theological reflection on servant leadership is followed by consideration of contemporary secular scholarship and links made between the theological and secular concepts in developing this lens through which *Leadership* has been examined.

---

5. Greenleaf, *Servant Leadership*, 7, 49.

6. Sendjaya and Sarros, "Servant Leadership," 58.

7. Sendjaya and Sarros, "Servant Leadership"; Udani and Lorenzo-Molo, "Servant Becomes Leader."

PART II: LENSES

Theological Reflection

The teaching of Jesus (Matt 20:26–28; Mark 9:35; 10:43; Luke 22:24; and John 13:1–17), as articulated by Paul (Phil 2:1–11) is the theological criteria for examining the servant leadership lens. This is emphasized by Kye who makes the point that instead of focusing on the needs of leaders, as many leadership programs do, they need to focus on Jesus, the "prototypical model of leadership . . . servanthood."[8]

From a Christian perspective, servanthood is an essential element of leadership, while leadership is also defined by servanthood. From a worldly perspective, although this has changed in some contemporary leadership theories, linking servanthood and leadership is seen as a paradox. It is one of the great paradoxes of the teaching and life example of Jesus. Jesus, the Son of God, has always held an exalted place. This is reinforced in the Revelation record of the many angels singing loudly: "Worthy is the Lamb, who was slain, to receive power and wealth and wisdom and strength and honour and glory and praise!" (Rev 5:12).

How then is he referred to as a servant? Jesus referred to himself as the example of servant leadership (John 13:15). The Isaiah 53 prophecy was that Jesus would be the Suffering Servant, as was borne out on the cross.

Biblical foundations of Jesus's servant leadership are found initially in the Old Testament. David Pettus recognizes *servant* as a key component of leadership in the Old Testament. In Samuel 15:1–5, King David's officials refer to themselves as the king's servants, "ready to do whatever our lord the king chooses," and the people of Israel are referred to by God as "my servants" (Isa 41:8–9); "servants of the Lord" (Isa 54:17).[9] Abraham, Isaac, and Jacob (Deut 9:17), Moses (Deut 34:5), and Joshua (Judg 2:8) are referred to as the Lord's servants. "Not surprisingly, the servant is expected to be obedient and faithful to the one he serves. First and foremost, the people are to 'fear God and serve him alone' (Deut 7:14; 10:12)."[10]

Yates contrasts "self-centred leaders who use their positions of power and influence for personal benefit" with "those leaders who embody faithfulness to God through service and servanthood to others."[11] Issues of the heart emerge again in considering the example of Jesus. Wolfe makes the

---

8. Kye, *Jesus Christ's Life*, 271.
9. Pettus, "Concept Study."
10. Pettus, "Concept Study," 37.
11. Yates, "Faithful Servants," 192.

point that, unlike the "teachers of the law and the Pharisees," Jesus's teaching was dealing with the "real issues," the "motives of the heart." "Jesus wasn't showing them necessarily 'what to do' but 'what to be.'"[12] In considering Matthew 23:8–12, Wolfe reflects, "A biblical leader, therefore, is not eager for titles, positions and power. He wants only to serve others. The posture of servanthood focuses on serving the needs of followers."[13]

Yates refers to Isaiah's suffering Messiah passage (Isa 52:13—53:12) as being "the ultimate example of sacrificial service for others."[14] He continues, "the Servant's mission is to be God's instrument of blessing . . . Even when serving others would involve subjugating himself to beatings, humiliation, undeserved punishment, even offering his own life as a 'sin offering,' the Servant would not turn away from his divine calling." "Jesus is the one who perfectly embodies and fulfils the role of Servant."[15]

Yates concludes that "the theology of leadership in the Major Prophets reflects the principle that 'God opposes the proud but gives grace to the humble' (Jas 4:6; 1 Pet 5:5),"[16] making a further link to the New Testament with the observation that "the servant trajectory that carries forward to the New Testament not only includes the prophets and Jesus, but followers of Jesus as well."[17] Paul refers to himself as a "'servant' of Christ (Rom 1:1; Gal 1:10; Titus 1:1)."[18] Returning the discussion to the servanthood model of Jesus, his teachings on links between servanthood and greatness and humility are now considered.

When the disciples were travelling along the road to Capernaum and were arguing about which of them was the greatest, Jesus, knowing what they were arguing about, turned the regular order of things upside down with his first/last reversal of the order; the one who wanted to be first, "must be the very last and the servant of all" (Mark 9:35; and a similar teaching in Matt 20:26–27, Mark 10:43, and Luke 22:24). Referring to Matthew 20:20–28 and Mark 10:35–45, Kostenberger and Crowther contrast "lording it over others" with "the pattern of suffering and service like

---

12. Wolfe, "Christian Leadership," 96, 98.
13. Wolfe, "Christian Leadership," 99.
14. Yates, "Faithful Servants," 194.
15. Yates, "Faithful Servants," 195.
16. Yates, "Faithful Servants," 197.
17. Yates, "Faithful Servants," 196.
18. Yates, "Faithful Servants," 197.

[Jesus]"—self exaltation contrasted with love and service.[19] The disciples were slow to learn and Jesus had to repeat the lesson, this time in action and words. It was the night before the crucifixion, so one can assume it was one of the most important lessons Jesus wanted to leave with them, as he carried out the traditional role of a servant and washed their feet. McManus adds weight to the importance and urgency of what Jesus was about to do, with his observation that "Jesus has about 72 hours to live."[20] He gave them an example in servanthood, in particular, the dimension of humility.

Humility

Humility is a key element of servant leadership,[21] although Jesus did not dismiss *power* or *greatness*. As stated by Russell, "Jesus acknowledged there would be exalted places of leadership but the Father had determined their designees."[22] While Jesus related greatness to servanthood, the issue is how these concepts are defined and translated into the work of God, through the church and in the world. Humility and other issues of the heart are good places to start.

Jesus had humbled himself and did something radical. He followed the practical lesson of washing feet with a challenge to his disciples to follow his example of humility and servanthood—to be prepared to take on the lowly role of servant leader; to give up something of themselves (e.g., status) for others, particularly for others they knew well, who were in their team. In discussing Jesus washing the disciples' feet from John 13:2–20, Hall-Harris considers that "the footwashing therefore represents an act of humble service for others, symbolic of the humiliating service Jesus will render in laying down his life for others—which is why the foot washing is *necessary* if the disciples are to have a share in him (13:8)."[23]

Hall-Harris continues that the ultimate standard for leadership is not just "servant leadership" (as often observed) but "sacrificial servant leadership," which means leading by example with humility, sacrifice, and vulnerability, rather than leading from a position of strength, authority, and

---

19. Kostenberger and Crowther, "Leading with Love," 480.
20. McManus, "Servant Heart."
21. Elmer, *Cross-Cultural Servanthood*, 27–34.
22. Russell, "Practical Theology," 3.
23. Harris, "Leading through Weakness," 356.

control.²⁴ Humility is also a key component highlighted by Kostenberger and Crowther: "Christ, in self-sacrificing humility and other-centred servanthood, demonstrated a willingness to be last"²⁵; and also Wolfe: "servant leaders lead with humility."²⁶

Humility is a hallmark of Jesus's exposition of servanthood, while in Paul's description of Jesus, "the need for humility within the character of the Philippian church leaders is prominent in the text." "We are never more like Jesus than when we serve others."²⁷

Servanthood as Being

The exhortation is to not just be a Christian and *do* servanthood out of duty for others; but to *be* servant-hearted in the image of Jesus and then *do* servanthood, a *doing*, born out of *being*; a simple biblically based reflection on *being* servant-hearted or *being* Jesus to others. Servant leadership is not merely a style of leadership to adopt; it is Jesus epitomized and is the kind of person a follower of Jesus is becoming and *being*. It is a stance of *being* in the world, that asks: Who are you serving? It is a gospel-in-action challenge, a paradoxical Jesus challenge, a practical theological challenge, to those outside of Christ—*being* a servant and a leader. Servanthood becomes our identity, our *being*.

Secular Scholarship on Servant Leadership

Servant leadership has found its way into the secular world of business and management, with many articles now being published in management, organizational, business, leadership, and public administration journals, including in the International Journal of Servant-Leadership.²⁸ Sendjaya and Sarros consider Jesus Christ's model of servant leadership in detail, isolating such dimensions as humility and equating greatness with a commitment to serve.²⁹ Five key points Sendjaya and Sarros drew from Greenleaf's

---

24. Harris, "Leading through Weakness," 361.
25. Kostenberger and Crowther, "Leading with Love," 480.
26. Wolfe, "Christian Leadership," 102.
27. Ayres, "Theology of Leadership," 20–21.
28. Spears Center, "International Journal."
29. Sendjaya and Sarros, "Servant Leadership," 59.

conceptualization of servant leaders were putting other people's "needs, aspirations and interests above their own," "making a deliberate choice . . . to serve others," serve first, then lead, seeking to "transform their followers to grow" and seeing followers become servant leaders themselves.[30]

In 2008, Sendjaya and Sarros joined with Santora to validate a measure of servant leadership, responding to the problems organizations were facing with other "value-laden leadership" approaches: "transformational leadership, authentic leadership, [and] spiritual leadership." They described servant leadership then as an "emerging leadership approach." Their emphasis was on "service, follower, and moral-spiritual dimensions."[31]

Two distinct, though overlapping, approaches taken by scholars are to describe servant leadership by comparing and contrasting it with other leadership models,[32] and to describe servant leadership through isolating its characteristics.[33] Some have attempted to distill these views into their own consolidated, or at times expanded, list. The methodology of several scholars has been to describe servant leadership through engaging in extensive literature reviews, leading to a synthesis and presentation of their own theoretical designs.

A constant theme among scholars on servant leadership is the identification of ethical, spiritual, and moral behaviour. Servant leaders "place a greater emphasis on morality and ethics than do transformational leaders."[34] Udani and Lorenzo-Molo quote Klamon as stating that "what makes servant leadership distinct from other leadership models . . . is the ethical motivation that inspires individuals to act."[35] Parris and Peachy take this closer to a Christian context when they refer to "spiritual and moral tenets" and to "humility, authenticity, interpersonal acceptance, and

---

30. Sendjaya and Sarros, "Servant Leadership," 57–58.

31. Sendjaya et al., "Defining and Measuring," 40, 403.

32. Sendjaya et al., "Defining and Measuring," 404, 405; Eva et al., "Servant Leadership," 2, 3; Parris and Peachy, "Literature Review," 262; Stone et al., "Transformational," 349; Van Dierendonck, "Servant Leadership," 1235, 1237.

33. Schwartz et al., "Servant Leadership," 1026; Carter and Baghurst, "Influence," 453, 454; Udani and Lorenzo-Molo, "Servant Becomes Leader," 377–80, 385; Kodish, "Paradoxes of Leadership," 45, 3; Sendjaya et al., "Defining and Measuring;" Eva et al., "Servant Leadership," 5.

34. Schwartz et al., "Servant Leadership," 1029.

35. Udani and Lorenzo-Molo, "Servant Becomes Leader," 374, quoting Klamon, "In the Name of Service," 9.

unconditional love."[36] In their subsequent work, they refer to "ethics, virtues, and morality."[37]

Eva et al. acknowledge "spiritual dimension" as "a distinguishing feature that "makes servant leadership a truly holistic approach relative to other positive leadership approaches,"[38] faithfully reflecting the theorizing of Greenleaf and Graham "that servant leadership relies on spiritual insights and humility as its source of influence." They recommend that future studies "examine spiritually-related constructs"[39]—a possible area of collaboration between secular and Christian scholarship.

Synthesis of Models of Servant Leadership

Sendjaya et al. examined a significant number and range of studies, "both qualitative and quantitative," in considering the "validation of a multi-dimensional measure of servant leader behaviour."[40] From their review of the literature, they identified twenty themes "pertinent of servant leadership" and these were "categorized into six different dimensions of servant leadership behaviour: Voluntary Subordination, Authentic Self, Covenantal Relationship, Responsible Morality, Transcendental Spirituality and Transforming Influence."[41] Sendjaya et al. reviewed four measures of servant leadership and then developed their own model. They noted "convergence among all models in the inclusion of servanthood (i.e., willingness to serve others) as a fundamental component of servant leadership."[42] They add being "driven by the leader's spiritual insights and humility"[43] and in particular add "spirituality and morality-ethics" into what they claim is "a more holistic model of servant leadership." Van Dierendonck considered models developed by several scholars and articulated an "operational definition" of the key characteristics of servant leadership. He claimed from his review that six characteristics "of servant leader behavior" can be distinguished and that they "give a good overview of servant leadership behaviour as

36. Parris and Peachy, "Building a Legacy," 259, 263, 367, 377.
37. Parris and Peachy, "Literature Review," 377.
38. Eva et al., "Servant Leadership," 5.
39. Greenleaf, "Servant Leadership"; Graham, "Servant-Leadership."
40. Sendjaya et al., "Defining and Measuring," 402.
41. Sendjaya et al., "Defining and Measuring," 406.
42. Sendjaya et al., "Defining and Measuring," 401, 410.
43. Graham, "Servant-Leadership."

experienced by followers. Servant-leaders empower and develop people; they show humility, are authentic, accept people for who they are, provide direction, and are stewards who work for the good of the whole."[44] Published in the same year, with Nuijten, Van Dierendonck's six characteristics had become eight, mostly overlapping but adding "authenticity," "standing back," and "courage," while omitting "provide direction" (though this may be encompassed within "accountability").[45] This set of eight characteristics has been cited and adopted by other researchers since[46] and was adopted for this study:

- Empowerment
- Accountability
- Standing back
- Humility
- Authenticity
- Courage
- Interpersonal acceptance
- Stewardship.

Eva et al. reviewed 285 articles on servant leadership spanning twenty years up to 2018. They propose that the trading of "hunter-gatherer small family-like tribes for large bureaucratic organizations with a globally mobile work force" has been moderated by servant leadership through "building a sense of social identity in their followers . . . and creating teams that are more like the kinship found in hunter-gatherer societies as team members assist and build capacity in others." Servant leadership has the characteristics of engaging followers in "relational, ethical, emotional, and spiritual dimensions," prioritizing the "well-being and growth" of followers.[47] These overlapping approaches have much in common but do leave synthesis of models of servant leadership a difficult challenge as we move to consider defining the concept.

---

44. Van Dierendonck, "Servant Leadership," 1232–35.
45. Van Dierendonck and Nuijten, "Servant Leadership Survey," 254–57.
46. E.g., Kieersch and Peters, "Inside Out," 161.
47. Eva et al., "Servant Leadership," 1.

Towards a Definition of Servant Leadership

Settling on a definition of servant leadership has been an elusive endeavor. Greenleaf did not clearly offer a definition.[48] Generally, scholars have been more inclined to be descriptive. As one example, servant leadership is "an employee [participant] and community focused leadership style." It involves role modeling, altruistic behaviours, and servant leaders producing servant leaders.[49] In addition to the approaches of description and definition, there are other common features of servant leadership described across authors. Some claim that servant leadership positively impacts the culture of an organization,[50] team effectiveness,[51] and the development of volunteers.[52]

Eva et al. offer the following definition of servant leadership, incorporating three features, "motive, mode, and mindset": servant leadership is (1) an other-oriented approach to leadership, (2) manifested through one-on-one prioritizing of follower individual needs and interests, and (3) outward reorienting of their concern for self towards concern for others within the organization and the larger community.[53]

This definition of servant leadership may be applied to both Christian and secular leadership—"other-oriented . . . prioritizing the needs and interests" of followers and putting concern for others ahead of concern for self. However, "Christian leadership development separates itself from secular theory . . . at the cross of Christ. Leadership development without the crucifixion of Self is not Christian."[54] There is a Christ/Christian dimension to leadership (and servanthood) going beyond any secular servanthood. It must confront the cross and move towards "identification with the Suffering Servant, and a confrontation with the paradox of death as the way to life."[55]

Complementing acceptance of the Eva et al. definition are the eight characteristics identified by Van Dierendonck and Nuijten.[56] That Van

---

48. Greenleaf, *Servant Leadership*.
49. Schwartz et al., "Servant Leadership," 1025.
50. Parris and Peachy, "Literature Review," 387.
51. Parris and Peachy, "Literature Review," 387.
52. Parris and Peachy, "Building a Legacy," 266.
53. Eva et al., "Servant Leadership," 3.
54. McKenna, *Christ-Centered Leadership*, 11.
55. McKenna, *Christ-Centered Leadership*, 22.
56. Van Dierendonck and Nuijten, "Servant Leadership Survey," 52.

Dierendonck has provided operational descriptions of his earlier six characteristics is a benefit in using them as a measure of servant leader effectiveness. This qualitative approach was preferred in this study over a quantitative approach using the measures developed by a number of scholars, including Sendjaya et al.[57] and Van Dierendonck.[58]

David McKenna recognized the millennial generation view that "servanthood has become the highest and best definition of secular leadership."[59] But then, based on Philippians 2:5 (identification with the mind of Christ Jesus), he reflected on whether there is not something more. He began to contrast his "career of upward mobility" with the "downward mobility of Christ," his "hidden drive for success" with the "sacrifice of Jesus." He concluded that there was a "critical disjunctive between the minimal self-giving of my servant-hood and the maximum self-sacrifice of the Incarnate Christ." He concluded this reflection with: "Servant leadership is the highest commendable option for the human mind, but sacrificial leadership is reserved for those who have the mind of Christ." "Servant leadership actualizes the self, serves others, and humbly denies credit. Incarnational leadership, however, dies totally to self, sacrifices to serve others, and gives the glory to God."[60]

Measuring Impact

Drawing on Greenleaf, Udani and Lorenzo-Molo suggest that authenticity of servant leadership is answered in response to the question, "Do those served grow as persons?"[61] Outcomes in followers experiencing servant leadership noted by Eva et al. in their review of 286 articles on servant leadership include: demonstrated "organisational citizenship behaviour,[62] focus on community and customers, employee engagement, thriving at work, innovation oriented outcomes, knowledge sharing between employees, trust in leaders, perceived leader effectiveness, integrity, quality relationships

57. Sendjaya et al., "Defining and Measuring."
58. Van Dierendonck, "Servant Leadership."
59. McKenna, *Christ-Centered Leadership*, xiii.
60. McKenna, *Christ-Centered Leadership*, 11.
61. Udani and Lorenzo-Molo, "Servant Becomes Leader," 384.
62. Organizational citizenship behaviour (OCB) refers to positive behaviour of an employee that is not in their job requirements. It is additional, voluntary, discretionary, and contributes to organizational effectiveness.

between leader and followers, teams task focused and person focused, effective teams, team creativity, and innovation."[63] The primary criteria for measuring positive change, initially from Greenleaf[64] and repeated by many others,[65] is whether servant leaders reproduce servant leaders.

For the purposes of this study, the measures of servant leadership that were used as the elements of this investigatory lens, as a guide towards determining whether servant leadership is critical to the apparent success of *Leadership* were:

- the three dimensions of the Eva et al. definition
- the eight characteristics identified by van Dierendonck and Nuijten
- whether leaders are reproducing leaders
- evidence of sacrifice in the service of others and the glory being given to God (McKenna); introducing the Christ/Christian dimension of servant leadership.

These elements are further informed by other servant leadership characteristics: building strengths in participants, organizational citizenship behaviour, encouraging innovation/creativity, trustworthiness, and integrity.

On the measure of reproduction of leaders, it is not surprising that the claim is made that servant leadership is contagious, as the behaviour that is modeled by trusted and respected leaders is likely to be emulated by followers. Within the servant leadership dimension of *transforming influence* that Sendjaya et al. identified[66] is the recognition that "those served by servant leaders are positively transformed in multiple dimensions (e.g., emotionally, intellectually, socially, and spiritually) into servant leaders themselves." The view that servant leadership is contagious is endorsed by Graham[67] and Udani and Lorenzo-Molo.[68] Parris and Peachy extend this thinking further, commenting that when servant leadership is lived it becomes "contagious" and when circumstances demand, it is found that

---

63. Eva et al., "Servant Leadership," 9–10.
64. Greenleaf, *Servant Leadership*.
65. Sendjaya et al., "Defining and Measuring," 408; Parris and Peachy, "Building a Legacy," 268; Carter and Baghurst, "Influence," 462; Schwarz et al., "Servant Leadership," 1026.
66. Sendjaya et al., "Defining and Measuring," 408.
67. Graham, "Servant-Leadership."
68. Udani and Lorenzo-Molo, "Servant Becomes Leader," 386.

others are able to and do take over, maintaining organizational mission, having "become servant leaders" themselves.[69] This is an outcome measurement that is important for *Leadership* and goes back to the original claims for servant leadership, as further articulated by Carter and Baghurst: "The success of servant leaders develops through committed employees who actively contribute to the success of the organization thus becoming leaders themselves."[70]

Findings of the Research

Servanthood is a key approach in *Leadership* and is articulated to participants at every level of the program.

Characteristics of Staff

Outlined in detail in chapter 2, one approach to assess the extent to which servant leadership is communicated and modeled at *Leadership* was to ascertain whether respondents recognized servant leadership characteristics in staff. Because of the large number of characteristics, two separate lists were put to respondents, inviting them to select up to five that they most noted in staff during *Leadership*. Characteristics identified by different theorists were grouped and assigned to lists. Neither list was more important than the other and, in both lists, other non-servant leadership identified options were included to test whether participants rated them more highly than the identified servant leadership characteristics. Responses to the first list, incorporating the dimensions of the Eva et al. definition of servant leadership and the eight characteristics identified by Van Dierendonck and Nuijten are outlined in table 26.

	CHARACTERISTIC	RESPONDENTS (%)
	Empowerment—believing in others and enabling others' development	59.5
	Humility—awareness of limitations and acceptance of any mistakes	51.9
	Authenticity—presenting one's true self	48.9

69. Parris and Peachy, "Building a Legacy," 268.
70. Carter and Baghurst, "Influence," 462.

CHARACTERISTIC	RESPONDENTS (%)
Standing back—giving others credit and support	48.1
Interpersonal acceptance—empathy and understanding	46.6
Accountability—developing clear goals then holding others accountable for achieving set standards	38.2
Stewardship—focusing on the common good above self-interest	38.2
* Showing respect for the Course Director	26.7
Courage—daring to take risks and challenge conventional practices	23.7
One-on-one prioritizing of follower individual needs and interests	22.1
Other-oriented approach to leadership	19.1
Outward reorienting of concern for self towards concern for others	14.5
* Being a visionary	10.7

Table 26. Servant Leadership Characteristics Most Noted in Staff—List 1

Those marked * were not identified characteristics of servant leadership but were included in the survey to expand the options.

The Van Dierendonck and Nuijten characteristics were selected in their top five by 23.7 to 59.5 percent of respondents:

- Courage (23.7%)
- Stewardship (38.2%)
- Accountability (38.2%)
- Interpersonal acceptance (46.6%)
- Standing back (48.1%)
- Authenticity (48.9%)
- Humility (51.9%)
- Empowerment (59.5%)

From this list of characteristics, according to respondents, *empowerment* (believing in others and enabling others' development) is the most highly observed servant leadership characteristic displayed by staff. Not only did participants generally believe they were empowered, but staff also believe this is the characteristic they were displaying most (staff respondents at 63.6 percent and a very high proportion of experienced staff at 92.9 percent).

According to participant respondents, Leadership staff *empowered* them, demonstrated *humility* and *authenticity, stood back*, and *gave credit and support to others, accepted them with empathy and understanding*, demonstrated *stewardship*, and expected *accountability*.

The Eva et al. statements were selected in their top five by 14.5 to 22.1 percent of respondents:

- One-on-one prioritizing of follower individual needs and interests (22.1%)
- Other-oriented approach to leadership (19.1%)
- Outward reorienting of concern for self towards concern for others within the organization and the larger community (14.5%)

All of these statements were selected in the top five by fewer than any of the Van Dierendonck and Nuijten characteristics. However, what might appear to be a relatively low proportion of participants selecting these characteristics, all *other*-related—between 14.5 and 22.1 percent—is contrasted with the high selection of *empowerment* as the most important of all characteristics at 59.5 percent. *Empowerment* was defined as believing in *others* and enabling *others*' development, demonstrating an *other*-oriented approach and a concern for *others*. Similarly, when examining the characteristics respondents described in their own leadership style, *others* was the most commonly used word, including the description, *proactively reaching out to others* (Stage 3, 2010). The reasons for the difference in rating between characteristics is unclear, but it is apparent that in selecting *empowerment*, respondents are acknowledging the focus on *others* of servant leadership.

Responses to the same invitation for a second list of characteristics, incorporating other identified servant leader characteristics, including *evidence of sacrifice in service* (McKenna), introducing the Christ/Christian dimension and characteristics expected to inform the dimensions of Van Dierendonck and Nuijten and Eva et al. included in List 1: *building strengths in participants, organizational citizenship behaviour, encouraging innovation/creativity, trustworthiness,* and *integrity* are outlined in table 27.

	CHARACTERISTIC	RESPONDENTS (%)
	Trustworthiness	55.0
	Modeling Jesus's servanthood standard (sacrifice in the service of others and giving the glory to God)	51.2
*	Pushing us towards our goals	51.2
*	Good communication skills	44.3
*	Acceptance of people for who they are	41.3
	Integrity	36.6
	Speaking about Jesus's servanthood standard	36.6
	Building strengths in participants	34.4
	Organizational citizenship behaviour	28.2
*	Providing direction	26.0
*	Working for the good of the whole	25.2
	Encouraging innovation/creativity	24.4
*	Having a strategic plan	15.3

Table 27. Servant Leadership Characteristics Most Noted in Staff—List 2

Those marked * were not identified characteristics of servant leadership but were included in the survey to expand the options.

From this list, *trustworthiness* was the servant leadership characteristic rated most highly by respondents. Selections of characteristics from this list were not as consistent across groups (participant respondents and staff respondents). Overall, survey respondents were more diverse in their selections. For example, the three selections made by more than half the respondents included one from the additional informing characteristics (*trustworthiness* at 55 percent), one from McKenna (*modeling Jesus's servanthood standard—sacrifice in the service of others and giving the glory to God* at 51.2 percent), and one from the non-identified characteristic list (*pushing us towards our goals*, also at 51.2 percent). The next most selected characteristics, in order, continues this mixed-source rating.

Considering the two lists together, some of the servant leadership models presented were highly recognized in staff by participants, particularly from the Van Dierendonck and Nuijten list. The narrow scope of the McKenna thrust: *modeling Jesus's servanthood standard (sacrifice in the service of others and giving the glory to God)* was also recognized. The Eva et al. statements were less highly recognized, although a possible explanation has been offered. Certain of the additional informing characteristics, in particular, *trustworthiness* and some of the characteristics included that were not necessarily identified as related to servant leadership were also recognized, most notably, *pushing us towards our goals, good communication skills,* and *accepting people for who they are*—the theme of *acceptance* again emerging. The differences may be accounted for as simply that fifteen- to seventeen-year-olds perceive more comfortably known one-word options. Nevertheless, simply relying on the Van Dierendonck and Nuijten characteristics is sufficient to see that servant leadership characteristics are recognized in staff.

Reproducing Leaders

A further and, for some, the most important measure of servant leadership, is the raising up others to become leaders, leaders reproducing servant leaders, or servant leadership being contagious.[71] Two survey questions sought to examine whether *Leadership* participants exercised leadership during the program itself (i.e., Were they being raised up as leaders?) and afterwards (i.e., Were they raising up other leaders?):

- Did you find yourself able to exercise a leader role during *Leadership*? (If they did, they were invited to give an example.)
- Since *Leadership*, what leadership roles have you been involved in—in BB, church, family, community?

On the first question, 79 percent said they were able to exercise a leader role during *Leadership*. As most *Leadership* participants are BB members and many are still under eighteen, there is no surprise that more than 50 percent of them are involved in leadership roles within the organization and their schools. The full spread of post-*Leadership* roles is outlined in table 28.

---

71. Graham, "Servant-Leadership"; Udani and Lorenzo-Molo, "Servant Becomes Leader," 386; Parris and Peachy, "Building a Legacy," 268; Carter and Baghurst, "Influence," 462.

LEADERSHIP CONTEXT	ROLE	NUMBER	%
BB local		63	56.8
School	School leadership e.g. School Captain (4)	13	12.0
University	Uni. club, etc.	6	5.4
Church—total		54	48.6
Church—specific	Church Council/Deacon	2	2.0
	Worship/Music/Creative/Tech support	19	17.1
	Pastor/Preaching/Prayer	5	4.5
	Kids ministry	16	14.4
	Youth ministry, including Youth camps	19	17.1
	Young adults' ministry	5	4.5
	RI in schools	2	2.0
	Outreach (e.g., Red Frogs)	2	2.0
Community	Community support (Support worker/Food bank)	2	2.0
	Arts	1	1.0
Family	Husband/Father/Self in family	13	12.0
Work/Business/Management	Manager/Team leader/Experienced staff member	24	21.6
	Mentor to new staff	3	2.7
	Army/Navy	2	2.0

Table 28. Leader Roles Exercised Post-*Leadership*

Particularly, if youth taking on leader roles is encouraged, their church is the other most likely opportunity to exercise or be mentored into leadership responsibilities. Worship and music roles are prominent, as are roles within kids or youth ministry—the latter a logical and natural extension to their BB leader roles. Very few mentioned taking on leadership in the wider community. As they move into the workforce, one might expect opportunities for leadership to arise there, as some respondents have reported. The other area of note is within family, reflecting a theme from *Leadership* dealing with a range of family and relationship issues. Examples of those mentioned by respondents were their leadership roles of husband and father—often a mission statement goal declared in Stage 3—and mention of self-leadership within their families—declaring independence or declaring a changed attitude within their family (e.g., "I've grown up"). Other personal statements about their approach to life and leadership were:

PART II: LENSES

> I am a leader wherever I go any day—family—work—self.
>
> I am my own leader.

The unknown question is how much of this acknowledged leadership development and taking up of opportunities is attributable to *Leadership*. One comment is cited from a participant respondent (now aged twenty-two or twenty-three) making links:

> I was leading NCO at BB until I was 18. I was part of a TEDx Youth Conference. I led 270+ people in a year-long competition in Melbourne (which we proudly won). I've led people on camping expeditions, hikes, in making a You Tube series . . . the list is long. And skills I've learnt from Leadership have been useful and applicable in every case. I'm very grateful for the experience. (Stage 3, 2015)

In a global survey conducted by Barna, among eighteen- to thirty-five-year-olds (with 15, 000 respondents from twenty-five countries), when asked about their spheres of leadership, 47 percent said they are a leader in their family, 34 percent in their job or workplace, 9 percent in their church or faith community, and 8 percent in the community (e.g., nonprofit or social causes). Thirty percent said they never thought of themselves as a leader.[72] It is not possible to conclusively compare the current *Leadership* survey with the Barna survey. However, it is of interest to note some contrasts. In the *Leadership* study, 96 percent of those who responded to the question on whether they had exercised leadership acknowledged that they had, while in the Barna study, 30 percent said they had not exercised leadership. Expectedly, given the respective cohorts, the proportion in the older age group Barna study who acknowledge they were exercising leadership in their families was higher (47% compared to 12%). Surprisingly, the relative proportions exercising leadership in their workplaces were closer (34% and 27%).

There is evidence that *Leadership* participants were exercising leadership—were being reproduced as leaders. A high proportion (79%) indicated that they were able to exercise leader roles during *Leadership*. Post *Leadership*, 56.8 percent indicated that they had exercised a leader role in their local BB companies; 17.1 percent that they had exercised a leader role in a youth ministry other than BB, and 48.6 percent in their churches. It was indicated by 17.1 percent that they had exercised a leader role in their schools or universities or were about to. Another 26.1 percent have

---

72. Barna, *Connected Generation*.

exercised a leader role in their workplaces. As a point of comparison, the 2020 Mission Australia Youth Survey found that 32 percent of young males aged fifteen to nineteen years had been involved in student leadership activities. Twenty-five percent of young males had been involved in youth groups/activities (not necessarily in a leadership role).[73] This data is too different to adequately compare, except to say that fewer *Leadership* graduates have been involved in student leadership activities in their schools or universities than in the general population—although some, at age fifteen, may not yet have had that opportunity. The challenge is to transfer their leadership into the community—although 26.1 percent said they had exercised leadership in their workplaces.

Interviewees were asked why they felt the characteristic of leaders reproducing leaders was not mentioned much. Interview responses lead one to conclude that the characteristic is substantially recognized as an attribute of servant leadership: the "idea of investing in [others] is very right; critical to humanity really"; it is recognized subconsciously; "a by-product or servant leadership"; "In the survey it might not have been mentioned because all of us felt it was happening"; "It comes back to discipleship and discipling someone is trying to build up another leader. So for me it's important"; "Reproducing leaders is a large part of servant leadership. It's one that I would link with servant leadership straight away." In summary, they believed the characteristic was present in their personal servant leadership practice.

Sacrifice in the Service of Others and Giving the Glory to God—The Christ/Christian Dimension

Interviewees were asked, "Why do you think survey participants did not openly identify very much the Christ/Christian dimension"? They provided a wide range of interpretative responses, including that it is assumed and that many may merely have selected items relating to the *physical aspects* or the *social benefit* of *Leadership* or that not everyone who attends is a Christian or a church attendee. One response is included in detail:

> I'm wondering if in the survey, have people responded in a very black and white, because often, bringing Jesus into the picture is emotive and when people are answering a survey it's emotional . . . what they've seen maybe in the survey they didn't go to that place. . . . Because Leadership is a Christian program it's assumed.

73. Tiller et al., *Youth Survey Report*, 126.

PART II: LENSES

> I felt that when I was doing a survey that I might just sound like a broken record if I keep bringing it up. Participation in worship and morning devotions is strong and is an obvious core component.

Any lack of recognition is contrasted with the response to worship—and this comment from a focus group participant:

> The Christian dimension is one of the fundamental successes of the course—compare this with other courses. Christ is servant leadership.

Evidence of Servant Leadership

While not all factors in all the models of servant leadership were immediately and equally apparent in the responses from *Leadership* participants, the data discussed suggests that the servant leadership characteristics adopted are evident at *Leadership* in program and staff. Complementing this data is that provided by survey respondents when asked to describe their current leadership style and what is important to them as they lead others. This evidence reinforces that servant leadership has been imparted to them as they are demonstrating servant leadership in their own leadership practice (i.e., that servant leadership has been reproduced in them). This data is summarized in table 29 using the servant leadership characteristics being examined as preset categories.

SERVANT LEADER CHARACTERISTIC	EVIDENCE FROM SURVEY RESPONDENTS (WORDS AND THEMES)
Other-oriented approach to leadership (including building strengths in participants)	"Other(s)" (42)—the most commonly used word in responses; proactively reaching out to others; investing in others; concern expressed for relationships and interaction between people; listening to others so all are heard; valuing other's ideas and opinions (13); everyone's voice heard; recognizing others' strengths and insights (3); bringing out the best in others
One-on-one prioritizing of follower individual needs and interests	Individualized consideration; help encourage people one-on-one

SERVANT LEADER CHARACTERISTIC	EVIDENCE FROM SURVEY RESPONDENTS (WORDS AND THEMES)
Outward reorienting of concern for self towards concern for others	Putting others needs and wants before your own; serving others rather than putting myself in the spotlight "I try to put others first. I care a lot about the team's feelings. This is how I was led during Leadership and it worked for me. I like to lead the same way" (Stage 1, 2008) Investing in others; empowering others; giving others the power to lead; happy to let others lead
Empowerment—believing in others and enabling others' development	Empowering others (2); encouraging others to develop their own strengths and abilities so they can grow (6); giving others the power to lead and grow; using praise and recognizing achievements; coaching and affiliative behaviour; encouraging others to work things out, towards their own independence
Humility—awareness of limitations and acceptance of any mistakes	Humility (2); admitting one's faults and errors
Authenticity—presenting one's true self (including trustworthiness and integrity)	Authentic (2); genuine (2); seeking to be authentic and to lead with integrity; trustworthiness; honesty; building mutual trust (2); practicing trustworthiness; integrity (3); practicing honesty; building a culture of honesty
Standing back—giving others credit and support	Supporting (7); giving space
Interpersonal acceptance—empathy and understanding; acceptance of people for who they are	Showing empathy (4); understanding (12); caring for others (6); getting alongside people; sharing struggles (2)—seeking mutual overcoming; being considerate of others (2); respecting and honouring others (8); respecting their views so they feel valued
Accountability—developing clear goals then holding others accountable for achieving set standards	Setting shared or group goals and helping to achieve them (7); communication skills (3); being task-oriented and looking for results (1); reach our goal (with everyone's input); guiding in the direction of the goal that has been set; encourage and push people to achieve things, but also happy to let others lead
Stewardship—focusing on the common good above self-interest (working for the good of the whole)	Recognizing group (13) or team (16); seeking group cohesion, consensus and a communal outcome; make it about everyone and not yourself; leading from a position of group wellness, instead of personal success; seeking collaboration and consensus; communal decision-making; valuing teamwork and a cohesive team; seeking group (not individual) success; using the strengths of others; desiring group success, not individual

PART II: LENSES

SERVANT LEADER CHARACTERISTIC	EVIDENCE FROM SURVEY RESPONDENTS (WORDS AND THEMES)
Courage—daring to take risks and challenge conventional practices (including encouraging innovation/creativity)	Allowing space for creativity
Modeling Jesus's servanthood standard—sacrifice in the service of others and giving the glory to God (the Christ/Christian dimension)	Self-sacrifice; Christ's standard (2); servant (5); modeling the example Jesus has set us; serve the group to point others to Jesus and not to myself "Lead a Godly and righteous life and by emulating Christ, become someone worth emulating" (Stage 1, 2015)

Table 29. Respondents' Descriptions of Their Current Leadership Style

(NB: Where numbers are included in brackets, this indicates the number of times this concept was mentioned more than once)

As indicated in the data, many characteristics of servant leadership were described. The evidence, although based on self-perceptions, is indicative of, at least, an understanding of servant leadership as it applies in a variety of contexts. The anonymous nature of the survey and the vulnerable tone demonstrated suggests that an assumption of a good degree of honesty is warranted.

No obvious evidence was found in the survey data that participants are demonstrating the courage to take risks and challenge conventions. This may be because respondents are aged between sixteen and twenty-eight, many in the younger age bracket, so this characteristic may be more sophisticated and take time to develop. However, in interviews, there was a different view expressed: that it is "second nature, normal, something we generally do," you "put yourself out there for the benefit of those you are leading, rewarding and honouring the commitment they are making to you"; it is "automatic."

Similarly, though they may have been leading as reproduced leaders themselves, there was no evidence in the survey data of an expressed awareness of the role of continuing to reproduce leaders from those they lead. Yet, interviewees said, "in the survey it might not have been mentioned because all of us felt it was happening"; "it's obvious," and, making a link to taking risks, being ready to "enable a new generation . . . to take up the challenge."

Many described their leadership style and what was important to them in a balanced and eclectic way, acknowledging the interests of those they lead.

Summary of Chapter

Servanthood has been examined in the light of Jesus's paradoxical teaching and his life example. When Jesus washed the disciples' feet, there was both a corporate teaching act taking place and an individual encounter of servanthood (e.g., with Peter). The servant leader adopts this focus too, towards those they serve, focusing on that individual at least in the moment of interaction. Secular scholarship has been explored recognizing a comparison of leadership models and characteristics approaches, which is linked to attempts to synthesize models of servant leadership.

Leadership viewed through a servant leadership lens includes consideration of the components of the Eva et al. definition, Van Dierendonck and Nuijten's eight characteristics, McKenna's concept of sacrifice and attribution of glory (the Christ/Christian dimension), and the issue of servanthood being contagious or self-reproducing, which are informed by other characteristics and combined to establish the standard of the Jesus model of servanthood. This was the criteria for the application of this lens to *Leadership* and discovery of whether it is an element contributing to the program's success.

The data providing insight into the lens of servant leadership has been presented and examined using criteria drawn from theological and secular literature. The evidence is that while the characteristics examined vary in their relative level of observation by participants, servant leadership is strongly presented, is demonstrated by staff at *Leadership*, and is observably replicated. Thus, it is concluded that examining *Leadership* through this lens has provided evidence that it is a factor contributing to the apparent success of the program. Linking to the emerging themes, the key observations are that staff are empowering participants, and participants are experiencing trust and acceptance. Staff are demonstrating, though imperfectly, the servant leadership of Jesus, and participants are taking their experience into the realm of where they can exercise leadership post-*Leadership*.

11

Masculine Spirituality

> It's easy if you've got a weakness to focus on that but looking at your spirituality as a whole is ridiculously important. (Stage 3, 2019)

MASCULINE SPIRITUALITY AND RITES of passage, as theoretical constructs, are considered separately, although Richard Rohr relates rites of passage to his consideration of masculine spirituality.[1] The challenge in dealing with the topic of masculine spirituality is recognized. One dimension of the challenge is reconciling Scripture with contemporary thinking, particularly in respect of the roles of men and women in the church. Keown proposes a "new masculinity" based on an interpretation of the household code of Ephesians 5:21—6:9.[2] His approach is considered through the eyes of various commentators and the issue of contemporary contextualization is considered. The key characteristics of masculine spirituality that are identified in *Leadership* are examined.

Reviewing the Theory

The male only nature of the *Leadership* program is suggestive of the fact that masculine spirituality might be an important factor in the success of the program. Masculine spirituality can be described as "a spirituality that

---

1. Rohr, *Adam's Return*; "Masculine Spirituality."
2. Keown, "Paul's Vision," 60.

offers a sacred path for the man to rediscover the nuances of their own line of life and redefine their lives according to the story of their hearts."[3]

The emergence of what became known as the *men's movement* has been linked to the concept of masculine spirituality—referred to by some, somewhat critically, as the "mythopoetic movement."[4] Many[5] link a critical view of masculine spirituality to the work of Robert Bly, who suggested that the emergent issue for men related to their remoteness from their fathers and "remoteness from their own masculinity."[6]

Rolheiser suggests that feminism be seen as a positive challenge to men and that in a "post-feminist understanding of themselves," men have become more sensitive, but also more tentative about their masculinity. Spiritually, men have been left with an inability to express their feelings, find a concept of God, or find "positive spiritual energy." Rolheiser recognizes the continuing concerns among men of "vicious competitiveness, violence toward women, the temptation to set money, power, and career above relationships," and a high suicide rate.[7]

Complementing this view are the views of Rohr, who suggests that an achieved and unique masculine spirituality is one that encourages a man to realize he "has life for others and knows it, he does not need to push, intimidate, or play the power games common to other men because he possesses his power with surety and calm self-confidence."[8] Rohr adds that "masculine spirituality emphasizes that doing, or acting, is the primary way of developing a spirituality—not hearing, not talking, not reflecting. Reflecting comes later after the action" and remains a critical part of the process.[9]

It is not proposed here to further examine the stimulus for the emergence of the men's movement, the various forms it took or organizations it spawned. What is critical for this present review is that, on the one hand, there was a response to the perceived position, interests and needs of men—and on the other hand, that it invited critique, including from feminism.

---

3. Good Men Project, "Understanding Male Spirituality."
4. Knuth, "Male Spirituality."
5. E.g., Rolheiser, "Masculine Spirituality"; Dalbey, *Masculine Soul*, ix.
6. Bly, *Iron John*.
7. Rolheiser, "Masculine Spirituality."
8. Rohr, "Masculine Spirituality."
9. Rohr, "Masculine Spirituality."

PART II: LENSES

Critique of men's movements from feminist academics and their claim to speak to masculine spirituality can be represented by Knuth,[10] who specifically examined the views of Rohr[11] and Arnold,[12] though she considers Rohr "not so adamant about sexual polarity as Arnold is." Knuth's critique of Rohr is focused upon, as his work is cited frequently in this study. Knuth takes issue with claims of Rohr and others that the church is "overly feminine" and questions his view of the need for boys to be initiated into manhood,[13] drawing Arnold back into the mix with a comment: "Why the plea to initiate boys into manhood, if personality characteristics are really determined by sex chromosomes?" Continuing with a feminist analysis, Knuth contrasts the position of women who have been oppressed and are "fighting for their lives" with the position of men who "are looking for some peace of mind." Rightly, she claims that "these are not equivalent."[14] It is not a woman versus man issue. Similarly, Knuth interprets Rohr's emphasis on dealing with power, suggesting that he is proposing a "quasi-divine authority" over "all he [man] surveys."[15] These positions remain in conflict.

Knuth concludes a feminist evaluation of male spirituality with a view that the movement is not "worthy of feminist support," that "from a Christian perspective, the idea that the spiritual realm is sexually polarized is a threat to soteriology," that "male spirituality, as it has been expounded" is not a "helpful approach," and that "it does not appear that there is any such thing as a specifically male path to God."[16] Rohr claims extensive support from women for his work, that there is evidence that men and women (boys and girls) do learn differently, and that their places in the world are different: "there are different paths [to God] because men and women pay attention to different things."[17]

There is a valid place for the views of Knuth and Rohr and their followers. Though in conflict, each sharpens the other. The debate is between a theoretical approach of feminist theology and a response to what emerged as a concern about men, which led to claims of a distinct *masculine*

---

10. Knuth, *Male Spirituality*.
11. Rohr and Martos, *Wild Man's Journey*.
12. Arnold, *Wildmen, Warriors, and Kings*.
13. Knuth, *Male Spirituality*.
14. Knuth, *Male Spirituality*.
15. Knuth, *Male Spirituality*, 6.
16. Knuth, *Male Spirituality*.
17. Rohr, *Wild Man*, 7.

spirituality. Knuth and others have caricatured masculine spirituality in a narrow manner and have then condemned their characterization. It is proposed that the debate, while important, should not cloud the theologically reflected views of a validly perceived need of contemporary men. That is the approach taken here. In an article that amounts to a response to criticism, Rohr referred to a vacuum caused by the loss of a transforming initiation for men and identified this as the space that "modern men's movements" came to occupy. He commented:

> Whether you agree with their message or style is not the important first question. Men are looking for spiritual experience; they are trying to submit themselves to "godfathers" in a country with very few of them. They are at least recognizing the need and the problem, and we do little good for them by simply dismissing and debunking them without offering a positive alternative for them.[18]

Rohr has been a voice in masculine spirituality for twenty years. He has answered criticism of his views, has survived time and criticism, and is still regarded as meeting the needs of contemporary men. There is no need to resolve the question of whether there is a specific masculine spirituality. True masculine spirituality takes seriously Ephesians 5 and 6 and is clearly in contrast with the dominating masculine spirituality that Knuth is critiquing.

The argument needs to be held in creative and respectful tension—ensuring that in the masculine spirituality argument, when linked to such passages as Ephesians 5 and 6, *submission* is seen as mutual and not used as an excuse to manipulate, put down, withhold opportunity from, or abuse women. Rather, it is an opportunity to serve and respect women before God and in the world.

Commencing with theological reflection, a specific article by Keown, interpreting the role of men through Ephesians 5:21—6:9 and making serious claims for the interpretation of this passage as a picture of contemporary scriptural masculinity,[19] will be examined to see if his concepts have any bearing on the effectiveness of the program being reviewed. This is followed by an examination of a contemporary application of the passage, including links to the lens of servant leadership.

---

18. Rohr, "Boys to Men."
19. Keown, "Paul's Vision."

Theological Reflection on Masculine Spirituality

Keown proposes a "new masculinity" or masculine spiritualty.[20] He proposes that "radical servanthood, gentleness, humility, sacrifice, and love should be the primary attitudinal marks of men in the church, the home, and all of life." This he refers to as the essence of "Paul's vision of a new masculinity," based on Ephesians 5:21—6:9. Keown considers the primary focus of this *Haustafel* or household code to be on the role of the "*paterfamilias* [husband, father, master]" and that "embedded in Paul's social vision is his fresh vision of what it means to be a man 'in Christ.'"[21]

In considering the roles of husband-wife, father-child, master-slave, Keown in the household code introduces the concept of servanthood, or what he refers to as "mutual servanthood" or "*paterfamilias* servanthood."[22] He links the Ephesians passage and the desired qualities of fatherhood with characteristics of Christ: gentleness, patience, and love, arguing for this pattern of Jesus. Keown acknowledges that this interpretation would have been a challenge to the social norms of first century, that it is a "radical picture of a new masculinity,"[23] which continues to challenge tradition today. The very concept of *mutual* servanthood and *mutual* submission imply a view that there are different but complementary masculine/feminine roles.

"Among New Testament scholars, sections of the Christian literature that cover domestic conduct are often labelled 'household code' material."[24] The Ephesians passage dealt with by Keown is the most detailed and is the one examined here. Broadly, a debate around the interpretation of the passage is outlined by Krause in these terms: "Many interpret the household code as instruction to follow the old patriarchal standard of Greco-Roman society. Others suggest it is teaching husbands to lead but with a softer and gentler patriarchy grounded in something called servant leadership."[25] Or, as put by Witherington, "What we see here is an attempt to provide a significant equalizing of the relationships within Christian marriage, altering the usual character and direction of a patriarchal marriage situation."[26]

---

20. Keown, "Paul's Vision," 60.
21. Keown, "Paul's Vision," 47, 49.
22. Keown, "Paul's Vision," 53–54.
23. Keown, "Paul's Vision," 57.
24. Thielman, *Ephesians*, 366.
25. Krause, "Household."
26. Witherington, "Letters to Philemon," 314.

Considering the preceding Ephesians passage (5:15–20), Paul gives the instruction to live wisely (5:15); to live in the Lord's will (5:17)—being filled with the Spirit (5:18). Then follows the instructions for Christian households—husbands and wives; parents and children; masters and slaves (5:21—6:9). Hoehner sums up the intention of the Ephesians expression of the code: "the instructions given in the household code are God's formula for the wise walk of spouses, children, parents, slaves, and masters. Each of these, linking back to v. 18, must be filled with the Spirit in order to consistently carry out the exhortations given."[27]

Slater acknowledges the considerable debate on the Ephesians Scripture. One view is that "the household code on marriage does not exhort Christians to equal relationships. Rather, along Greco-Roman cultural expectations, it teaches unequal mutual relationships," relationships that are not equal as "men have more responsibility but also more power."[28] Slater also refers to a view that makes some concession, based on the comparison of Christ and the church with husbands, fathers, and slave-masters and where "order is established in the Christian community when the more powerful person relinquishes some power for the well-being of subordinates."[29] Bruce, writing many years earlier, suggests that in the fellowship of the Christian household, "Here pre-eminently should mutual consideration and deference be shown, between husbands and wives, between parents and children, between masters and servants."[30] Bruce continues: "The obligation of husbands" are "no lower" than the "duties of wives." The love of husband to wife should involve "his active and increasing and self-sacrificing concern for her well-being."[31] Another balanced view is proposed by Lincoln, though written earlier than most other commentators cited. Lincoln acknowledges that the household codes "can be seen as part of the process of stabilizing communal relationships in the Pauline churches."[32] He is of the view that "*all* the members of the household [are] to submit to one another" (v. 21). Whatever their roles and the household structures, "there remains the overarching demand that in all lowliness and meekness with patience, believers should bear with one another in love."

27. Hoehner, *Ephesians*, 816.
28. Slater, *Ephesians*, 149, 154.
29. Slater, *Ephesians*, 152.
30. Bruce, *Epistle*, 113.
31. Bruce, *Epistle*, 115.
32. Lincoln, *Ephesians*, 360.

PART II: LENSES

"Whatever their status in the household, to display the selfless regard for others which puts oneself at their disposal, sits perfectly compatibly with the requirements for particular subordination."[33]

A literal interpretation of the household code, particularly any strict interpretation of the instruction to wives to *submit* to their husbands (Eph 5:22–24), is countered by a view that the early church emerged in a society which already had a patriarchal structure, so they were given instruction on how to live as Christians in their households. Christians had to deal with accusations that they were destroying the society.[34] As put by Fowl, "to the extent that Christians found themselves in conventionally structured patriarchal households, Ephesians gives them guidance about how best to live in those households as followers of Christ."[35] Lincoln and Slater also propose views that support contextualization: "The specifics of the code are tied to their own time and social setting."[36] "These codes reflect their time and place. They represent a Christian version of the most enlightened views of the time."[37]

Thielman and Hoehner introduce a family-focused interpretation. Thielman conjectures that Paul "envisions members of each group [husbands and wives, fathers and children, masters and slaves] gathered within a house for worship and listening to this letter as it is read aloud," thus closely sharing life and worship.[38] In a similar vein, Hoechner, while acknowledging that the different categories of people are to submit to one another, considers there is a connotation of "mutual submission," implying "humility."[39] Likewise, Thieman considers alternate interpretations of this vision of the household code, preferring a view that "submitting to one another" carries a "hint that there is a sense in which everyone is involved in serving others."[40]

O'Brien refers to a "widely held view that v. 21 states a general principle of *mutual submission* by all Spirit-filled Christians to others in the body of Christ," including "specific kinds of mutual submission" involving

33. Lincoln, *Ephesians*, 385.
34. Fowl, *Ephesians*, 293; Snodgrass, *Ephesians NIV*, 304.
35. Fowl, *Ephesians*, 181.
36. Lincoln, *Ephesians*, 409.
37. Slater, *Ephesians*, 164.
38. Theilman, *Ephesians*, 366, 370.
39. Hoehner, *Ephesians*, 717.
40. Theilman, *Ephesians*, 366, 373.

the relationships husband-wife, parent-child, and master-servant. "Mutual submission requires that all Christians, regardless of status . . . are to serve one another in love (Gal 5:13)."[41] O'Brien quotes Bilezikian that "mutual subjection as defined on the basis of Ephesians 5:18–21 refers to relationships of reciprocal servanthood under the sole lordship of Christ," rendering "hierarchical distinctions irrelevant within Christian communities of church and family."[42] Others argue a different interpretation—that it is not mutual submission but "submission to appropriate authorities."[43] The strength and relevance of this interpretation revolves around the definition of *submission*. These two interpretations have a different emphasis, but there is no reason to regard them as irreconcilable. Both are possible. Mutual submission can incorporate submission to appropriate authority.

The argument to recognize change over time and culture is supported by Wilson, who in his study of the Hebrew Bible identified a "diachronic change . . . in Israelite views of masculinity." This is based on an examination of the coming-of-age experiences of David and Solomon incorporating "qualities like strength through physical force and the combative defence of honor."[44] An "alternative masculinity"[45] was recognized and "the exile context . . . engendered a reconstruction of manhood that diminished certain qualities previously central to Israelite masculinity, most notably strength as expressed through bellicose force." Such qualities diminished with the later experiences of Samuel and Solomon that "differ to such a great extent from the overall construction of masculinity in the Hebrew Bible."[46] This recognition of change in the view of masculine spirituality over time and culture is important in considering contemporary examples and as an informing theory through which to consider *Leadership*.

Contemporary Application

Lincoln leads the way for a contemporary contextualization of the household code. This is firmly established in relation to masters and slaves, followed by a new approach to male/female, particularly husband/wife

41. O'Brien, *Letter to the Ephesians*, 400.
42. O'Brien, *Letter to the Ephesians*, 401, quoting Bilezikian, *Beyond Sex Roles*.
43. O'Brien, *Letter to the Ephesians*, 401.
44. Wilson, *Making Men*, 153.
45. Wilson, *Making Men*, 225.
46. Wilson, *Making Men*, 152–53.

PART II: LENSES

relationships, and less remarkably, relationships between parents and children. Cohnick takes a forthright view, suggesting that in interpretation of the household code, there is a "need to keep an eye both on the historical past and on our own context."[47] Cohnick proceeds to the views that "Paul has introduced reciprocity in marriage" and "that the institution of patriarchy, which infused the social ordering of men and women is destabilized by this passage."[48] Fowl also provides a clear contemporary view that "most of us no longer believe in the biologically inscribed hierarchies such as those Paul and his contemporaries assumed."[49] Fowl adds that "the most important thing Paul offers the Ephesians is the example of seeing and interpreting the world through Christological ground lenses rather than lenses ground by Roman social custom and convention."[50] Fowl provides a conceptual interpretation that "these relationships of ordered interdependence reflect our fundamental dependence on God in Christ: they are honoured as Christian relationships to the extent that they reflect the divine-human relation."[51] It is concluded therefore that a contemporary view of Ephesians 5:21—6:9 is a proper view to take and this supports the *new masculinity* or masculine spirituality thesis of Keown that "radical servanthood, gentleness, humility, sacrifice, and love should be the primary attitudinal marks of men in the church, the home, and all of life,"[52] qualities that are also characteristics of servant leadership.

Research Findings

Of all the lenses, this is the most contested. For the purposes of this study, it has been accepted that there is a definable masculine spirituality and that it is a valid lens through which to view *Leadership* where terms such as *Christian man* are used.

In preparation for the examination of this lens, it was put to survey respondents that during *Leadership* they hear the expression "Christian man" or "man of God" and receive input on what God wants of a man. They were then asked to select from a list of twenty-two (informed by Keown),

47. Cohnick, *Ephesians*, 27.
48. Cohnick, *Ephesians*, 141–42.
49. Fowl, *Ephesians*, 197.
50. Fowl, *Ephesians*, 198.
51. Fowl, *Ephesians*, 145.
52. Keown, "Paul's Vision," 60.

up to five characteristics they consider the most important indicators of the spirituality of a Christian man today. Consideration of different views of older men was thought to be important. Participant responses, staff responses (where there is some overlap of age/experience), and experienced staff (tending to be older and likely to be husbands and fathers) responses are presented. Their choices are set out in full in table 30, and a comparison of top ten choices in table 31.

CHARACTERISTIC	ALL RESPONDENTS (%)	PARTICIPANT RESPONDENTS (%)	STAFF RESPONDENTS (%)	EXPERIENCED STAFF (14) (%)
Humility	50.8	48.4	57.6	71.4
Godliness	49.2	47.4	54.6	28.6
Servanthood	46.9	37.9	72.7	85.7
Love	46.9	49.5	39.4	85.7
Wisdom	43.0	44.2	39.4	7.1
Being responsible	39.9	42.1	33.3	42.9
Sacrifice	36.7	40.0	27.3	42.9
Strength in times of testing	35.2	36.8	30.3	0.0
Gentleness	31.3	31.6	30.3	50.0
Being a leader	27.3	24.2	36.4	0.0
Treating his wife as an equal	20.3	24.2	9.1	28.1
Husband and wife relating together in mutual submission	17.2	15.8	21.2	14.3
Managing power	13.3	9.5	24.2	7.1
Letting go of power	10.2	13.7	0.0	7.1
Being a warrior	9.4	7.4	15.2	14.3
Reflecting	8.6	9.5	6.1	7.1
Preference for doing or acting as the primary way of developing spirituality	7.0	6.3	9.1	0.0
Age	2.3	3.2	0.0	0.0
Broad experience	1.6	2.1	0.0	0.0

PART II: LENSES

CHARACTERISTIC	ALL RESPONDENTS (%)	PARTICIPANT RESPONDENTS (%)	STAFF RESPONDENTS (%)	EXPERIENCED STAFF (14) (%)
That his children obey him	1.6	2.1	0.0	0.0
Expectation that his wife will submit to him	0.8	1.1	0.0	0.0
Being in charge (the master)	0.0	0.0	0.0	0.0

Table 30. Indicators of the Spirituality of a Christian Man

	PARTICIPANT RESPONDENTS		STAFF RESPONDENTS		EXPERIENCED STAFF	
	CHARACTERISTIC	%	CHARACTERISTIC	%	CHARACTERISTIC	%
1	Love	49.5	Servanthood	72.7	Servanthood	85.7
2	Humility	48.4	Humility	57.6	Love	85.7
3	Godliness	47.4	Godliness	54.6	Humility	71.4
4	Wisdom	44.2	Love	39.3	Gentleness	50.0
5	Being responsible	42.1	Wisdom	39.3	Being responsible	42.9
6	Sacrifice	40.0	Being a leader	36.7	Sacrifice	42.9
7	Servanthood	37.9	Being responsible	33.3	Godliness	28.6
8	Strength in times of testing	36.9	Strength in times of testing	30.3	Treating his wife as an equal	28.6
9	Gentleness	31.9	Gentleness	30.3	Being a warrior	14.3
10	Being a leader Treating his wife as an equal	24.2	Sacrifice	27.3	Husband and wife relating together in mutual submission	14.3

Table 31. Indicators of the Spirituality of a Christian Man—Comparison of Choices

The top nine selections were closely clustered together (spread between being selected by 31.3 percent and 50.8 percent of respondents). To respondents, masculine spirituality is a multifaceted domain, with no clear characteristic or group of characteristics emerging. The lack of a clear top choice and the weak discrimination between consecutive choices may be explained through comparing responses of participant respondents with those of staff respondents and those of experienced staff. For some characteristics there is a significant difference. *Humility* is the only characteristic rated in the top three by all groups. The next closest to a consistent ranking is *love* (given the top ranking by participant respondents).

However, there is divergence amongst the groups in their other responses. Participant respondents are more diverse in their choices, which are spread across more characteristics (hence the lower percentage) than experienced staff in particular, whose top four (top five for staff respondents) have a higher percentage score than any choice of participant respondents—with staff respondents and experienced staff not choosing some characteristics at all. It is concluded that staff respondents and experienced staff have a more focused view on what they see as the most important characteristics for masculine spirituality, a concept that is still developing in clarity for younger participant respondents. As participant respondents were weighted towards the lower end of the range of ages, this may have affected their selections. Reflecting on whether there is any change over time and with maturing, the views of staff respondents are further examined. They rate *servanthood* more highly than do participant respondents (72.7% compared with 37.9%), yet surprisingly, they rate *sacrifice* significantly lower (27.3% compared with 40%). When the views of experienced staff are examined, it is seen that their views are more consolidated into a small range of choices, the highest being *servanthood* and *love* and, in fact, their top five corresponding exactly with the Keown (2016) list.

In interviews, a number shared their insights on whether masculine spirituality was multifaceted and proposed that it should be:

> Being singularly focused is a shallow and naive way of living your life. (Stage 1, 2019)

> I think, at the end of the day, it's all about following God's word and reaching out to others, but I think there are no qualities of a person that should really stand out. It should be their actions and what they do that should identify them. (Stage 2, 2019)

> There's not one thing that makes a man a man; that makes a Christian man. There are a lot of things. Ultimately being like Jesus is the goal. There are so many different levels and Jesus wasn't just one thing; he was so many different levels; he was multifaceted, so we should be multi-faceted. (Stage 3, 2019)

The five Keown characteristics of servanthood, gentleness, humility, sacrifice, and love all appeared in the top seven selections of survey respondents.

Given the theory of masculine spirituality being drawn from a consideration of the household code and its dealing with relationships between husbands and wives and fathers and children, it is interesting that respondents, including staff respondents (the group most likely to have marriage and family top of mind), did not rate highly the options of treating their wife as an equal or husband and wife relating together in mutual submission. On the issue of *submission*, the option of expectation that a wife will submit to her husband scored the second lowest rating of 0.8 percent.

Summary of Chapter

The chapter acknowledges opposing views on masculine spirituality, including those arguing from a feminist perspective and those responding to the perceived needs of men. It was concluded that the opposing views should be held in creative and respectful tension.

Ascribing caring, gentleness, and mutual recognition dimensions to the role of husband, father, and master is paralleling Christ's example of servanthood. In reflecting on "the state of masculinity" today, Keown proposes that the Ephesians 5–6 passage should be recognized as "primarily targeting *men* to pattern their lives on the consummate image bearer and new Adam, Jesus Christ as Lord."[53] Referring again to Keown, the focus of the Ephesians passage is on "attitude," particularly "servanthood, humility, and giving up oneself for the good of the other"—"a radical, socially submissive portrait of manhood that challenges traditional structures."[54] This is the defining statement of masculine spirituality, suggesting a link with an emphasis of *Leadership* (servanthood, humility, and being other focused).

This supports the *new masculinity* or masculine spirituality thesis of Keown that "radical servanthood, gentleness, humility, sacrifice, and love should be the primary attitudinal marks of men in the church, the home, and all of life," whether this be as husband, father, or master, or any leadership role in the church or the community.[55] This view respects the views of those who critique the concept of a masculine spirituality and excludes any hint of male superiority, particularly involving violence to women. It is not considered any more radical than Christ was.

---

53. Keown, "Paul's Vision," 59.
54. Keown, "Paul's Vision," 59.
55. Keown, "Paul's Vision," 60.

Research findings are that young men recognize a masculine spirituality, and their views accord with those of Keown, that it is characterized by servanthood, gentleness, humility, sacrifice, and love. This view is further consolidated as men mature and their views become more keenly focused on what it is to be a spiritual man—becoming mature being a key understanding; not yet perfect, but *acceptance* by others and accepting in themselves of their *imperfection* on the journey to a masculine spirituality, an understanding that is *freeing*. This contributes to recognition of the elements of the emerging substantive theory that responds to the research question. The consistency between respondents and the links to their views of servant leadership make this lens a useful one through which to view *Leadership* as it contributes to isolating those factors that contribute to the apparent success of the program.

12

Lenses of Outpouring

Servant Leadership and Masculine Spirituality

THE SECOND COALESCENCE OF lenses brings together the lenses of servant leadership and masculine spirituality, the lenses of outpouring. These two lenses have been dealt with in detail in chapters 10 and 11, with a review of the theory and theological reflection. This is continued here to demonstrate the correlation between theological and social science understandings, establishing a high level of correlation particularly in relation to servant leadership. Servant leadership is such a central teaching at *Leadership* that it is also featured as an important element of the uniqueness of the program (chapter 13) and contributes heavily to the categories forming the substantive grounded theory outlined in chapter 14. Servant leadership and masculine spirituality share characteristics, mirroring one another and the character and teachings of Jesus, but they are treated as separate and stand-alone lenses.

Theology informs the insights generated by the two lenses of outpouring through their clear and direct links to theological principles. The characteristics and theology of servant leadership are increasingly informing the secular world of management and leadership practice. An often-mentioned characteristic is humility—a consistent theological theme throughout Scripture. However, theologically informed servant leadership also has insights related to attitudes towards bias, discrimination, and dealing with the marginalized. The theology of masculine spirituality, as carefully developed in *Leadership* informs the insights relating to all who deal with others, particularly in family or other close relationships—including the intergenerational discipleship demonstrated by Jesus and adopted at *Leadership*.

The examination of servant leadership brought together the literature from theology and organizational/management practice. In chapter 10, biblical foundations of Jesus's servant leadership were traced, beginning with the recognition of *servant* as a key component of leadership in the Old Testament (e.g., 2 Sam 15:1–5; Isa 41:8–9; Isa 54:17; Deut 9:17; Deut 34:5; Judg 2:8; Deut 7:14; 10:12). Gary Yates introduced the concepts of heart examination and leaders motivated to act as faithful servants towards others.[1] Yates links the Old Testament and the New Testament by including Jesus and his followers in a humble "servant trajectory" (e.g., Rom 1:1; Gal 1:10; Titus 1:1).[2]

The servanthood model of Jesus and his teachings on links between servanthood and greatness and humility were considered through the passages of Mark 9:35, Matt 20:26–27, Mark 10:43, and Luke 22:24. The teaching of Jesus in those passages and in John 13:1–17 was acknowledged as the theological criteria for examining the servant leadership lens.

The origin of servant leadership in Jesus is acknowledged, even to a limited extent in management literature, and it was noted that many secular organizations are adopting a servant leadership model as their preferred leadership style for staff and management. The correlation between theological and management approaches, in particular, the work of Eva et al.,[3] Van Dierendonck and Nuijten,[4] and Mc Kenna,[5] led to a conclusion that these models were recognized and adopted by *Leadership* participants.

Servant leadership does not, and neither did Jesus, mean simply serving others in an obvious manner. It includes aspects of service that are tough, that involve challenge, drawing people towards something better and at times, something countercultural. It involves *demanding* transformation, equipping, and sending out. Servant leadership disciples followers spiritually but also in developing understanding, attitudes, and relationships. Examples of *Leadership* program elements have a clear theological relevance, including facing participants with an examination of issues of bias and discrimination towards those with certain attributes or conditions.

1. Yates, "Faithful Servants," 185.
2. Yates, "Faithful Servants," 196.
3. Eva et al., "Servant Leadership."
4. Van Dierendonck and Nuijten, "Servant Leadership Survey."
5. McKenna, *Christ-Centered Leadership*.

PART II: LENSES

Jesus did not discriminate on these bases (e.g., his concern for widows and orphans—Matt 18:6; Mark 9:42; Luke 17:2). In fact, people with these conditions were the ones he welcomed. He welcomed, touched, and healed those who were ill or disabled (Luke 14:12–14; John 5:1–15). He demonstrated understanding and care for the poor (Mark 12:41–44; Luke 14:12–14). He mixed with those who were most disliked and possibly discriminated against—the tax collectors (Luke 19:1–10). He did not consider ethnic difference an obstacle (e.g., a Samaritan woman—John 4:7–26). He showed no gender bias. On the question of age, he bypassed the wise and mature to call young men to follow him, and then set about training them (the whole essence of *Leadership*), to the point where Jesus acknowledged them not as *servants*, but "I have called you friends, for everything that I learned from my Father I have made known to you" (John 15:15)—an example to the church of "intergenerational-discipleship in the church and in the home."[6] Responding to these concerns is important to young men. To cite just one example, as noted in chapter 1 in considering the justification and importance of the research, in the 2020 Mission Australia youth survey, 31.7 percent of young males listed "equity and discrimination" as an issue of concern, second only to COVID-19.[7]

Strong evidence emerged from the data that the characteristics of *servant leadership* were adopted and demonstrated by *Leadership* staff and participants. *Empowerment* of *others* and *humility* were strongly recognized, and the model of the servant leadership of Jesus was adopted. Thus, it is concluded that servant leadership at *Leadership* is soundly based theologically and correlates highly with contemporary management literature and practice in many organizations.

Servant leadership is also considered as an attribute of masculine spirituality. Keown has proposed a *new masculinity* or masculine spiritualty, incorporating the characteristics of "radical servanthood, gentleness, humility, sacrifice, and love," based on his interpretation of Ephesians 5:21—6:9.[8] Examination of the survey data led to a conclusion that young men recognize a masculine spirituality, and their views accord with those of Keown. This view is consistent with the view of Tidball, who set about resolving the tension between leadership and servanthood. He presents a New Testament "parental model" for servant leaders—a model where

6. McGarry, *Biblical Theology*.
7. Tiller et al., *Youth Survey Report*.
8. Keown, "Paul's Vision," 60.

acknowledged imperfect fathers "were in charge [and] they were, because of Christ, simultaneously the family's servant." They made decisions and provided direction, but also "support, maintenance, encouragement, and practical service," but they were not and did not have to be perfect—not even in the important role of father—just as young people do not have to be perfect to follow God.[9]

A coalescence between the lenses of servant leadership and masculine spirituality is informed by theology and is established through sharing common characteristics, particularly empowerment and humility and recognizing the model of Jesus as the standard. Servant leadership has become a preferred leadership style in many secular organizations, so it is useful that *Leadership* adopts this as its style, both exemplified by staff and as a challenge to participants to reproduce. The concept of masculine spirituality occupies a more contested space, but it is a useful concept for young men through which to consider their personal and leadership qualities, consistent with faith and mission commitment.

Summary of Chapter

This chapter brings the lenses of servant leadership and masculine spirituality together, after these two lenses were extensively examined separately in the preceding chapters. It supplements the theological application and reflection, reinforcing their importance as lenses through which to view *Leadership*. It makes the point that they share characteristics but operate as stand-alone lenses that inform the emerging theory.

---

9. Tidball, "Leaders as Servants," 46, 47.

Part III

Uniqueness Characterization

THROUGHOUT THE SURVEY, RESPONSES of participants citing examples of difference and uniqueness of *Leadership* were noted, providing scope to explore how this contributes to the apparent success of the program. There is frequent reference to uniqueness recorded by survey respondents, interviewees, and focus group members. These are further examined and discussed in chapter 13 as a step in the development of the theory as to what factors contribute to the apparent success of *Leadership*.

13

Uniqueness of *Leadership*

> I felt I had accomplished something bigger than myself that not every boy has accomplished.

> Leadership is countercultural. It's not what normally goes on in the world.[1]

LEADERSHIP IS FREQUENTLY IDENTIFIED as a unique experience, even though it is possible that some aspects of *Leadership* may be able to be experienced in other situations (e.g., youth camp; long-term BB membership). The combination of components of the *Leadership* program across three stages is significant, though for some participants, one element or event is what makes it unique. Specific characteristics of *Leadership* have been identified as unique in themselves.

The uniqueness of *Leadership* emerged as a powerful link in the chain of grounded theory[2] development. This theme arose during the process of theory development, not from prereviewed literature, but from the research data. Six identified properties[3] of uniqueness, often linking to one of the lenses and themes, are discussed in this chapter.

---

1. A comment offered by a visiting staff member from a course developed in the US.

2. The methodology is outlined in Appendix I.

3. *Properties* is a grounded theory term, and as with others, has a specific meaning in that methodological context. A glossary of terms is included.

PART III: UNIQUENESS CHARACTERIZATION

The theme of uniqueness, appearing in both key component and application of lenses data categories, is of a different genre to the other themes and is considered here, defining its component properties, to support an increasing level of abstraction from data coding and analytical strategies. Uniqueness tends to incorporate other emerging themes and sits between intermediate and advanced coding in the grounded theory design summary, demonstrating "the interplay between the essential grounded theory methods and processes."[4] This confirms and consolidates the emerging themes, leading into the final grounded theory, as presented in chapter 14.

From the Research Data

There is a constant theme in the data, reflected and confirmed in surveys, interviews, and focus groups through theoretical sampling and constant comparative analysis, that there is a uniqueness about *Leadership*—different from any other experience participants have had.

Characterization of Leadership as Unique

Table 32 sets out the participant-identified unique characteristics of *Leadership* in broad groupings. Examples of the characteristic are provided and where direct quotes from respondents are used, they are in italics.

THEMES, ETHOS, APPROACHES	
CHARACTERISTIC	ILLUSTRATION
Servanthood and acceptance	These two characteristics are among the most identified as unique at *Leadership*
The facilitator relationship—and older men as well; strong Christian men	*My group had a facilitator who is pretty young, has done Leadership, not that long ago, who is prepared to share their story and guide us through the week. They, and we, also have older men with much experience who can be asked questions and who will support us in reaching solutions to situations that arise, including faith/spiritual, family, or personal.* *Being able to look up to good strong Christian men.*

---

4. Tie et al., *Grounded Theory Research*, 6.

THEMES, ETHOS, APPROACHES	
CHARACTERISTIC	ILLUSTRATION
Staff exampling servant leadership not just talking about it	*They are not just mouthing it; they are authentic and open. Their lives are exposed to one another and to participants. They demonstrate this through their through-the-year and annual commitments to Leadership.*
	Participants identify servant leader characteristics in staff.
The clean slate phenomenon	*It definitely makes an impact (being placed in a group where you don't know anyone). A number of the boys were comfortable and it was easier to share openly due to the lack of connection with others back home, it would be taken without judgement and that definitely helps with the openness.*
	It was a complete batch of strangers if you like. And I think because again that sort of principle of everyone's a stranger so it's a clean slate and you sort of can be honest with people if you so choose and present yourself.
	Being thrown into a group you have no idea about.
With an individual staff member or in my group, I can talk about anything, tell my personal story, or ask any question I want to and I know my *secrets* are safe	Participants frequently say that they can share or ask anything they want to at *Leadership*, usually in their small group, a safe and accepting environment. They have never had the opportunity to do this anywhere else. This includes topics of faith, relationships, family, sexuality, self-harm, inadequacy, self-image, and much more—usually something they have been worried about and now find they are not alone or unique in having those issues and questions.
	Members become buddies for life and are often the only ones that know "my secrets."
	Referring to Stage 3 Duo: Getting to know someone more deeply, more intimately; *journeying deeply with another man*; developing trust sufficient to tell *my deepest and darkest secrets.*
Liminal space (along with isolation and self-reflection)	Although the concept of liminal space was often not well understood, one who had only completed Stage 1 highlighted it as a unique feature of *Leadership*:
	Liminal space, isolation and self-reflection. I haven't seen this on any other leadership course and definitely something that other premier leadership training organizations don't do. Self-reflection—the opportunity for—which ties back to liminal space is very different.
Critical thinking	This was listed as a unique feature by one interviewee:
Through instant feedback	*Frequent appraisal of your own activity is very important (e.g., teamwork) for healthy critical thinking rather than cynicism.*

PART III: UNIQUENESS CHARACTERIZATION

THEMES, ETHOS, APPROACHES	
CHARACTERISTIC	ILLUSTRATION
Parents/family	As well as arising in dealing with relationships, there are two unique opportunities for communication between participants and their parents, both through a mode that itself has become unique. In Stage 1, participants write an (anonymous) letter to their fathers. It is not delivered, unless a participant asks for and identifies his letter to take home. It allows expression of desires, with some value for the writer and possibly giving confidence to communicate in person to their dads later. The second, the most highly significant event on Stage 2 Solo, are letter(s) they open from their parents and read while alone in the wilderness—again an unusual and unique event in their lives—letter(s) that in some cases are the first or only letter they have ever received from their parents, particularly their fathers.
Encouragement to be a leader now—not just later	Many opportunities in their groups, Overnight Expedition; Stage 2—leading self, feeding into Stage 3—Mission Statement.
SPECIFIC ACTIVITIES AND THOUGHTS	
CHARACTERISTIC	ILLUSTRATION
Letters—writing and receiving	The written word—to father/from parents/from BB Captain/to self.
The community or *family*	The *Leadership* community is recognized, both at and after the experience. Participants draw on *family* related terms to describe their unique relationships and friendships developed, often with a speed that surprises them.
Brotherhood	Becoming brothers is a common expression used and is a specific example of the community or *family* experience.
Group [My Group] *Communitas*	The group experience is new and unique to them and surprises them at how their group develops and invites engagement so quickly and deeply—experiencing *communitas*. *I definitely think that group and that emphasis. Rather than the macro level, the micro level details and getting to know quite intimately six people as opposed to getting to know averagely thirty people.*
The Anzac phenomenon—having experienced something serious and significant together	Like those who enlisted in the First World War, including many the same age (underage for war at fifteen to seventeen years), *Leadership* participants develop a connection with one another, sharing time in the *trenches* that only those who experienced it can understand—a comradeship that is totally loyal and is unbroken by time apart, spontaneously re-emerging whenever two or more meet, like veterans meeting up on Anzac Day—the spirit of *Leadership* mirroring the spirit of Anzac.[5]

5. Something that can be drawn from the title of Patrick Lindsay's book *The Spirit of the Digger* (Lindsay, *Spirit of the Digger*).

SPECIFIC ACTIVITIES AND THOUGHTS	
CHARACTERISTIC	ILLUSTRATION
Problem-solving	A different experience of problem-solving—where strategies are taught, debriefing is practiced with encouragement which leads to the development of critical thinking.
Wilderness as a location for certain activities	Not like at any other camp Includes outdoor problem-solving
Overnight Expedition	It is unfortunate in many respects that this activity is labelled as unique, but the reality is that fewer boys are getting such wilderness experiences elsewhere. Even for those who are experienced, however, there is a unique aspect that they highlight—that as fifteen-year-olds in their group, they were given the authority to do all the planning and make all the decisions.
Solo Solo celebration	No one else they know, except *Leadership* mates, have ever done it—three nights/four days alone in the bush. No school or church mates; just them. They expressed a sense of having completed something that was difficult; *something major in my life*; something hard and worthwhile; something to be proud of; a big step with a new chapter now beginning. Some comments in greater detail: *The feeling of truly accomplishing something that is no small feat for a 15/16-year-old in today's age.* *Finally it settles in: I've done something hard and worthwhile—something worthy of celebration. Being endorsed, not superficially, and generally, but truly and deeply was an experience and feeling that has stayed with me.* *Solo was actually something significant and important in my life, and should be something that I am proud of.* *I had achieved something major in my life.* *This was an amazing feeling, knowing that I had just completed a very difficult task and sharing the experience with people who had gone through it too.*
Mission statement	Many develop goals; few young men develop a mission statement for the rest of their lives. This they do at *Leadership*, declaring it in a unique context, in front of their cohort holding a real and symbolic sword. They appreciate the unique opportunity of being given the time they need to develop their statement and share it with those with whom they have shared three stages of *Leadership*. Where else would they stand and deliver a statement for the rest of their lives in front of peers?

PART III: UNIQUENESS CHARACTERIZATION

EVENTS	
CHARACTERISTIC	ILLUSTRATION
Rites of passage	Though here is a growing interest in rites of passage for young men, the *Leadership* experience is uniquely developed, planned, and delivered over three years, with all the ingredients of liminality, isolation, a cohort together, in the wild, and affirmation from respected older men.
Formal dinner	Identified as a highly significant event in every stage, the formal dinner is a new experience and enjoying it with their group members makes it more significant. *I'm sure the formal dinner [is unique] for lots of people.*
IT JUST HAPPENS	
CHARACTERISTIC	ILLUSTRATION
New things	Many camps or other programs offer new experiences, so this is not claimed as unique. Yet it is mentioned. *There were things that I did at leadership that I'd never done before. I played European handball. I'd never played European handball before so there's that sort of, you know the porridge.*
The porridge phenomenon (an *in vivo* code); a symbol that draws people into community Symbols Porridge Rocks Good food; not "camp food"; restaurant quality Cereal and hot breakfast; two course lunch; two course dinner; supper	It's mid-winter and the *Leadership* caterer serves porridge for breakfast. It's an option but after only a few days, practically everyone is eating porridge (with brown sugar). A plain plate of porridge has been elevated to iconic status and is frequently mentioned by participants post-program as something they remember: *(What elements are unique?) Did I say this in the survey, the porridge? Helen's porridge?* This phenomenon lends itself to similar iconic and unique *Leadership* experiences, such as Stage 2 participants collecting and adding their rocks to the growing cairn during their post-Solo recognition activity, in some cases even this simple action being linked to becoming a man. As with the saying that an army marches on its stomach; maybe young men being intensely challenged (intellectually, physically, spiritually, attitudinally, learningly) march on their stomachs.

THEOLOGICALY INTEGRATED, GROUNDED	
CHARACTERISTIC	ILLUSTRATION
Worship	*For me, the worship would be up in there as well. It was unlike anything I've ever done.*
	The worship and the relationships; it's just amazing.
	I would say it's some of the most significant worship ever in my life. I've been to . . . camp and worship is like party, party, party. The worship at leadership feels like we're not singing for ourselves. We're singing to God. It's all worship when we all sing together, there's something really beautiful about that. It feels intentional and from God.
Life changing/ transformative	Many examples are cited in different chapters, including the unique experience of Solo and meeting Jesus in solitude.

Table 32. Unique Characteristics of *Leadership*

These characteristics were collapsed into six properties, presented in diagram (figure 6) and narrative. Each of these properties is an abstraction, combining many codes and concepts (dimensions). In the descriptions that follow, dimensions of these properties are *italicized*. Many are dimensions of more than one property and link to the identified categories. Brief descriptive statements for each property are followed by theological reflection on each.

PART III: UNIQUENESS CHARACTERIZATION

Uniqueness—A Step in the Development of the Substantive Theory

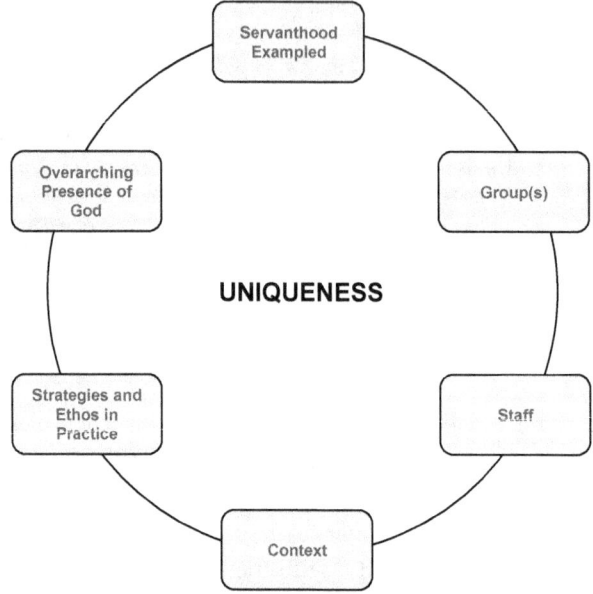

Figure 6. Properties of Uniqueness

Servanthood Exampled

Participants identified that the servanthood (of Jesus) is not just talked about, but is lived and modeled by servant leaders, not lauding it over participants, but sharing the journey of life together—living the example of *servant leadership*, not just talking about it. Characteristics of *servant leadership* are being reproduced in *Leadership* participants, but they want to be sure they are doing it *authentically* and are happy to acknowledge their *imperfection*.

Group(s)

They start with a *clean slate*,[6] leading to total *acceptance*, which *empowers* and generates a sense of *trust, freedom,* and *safety* in sharing. They move to a *communitas* experience (*My Group*) and then to a recognized *brotherhood* and *community* (*family*), which is *empowering,* and which extends long-term, mirroring the *spirit of the Digger* (*the Anzac Phenomenon*).

In the community and the group, participants find themselves with *diverse* but strangely similar people, with similar struggles; there is an instant *brotherhood* formed and love shown between members of the whole community, who look forward to meeting again in twelve months, or unexpectedly in their life journey, immediately rekindling their *Leadership* experience.

Staff

Relationships are formed, with and through facilitators who share life and *story* (links to My Group), and this extends to the full *Leadership* community which is described as a *multigenerational, nonhierarchical, servant-led community of men.* The staff team are committed to the long-term, and the team is *ever-renewing,* through adding to the community annually a new cohort of young men as participants and *seamlessly transitioning* others into the staff *community.* The staff group is seen as *authentic* and is prepared to be seen as *imperfect* and *vulnerable*—as revealed in their personal *story sharing.* The team *comes together for purpose* and does not place high value on *differentiation of status.*

The *cross-generational* staff and their *longevity* is seen as different from that in many churches and other parachurch ministries. "People on the journey have stuck through for a long period of time. There are many people who have stayed the course. I remember when my kids were born, I wanted a course that mine could go to that would be worthwhile, so part of my investment was that."[7]

---

6. This phenomenon is identified and explained in chapter 2. Briefly, when participants use this term, they are referring to the situation in Stage 1, where they are placed in a group with no one they know or have met before. So they are free to be themselves, without baggage, and to construct the persona they desire in their group. The positive explanation is that they see it as an opportunity to be their real selves and to engage in conversation they do not feel free to engage in, in other situations where they are *known*—but not really *known.*

7. Comment from a long-serving staff member.

PART III: UNIQUENESS CHARACTERIZATION

Context

The location is away from the pressures and circumstances of normal life, in a new closed community, at times in *liminal space* and in *wilderness*. Participants are at various times in *solitude*, with one other participant, in their group, in their stage group, or in the whole course community. *Symbols and traditions* (e.g., *The Porridge Phenomenon*) are recognized.

Strategies and Ethos in Practice

Strategies and ethos are reflected in a wide variety of program elements and activities. The strategies and ethos include:

- providing challenge and space for *self-reflection, affirmation*, declaring *life mission*, and enjoying *celebration* with mates
- recognition of the importance of participants' *families*
- total *acceptance*; nonjudgmental acknowledgment of *imperfection*
- *empowering* participants through *freedom* and being given real *responsibility*
- giving permission and opportunity to exercise *leadership now*—practicing this safely at *Leadership*, then at home.

Leadership is *progressive* in nature. At home, younger boys (e.g., in BB groups) see older boys returning and they want the same experience. At *Leadership*, the three-year progression between stages is clear and is experienced with expectation and excitement as they look ahead to the next stage.

Overarching Presence of God—Engagement and Celebration

The recognized *spiritual hunger* of young men is responded to through integrating it into whole of life through shared living, a modeling and teaching/learning experience, and a *unique worship* experience that is *authentic* and real, though *imperfect*. *Authentic* Christian manhood and a masculine spirituality distinguished by *servanthood*, gentleness, humility, sacrifice, and love is promoted, leaving space for the Spirit to move in the place of *mystery*. This explains the *mystery* of how boys become so close with one another and experience *communitas* so quickly, deeply, and long-lastingly; how boys change so substantially in one week—God in action in the world of younger and older men together, in *the community* that is *Leadership*, leading to life change/*transformation*, spiritually, relationally, and practically.

Theological Reflection on the Characterization of *Leadership* as Unique

Throughout this discussion the concept of mutual critical correlation (between theology and the social sciences) will be evident, as in other chapters.

Servanthood Exampled

Servant leadership has been discussed and linked with the lens of masculine spirituality, bringing together understandings from multiple disciplines and contemporary applications. The extension that uniqueness of *Leadership* adds to the findings and the theory is the uniqueness of *servanthood exampled*. Participants say the *Leadership* staff are different from other people, even other leaders they have encountered. In particular, it is that staff not only are themselves hearers of the word, but they are exemplars, and doers, resonating with James 1:22: "Do not merely listen to the word . . . Do what it says"; or Paul's charge to Timothy to "be an example for the believers" (1 Tim 4:12); and, above all, the clear instructions of Jesus to his disciples to be an example of his servanthood to others: "I have set you an example that you should do as I have done for you" (John 13:16). These theological principles enhance understanding of what happens at *Leadership* in the interactions between participants and staff as participants experience staff speaking *and exampling* servant leadership, recognizing as well that in education and training practice, it is well-established that providing examples and demonstrations is much more effective for learning than just telling.

Group(s)

A unique theology of fellowship surrounds the *Leadership* groups, including raising the relationships to the status of brotherhood and family.

Groups and group dynamics have long been an area of study in the social sciences, for example, anthropology in understanding cultures, sociology in understanding characterization of communities, and psychology and social work in understanding group formation and as a strategy for therapeutic intervention. My Group, particularly as this is experienced in Stage 1 of *Leadership*, is a key essential factor contributing to the apparent success of the program. It is one of the most unique experiences, something participants report that they have never experienced anywhere else, not even in their other Christian groups. Starting with the essential *clean slate*, acceptance leads to a feeling of safety, freedom, and empowerment, even in the realization of imperfection (key categories in the substantive grounded theory).

The initial liminal experience leads to spontaneous *communitas*, just as Jesus put people, especially his disciples, in a liminal space. Jesus invited spontaneous *communitas* simply through his character and ministry, something that was later reflected in Paul's description of the early church (Acts 2:44; 4:32). The *Leadership* experience of *communitas* mirrors the experience of the early church, seen through a theology of fellowship; a spiritual experience. Following Pentecost (Acts 2), the believers devoted themselves to the apostles' teaching, fellowship, breaking of bread, and prayer (Acts 2:42). They broke bread in their homes (Acts 2:46), indicating they shared the fellowship of a meal. Christians are called to fellowship with Jesus (1 Cor 1:9) and the Holy Spirit (2 Cor 13:14). There is recognition of partnership in the gospel (Phil 1:5) and to their generosity, including to the poor (2 Cor 9:6–15). The unique *Leadership* group experience that participants describe incorporates this New Testament fellowship, even the sharing of meals, and leads to an experience of *brotherhood* or *family*, that is likened to the experience of those who fought together in wars—referred to in the Australian context as the *Anzac phenomenon*, the unique experience reported by the *Aussie Digger*. The theological and social science insights from group dynamics combine in correlation and assist in understanding what is occurring in the *Leadership* community experience.

Staff

Insights generated by considering the roles of staff are informed by a theological consideration of teaching with authenticity, adopting Jesus's strategy of story sharing, and the body metaphor.

The unique characteristics of *Leadership* staff are able to be divided into two distinct areas: staff attributes and the staffing structure. It has already been noted that staff are recognized by participants as exampling servanthood, and as examples of integrity and authenticity, something they do not always experience in other adults. It was reported by 32.8 percent of participants that "staff presented themselves authentically through openly sharing information and feelings."

They model the discipleship model of Jesus in working with young men to prepare them for mission and ministry and to teach them spiritual truths, living out the essence of the identified themes, in particular, acceptance, worship, empowerment, and transformation, while acknowledging their imperfection, something with which participants are able to identify. The characteristics that participants identified most highly in group facilitators were:

- They shared their stories (33.1%)
- They embraced openness and transparency (29.3%)
- They accepted me as I was (27.8%)
- They did not put others down or act as though they were better than others (27.1%).

The power of sharing personal stories has been discussed previously, drawing on the theory presented by Hernandez in examining the spirituality of Henri Nouwen, clearly explained through Nouwen's "logical relationship of spirituality with psychology, ministry, and theology."[8] From a theological perspective, Jesus models storytelling both in telling his personal story and as a strategy in delivering his message to his hearers. His story was not always understood, which provided opportunity for teaching. This illustrates a correlation between theology, educational practice, and psychology that backgrounds a developing understanding of why this characteristic, identified in staff, is effective.

The unique nature of the *Leadership* staffing structure has been described as being a multigenerational, nonhierarchical, and servant-led community of men who come together for purpose and do not place a high value on differentiation of status. Two related features are the annual recruitment of new staff from the graduating Stage 3 group and the longevity of many staff—guaranteeing a cross-generational and regularly refreshed staffing team. Theologian Henri Nouwen subscribes to a nonhierarchical structure in ministry, his view referred to by Hernandez as a "commitment

---

8. Hernandez, *Henri Nouwen*, xvi.

PART III: UNIQUENESS CHARACTERIZATION

to dismantle the constant elevation of hierarchy in ministry,"[9] quoting from Nouwen that "we are all healers" and "we are all patients in constant need of help," a realization that keeps "professionals from becoming distant technicians and those in need of care from feeling used or manipulated."[10] The perceived nonhierarchical structure of *Leadership* avoids any feeling of manipulation, keeps staff grounded in reality and humility, contributes to the program uniqueness and is a significant element in its apparent success. It also facilitates a seamless transition from Stage 3 to staff for those who follow that pathway.

Paul's message to the Romans (12:3) assists further in understanding what happens at *Leadership* in the staff space as they strive, imperfectly, to follow the principle, "Do not think of yourself more highly than you ought, but rather think of yourself with sober judgement." It is no accident, that this instruction from Paul is followed (12:4–8) with teaching using a body metaphor, that "in Christ we who are many form one body and each member belongs to all the others." Our gifting is different, and individuals should be allowed to exercise their gifts, including serving, teaching, contributing to the needs of others, and leadership: "if it is leadership, let him govern diligently." The theology of Paul enhances our understanding of *Leadership* and the staff role within a community that is a united body, recognizing, giving permission, and empowering each, staff and participants, to exercise their different gifts (recognized in Stage 1 as style differences and acceptance of diversity and in Stage 2 through differentiation of a gifting drawn from the fruit of the Spirit).

It must be expected that serving on the staff team has an impact on staff themselves, from personal and spiritual formation perspectives. It also impacts their developing gifting and vocational trajectory, as observed by Douglass and Dean in the US HSTP: "we powerfully witnessed the vocational significance these programs had for college graduate students serving as staff, as well as for teenagers themselves . . . we came to recognize how programs that are intentionally designed to foster leadership among youth have a 'spill over' effect that influences the vocational discernment of young adult program leaders as well."[11]

---

9. Hernandez, *Henri Nouwen*, 69.
10. Nouwen, *Reaching Out*, 93.
11. Douglass and Dean, "Research Methods," 290.

Context

Although *context* in *Leadership* is a broad topic, discussion here is limited to those aspects that were identified and highlighted in the findings, including separation (from normal life), a new community, liminal space, and wilderness. The spiritual context is dealt with separately. Other contextual features were the varying groupings, from Solo to Duos, small groups, and the whole community. Group(s) and the emergence of spontaneous *communitas* have been dealt with as a separate property of uniqueness. In this section, it is wilderness that will be given most attention, extending the earlier discussion where wilderness (solitude) was considered in coalescence with *communitas*, liminality, and rites of passage.

Those who work in the areas of masculine spirituality and rites of passage view wilderness as an essential context and place. For Jesus, wilderness was a significant place for retreat, prayer, and preparation for ministry or life. Often his wilderness was desert or mountain. This and the potential of wilderness to heal and inspire were discussed in chapter 8. It was concluded from the literature that time in wilderness was likely to be positive and to stimulate transformation and preparation for something still to come. This was confirmed in the research findings. The context of a wilderness location for certain *Leadership* program elements was regarded as positive. These were the places where personal and spiritual growth and transformation occurred. The key descriptors of their wilderness experience were a sense of God's presence, a place to do some deep thinking, and just being in the outdoors. The personal and group freedom that wilderness provided became one of the emerging key themes that contributed to theory development. Drawn from an interviewee was the insight that wilderness represented separation, which led to closeness to God, making a conceptual link with liminality theory, and a critical step in rites of passage. It is not just *going into the bush*, but the whole wilderness experience that is significant, including links to the wilderness of one's relationship with self, others, and God, for example, in the parable of the prodigal son, who rejected family and travelled to "a distant country" (Luke 15:13)—a *wilderness*.

The emerging literature of desert, mountain, and wilderness as a place for exploration of spirituality[12] may be a pathway not everyone wants to take, but its value and insights are worthy of further exploration and is an area for further research in relation to *Leadership*.

---

12. E.g., Lane, *Fierce Landscapes*.

PART III: UNIQUENESS CHARACTERIZATION

Finally, on the uniqueness of context, are references to rituals, symbols, and traditions, which have been related to liminality, the development of *communitas*, and to the stripping away of status and identity so "the individual is free to be immersed in and effected by their environment."[13] As in other retreats, this is part of the context of *Leadership*.

Strategies and Ethos in Practice

Many strategies have been mentioned and the ethos of *Leadership* has been described. Key strategies are the use of dialectic, rather than didactic teaching/learning approaches. This involves the introduction of critical thinking skills, self-reflection, affirmation, and celebration—well established as effective strategies in the theory of teaching and learning. Though away from family, the place of family is highly regarded, consistent with the 2020 Mission Australia Youth Survey where 74.7 percent of young males indicated that family relationships were extremely or very important to them.[14] Also high on the ethos agenda are the expression of consistency, unconditional acceptance, celebration of diversity, and recognition of imperfection. Giving the invitation to take responsibility and exercise leadership *now* is highly promoted. And nonhierarchical, intergenerational leadership is practiced. Though recognizing contrary views and with the recognition of the negative impacts of misogyny, the existence of a distinct masculine spirituality is accepted. Jesus encouraged children and involved them in ministry, at the same time as seeing training towards adulthood as important—preparing for a rite of passage that was recognized by commissioning for ministry.

Following a review of youth ministry in the New Testament, and drawing on theological and educational/psychological (youth development) theory, McGarry makes the observation that today: "too many teenagers are given the impression that serving in the church means serving in the youth or children's ministries," viewing them as "members in waiting," whereas "the biblical witness consistently affirms their value and reflects a shared commitment by the community of faith to the next generation." Those who "overlook the young are in blatant disregard of the biblical pattern of ministry."[15] It is not just about exercising leadership; more importantly, it is about Christian youth having "a role to play in the body of Christ"; it is

13. Nagy, "Lens of Liminality," 47.
14. Tiller et al., *Youth Survey Report*, 26.
15. McGarry, *Biblical Theology*, 56.

about "mentoring and discipleship" and "empowering them for a lifetime of ongoing ministry in the church."[16] The *Leadership* ethos of empowerment to exercise leadership *now*, reinforces these insights and theories from a variety of disciplines and confirms their standing in mutual correlation.

Overarching Presence of God—Engagement and Celebration

It may well be that the overarching presence of God and the spiritual dimension of *Leadership* is the key point of uniqueness that provides the distinguishing factor between *Leadership* and other leadership development programs. Participants are challenged to consider how serious they are about their faith, somewhat similar to Jesus's story of the rich young ruler (Matt 19:16–21; Mark 10:17–23; Luke 18:18–25), challenging people to be willing to surrender what they have to follow him.

Participants and their spiritual interest, even hunger, are respected and provided for through shared living, a modeling and teaching/learning experience and a unique worship experience that is regarded by participants as authentic and real, though imperfect. Promoting authentic Christian manhood and a masculine spirituality is distinguished by servanthood, gentleness, humility, sacrifice, and love. While not always articulated, participants are clearly of the view that the Christian/spiritual dimension of *Leadership* is assumed, always present and, as one respondent put it, is "one of the fundamental successes of the course compared with other courses."

Returning to the observation that *Leadership* participants have a spiritual interest, even hunger, one might compare this with the criticism of some youth ministry programs that they have moved away from the theological. There is a strong push towards remedying this and towards including theology (the term as used in the US) in youth ministry programs at all levels, including the local church.[17] The last reference is to a review of the HSTP, which expressly involves theological colleges and theological teaching. The call is to recognize the capacities of youth for commitment, leadership, and theological engagement. This is dealt with in the general context of youth ministry in chapter 20.

The most frequent unique spiritual activity mentioned at *Leadership* was worship, which participants clarified is not just singing, but the message,

---

16. McGarry, *Biblical Theology*, 89.

17. Root and Dean, *Theological Turn*; Dean et al., *Starting Right*; Fritz, *Art of Forming*; Dean and Hearlson, *How Youth Ministry*.

and on the final night sharing a dinner and communion with their mates. Because of its significance, worship is now given additional attention.

Worship

Classic quotes from the survey/focus group data are that worship is unique and different, because "I can't sing. A lot of the boys next to me can't sing [but we sing]." "The kid beside me can't sing, and that's okay. Some of the people with microphones can't sing, and that's okay." Worship is happening outside the usual worship box of their home churches and other camp experiences.

Stephen Newby examines the theology of music and worship, which he applies to multiethnic ministry. He advocates for change—for "worship outside the music box."[18]

While Newby's focus is on ethnic diversity, he also makes a link into the context of *Leadership* and youth worshiping, suggesting that "intergenerational worship is multicultural." Theologically speaking, Jesus modeled an inclusive community, in which all could participate and without bias (except sometimes positive bias) on the grounds of age or culture. Jesus established a unique teaching/learning community with his disciples, and this can be viewed more broadly to include other connected persons—connected through relationship and connected through sharing the doing or receiving of ministry. Jesus's community was multiage and multicultural. Jesus drew others in as participants to whom he gave great responsibility, finally in the Great Commission (Matt 28:16–20), which was given directly to the disciples, but with the implication that they would make disciples who would make disciples, one of the characteristics of servant leadership explored in this research—leaders raising up other leaders. The strong sense of community of believers recorded in Acts 2:42–47, where teaching, fellowship, possessions, and meals were willingly shared was attractive and drew others in. It is well established in social science, for example, in organizational and management theory and practice, that participation and commitment are related. *Leadership* is highly participatory, including in worship. This contributes to the enthusiasm, commitment, and transformation that occurs, even in participatory worship.

Newby extends this thought to advocating for youth to lead and share leadership responsibilities in churches—equipping the next generation "to

---

18. Newby, *Worship Outside*.

become change agents for God's Kingdom."[19] The intergenerational worship experience at *Leadership* may partly explain its uniqueness and may be a model for churches to adopt: "when diverse worship styles are lifted up to God... something new and different gives rise. The Holy Spirit who teaches all things, creates something new that has not been experienced before."[20] The worship does not have to be traditional: "our worship gatherings can reflect this theology of incarnation [of Christ] by simply taking time to be in the presence of others." In fact, Newby claims that worship gatherings must be diverse if they "are to shape and form us in the image of Christ."[21] His concept of worshiping outside the box is "allowing Jesus Christ to be our pastoral worship leader and the Holy Spirit to be our teacher,"[22] a position *Leadership* approaches and is discussed in chapter 14 as part of the mystery of the effectiveness and uniqueness of *Leadership*.

Summary of Chapter

Uniqueness is a distinguishing characteristic of *Leadership*. Participants frequently articulate aspects that to them were unique—different from all other experiences. Uniqueness is attractive, and it was affirming that they were part of it. Many examples of uniqueness have been identified and these have been collapsed into six characteristics or properties of uniqueness: servanthood exampled, the group, staff, context, strategies and ethos in practice, and the overarching presence of God (particularly in worship).

A similarity of experience can be drawn between *Leadership* and the US HSTP:

> While HSTPs must surely be counted among the groups nurturing leadership, what is unique about these programs is that they are intentional about developing *Christian* leaders: leaders who are vocationally compelled by the good news of Christ and who acknowledge a calling to use their gifts for ends other than economic gain or social prestige... disoriented from the dominant values of the wider culture but who are also reoriented toward the emerging

---

19. Newby, *Worship Outside*, 45.
20. Newby, *Worship Outside*, 16.
21. Newby, *Worship Outside*, 34.
22. Newby, *Worship Outside*, 98.

Kingdom of God in which all Creation has been reconciled with the Creator.[23]

This too could readily be adopted as a summary of the uniqueness of *Leadership*.

---

23. Kaethler, *Turned Around*, 153.

Part IV

Theory Development

THE GROUNDED THEORY METHODOLOGY has led the researcher through a detailed pursuit of coding, sampling, and progressive abstraction. Figure 7 provides a glimpse of the process of theory development, through properties, dimensions, and themes to the identification of the core category, *acceptance*, the subcategories, *imperfection*, and *freedom and empowerment*, with the *spiritual dimension* being the central organizing or all-encompassing concept or contextual category.[1]

The final substantive theory that answers the research question—*What factors contribute to the apparent success of the Boys' Brigade Leadership program?*—is outlined in chapter 14; then the identified categories are examined in chapters 15–18.

Theology informs the insights generated by the substantive theory through each of the categories. A theological understanding of acceptance highlights a mindset for relating to others: brotherly love. The acceptance modeled by Jesus's acceptance of others was immediate and spontaneous and was acceptance despite imperfection. Participants come to realize that we are only made acceptable through Jesus's sacrifice, and this can then lead to acceptance at a *my family* and *brotherhood* level. An acceptance of imperfection fosters humility and self-acceptance, towards Christlikeness. Spiritual freedom is a gift from God and the key proposition is that "the truth will set you free." Freedom is seen to expressly link with empowerment and then to link with imperfection. Just as Jesus empowered the disciples,

---

1. For more detailed information on the methodology of the research, refer to Appendix II (Research Methodology and Methods) and the glossary of grounded theory terms.

so freedom in the Spirit is empowering. The spiritual dimension is the contextual category, underpinning the theory and creating the mystery.

Taking a brief summary look into the methodology, commenced in parts I and II, and continued in part III, part IV also continues to address the second and third core tasks in Osmer's[2] framework for practical theological interpretation: the interpretative task, which asks the question, "Why is this going on?" and the normative task, which asks the question, "What ought to be going on?" The focus of the interpretative task is "drawing on theories of the arts and sciences to better understand and explain why these patterns and dynamics are occurring." The focus of the normative task is, "using theological concepts to interpret particular episodes, situations, or contexts, constructing ethical norms to guide our responses, and learning from 'good practice.'"

---

2. Osmer, *Practical Theology*, 4.

PART IV: THEORY DEVELOPMENT

CORE CATEGORY

ACCEPTANCE—
unconditional; belonging; nonjudgmental; diversity; trust; brothers/family

SUBCATEGORIES

IMPERFECTION	FREEDOM AND EMPOWERMENT	SPIRITUAL DIMENSION
		CONTEXTUAL CATEGORY

PROPERTIES

- staff and their stories
- self-reflection
- from the spiritual, to God, to worship
- faith development
- mystery
- always striving; never there

- clean slate
- challenge (opportunity)
- permission (to have a go)
- worship
- affirmation ("you've got what it takes")
- trust

- spiritual hunger recognized
- servanthood
- group(s)/*communitas*
- staff open and vulnerable
- overarching presence of God
- worship
- mystery

DIMENSIONS

- authenticity/imperfection
- brotherhood and community
- intergenerational staff
- solitude
- acceptance of difference

- to be; to be me
- to be a man and to be masculine, yet spiritual
- to serve and be a servant leader *now*
- to take risks and to question

- God—his terms and my terms
- drawn to worship
   - it's different here
   - it's real, spontaneous, and meaningful
   - it's with mates

THEMES

CRITICAL THINKING AS A CATALYST FOR GROWTH
AUTHENTIC SERVANT LEADERSHIP
PATHWAY TO MANHOOD/SPIRITUAL MANHOOD

TRANSFORMATION CELEBRATION

Figure 7. Theory Development—Core Category, Subcategories, Contextual Category, Properties, Dimensions, and Themes

14

The Substantive Theory

IN THIS CHAPTER, THE final substantive theory that answers the research question—*What factors contribute to the apparent success of the Boys' Brigade Leadership program?*—is outlined in diagram and narrative and is followed by a summary of the narrative.

The Theory in Diagram

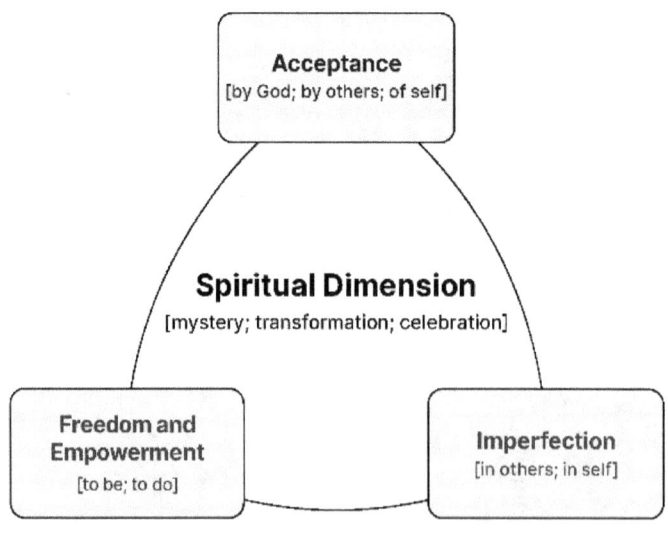

Figure 8. Substantive Grounded Theory

In the diagram (figure 8), the contextual category of *spiritual dimension* is the central organizing subcategory and is transposed into the interactive diagram incorporating the core category of *acceptance* and the other subcategories: *imperfection*, and *freedom and empowerment*. However, this contextual category is unbounded. Each category interacts with all others, as is observed in the specific analysis of the respective properties and dimensions of each. The spiritual dimension is reflected in acceptance, imperfection, and freedom and empowerment. Acceptance is offered despite imperfection and is a trigger towards freedom and empowerment. Imperfection does not diminish acceptance or inhibit freedom and empowerment. Freedom and empowerment are experienced because of acceptance and despite imperfection.

The Theory in Narrative—Storyline

In broad terms, the core category, *acceptance*, the subcategories, *imperfection*, and *freedom and empowerment*, and the contextual category, *spiritual dimension*, encompass the factors that contribute to the apparent success of the Boys' Brigade *Leadership* program and thus answer the research question. As a narrative to support and explain the diagram, the properties of each category are expanded.

Acceptance—By God, by Others, of Self

Acceptance is the first and fullest characteristic of *Leadership* that emerged from the data. Acceptance was the most common description participants used in speaking about their Stage 1 group. They also noted acceptance highly as a characteristic of their facilitators. In analyzing data, acceptance was noted as the most powerful theme. The experience of unconditional acceptance in their group stimulates spontaneous *communitas*. The importance of the theme, acceptance, continued to be confirmed as the developing core category of the theory through responses of those interviewed. Speaking of his Stage 1 group, one interviewee said, "I was able to engage, I felt accepted. I was really shocked by how quickly things opened up."

Acceptance incorporates the theme of being brothers and this continues throughout, being accorded the status of family. When explored further in interviews, the theme continued.

Diversity is a property of acceptance. Learning from diversity and growing in understanding of those with different life experiences, are linked in comments such as someone from an intact family being shocked that one member of his group "didn't know his dad ... which was quite heartbreaking for me." As this and other family (particularly father-son) experiences were shared, it became an "eye-opening and learning experience; meeting people who were different (diverse); and hearing other people's [difficult] stories." Acceptance, even celebrating the value of diversity in their group, becomes relevant. They accept those who themselves or in their families are living with difference.

Acceptance by God and by others leads to self-acceptance, putting to rest the unacceptance they find in themselves. They are positioned to vicariously accept Jesus through accepting those he accepted (the sick, the poor, the imprisoned).

Imperfection—In Others, in Self

Imperfection is a subcategory of the core category, *acceptance*, not that imperfection is taught or encouraged. Striving for wholeness as a person is a goal personally and in relationships. Striving for spiritual wholeness, for holiness and sanctification, is a shared endeavor that those on staff (younger and older) acknowledge is for them too an ongoing challenge in which they sometimes fail.

Participants come to *Leadership*, outwardly presenting themselves as *perfect*, though they and their parents (and probably others) know they are not. And, in the safety of their small group, they begin to share their stories and thus acknowledge to others that they are not perfect, and they find out that no one else is perfect either. Their imperfections are the same or similar to those of others. They are united in their imperfections. They are *accepted* in their imperfections. They learn also that their facilitators and other staff (as they hear their story) are also imperfect. Though they are taught at home that they must outwardly reflect the perfect family, they acknowledge the imperfections in their family, in their relationships with their fathers, mothers, and siblings.

They return in subsequent years, still *imperfect*, having tried and failed, but back again to the safety of a place of *acceptance* and shared imperfections of those that constitute the *Leadership* community.

In Stage 2, they receive letters from their parents—perhaps parents acknowledging their own imperfections and they realize their parents, like them, are imperfect. On Solo, they reflect deeply on their imperfections and often start to measure themselves by God's standards. They are told they have what it takes to be a godly man, yet some know they've got a long way to go; they are imperfect. In Stage 3, they've got it all together. No, they haven't; and on Duo they share more deeply and honestly about their imperfections and see this as a step towards leaving some of the memories and impacts of their imperfections behind. All this is happening while they are writing their *perfect* personal mission statement—their aspirations for their future for themselves, with God and family—yet they are still struggling with their own present imperfections, including unresolved conflicts in their personal space and within their family.

The whole time, across all stages, they have become part of the *Leadership* community, a community of imperfect people (fellow participants and staff) and here they feel safe, *accepted*, and free. Drawing on Andrew Root's concept of "place-sharing,"[1] *Leadership* brings people together as place-sharers. For a week or maybe just a brief moment, members of the *Leadership* community place-share with each other. Group members place-share with one of their team at a moment they need that. They along with staff place-share all week with one of the community who is struggling in their present place. They are inhabiting "the concrete location of God's action in the world."[2] They place-share imperfectly, but they direct one another to the perfect Place-Sharer, just as Jesus place-shared with the woman caught in adultery (John 8:1–11) during her moment of need, embarrassment, accusation, and fear. As she was, they too are *accepted* without judgment.

Root describes the role of a place-sharer as:

> One person must stand in the place of another, acting fully on his behalf, like a noble leader for her citizens, a thoughtful teacher for his students or a loving father for his children . . . Just as Jesus incarnate, crucified and resurrected was fully our place-sharer, so we too, as Jesus disciples must ourselves become place-sharers, suffering with and for young people . . . [and be] able to see human-to-human relationships as the location of God's presence in the world.[3]

1. "One person must stand in the place of another, acting fully on his behalf . . . Just as Jesus . . . was fully our place-sharer, so we too, as Jesus disciples must ourselves become place-sharers, suffering with and for young people" (Root, *Revisiting*, 83).

2. Root, *Revisiting*, 83.

3. Root, *Revisiting*, 83.

The *Leadership* community comes to worship, and they realize that it too is imperfect. It is nothing like their normal church where the practiced musicians and worship leaders put on a *perfect* show; where only the adults sing and they, if they still go, stand (or sit) in disengaged silence. At *Leadership* they stand and sing together, with their mates and with staff, men together, all imperfect. They are free to try themselves out and are *accepted* and *empowered*, despite their imperfection. All is imperfect, and that doesn't matter; but all is authentic, honest, and real and they engage with God. They sing to a perfect God, not to the imperfect people around them.

On the last night, they enjoy the formal dinner, not like at the school formal, but another imperfect *Leadership* experience. They feast, worship, and celebrate together with an imperfect but highly significant group of mates. They are *accepted* in their imperfection as they likewise *accept* others in their imperfections. And even imperfection can be celebrated.

Freedom and Empowerment—To Be, to Do

The experience of *acceptance* communicates trust, leads to a freedom and is empowering—*free and empowered* to reveal oneself and one's struggles; free to *have a go* at new challenges (e.g., on the Stage 1 Overnight Expedition). They are *empowered* by staff who demonstrate that they believe in others (them) and are concerned to enable others' development. They see this as the most noted servant leadership characteristic in staff—by 60 percent of participants. The invitation to exercise leadership *now* empowers participants to do this. Participants are *empowered* in all areas of life and thus gain confidence; empowered to solve problems; to conquer spiritual and physical wilderness; to practice being a man; to consider life direction. The expression of *freedom and empowerment* is in part facilitated by the *clean slate* phenomenon and the *acceptance* of them for who they are. They develop a simple freedom just to *be*, a freedom to be *me*, a freedom to *do*. They experience the empowerment that Jesus gave to his disciples; that Paul gave to Timothy and Titus.

Spiritual Dimension—Mystery, Transformation, Celebration

One of the unique features of *Leadership*, the overarching presence of God, is captured in the *spiritual dimension*. So accepted and embedded throughout the program is the spiritual dimension, that participants say they assume this and see it particularly in servant leadership. The most common reference to the spiritual dimension is through the worship experience at *Leadership*—its uniqueness and its spontaneous engagement of young men who rarely become, or even feel motivated to become, so enthusiastically engaged in worship. They draw other concepts into their spiritual engagement, particularly Jesus's example of servant leadership, the importance of solitude, and the example of staff. Yet there remains a mystery, with only the Spirit as an explanation of community and transformation, which they can celebrate.

Summary of Theory Narrative

The following table provides a succinct summary of the narrative of the substantive theory.

CORE CATEGORY
Acceptance
by God, by Others, of Self
that is real, authentic and survives testing
SUBCATEGORY
Imperfection
in Others, in Self
that is acknowledged and celebrated
SUBCATEGORY
Freedom and Empowerment
to Be, to Do
that is encouraged, practiced and vulnerable
CONTEXTUAL CATEGORY
Spiritual Dimension
Mystery, Transformation, Celebration
that is young-man-appropriate, God-attractive, transformative, celebratory, and community invoking; and that explains the mystery

Table 33. Summary of Theory Narrative

PART IV: THEORY DEVELOPMENT

Summary of Chapter

This chapter has presented the final phase of the grounded theory development, towards answering the research question: *What factors contribute to the apparent success of the Boys' Brigade Leadership program?* It presented the substantive grounded theory in diagram and narrative (storyline), identifying the core category (acceptance), two subcategories (imperfection and freedom and empowerment), and an overall contextual category (spiritual dimension). Linkages between each category were described. The substantive theory draws the categories together in an abstract theory that answers the research question and forms the basis for the discussion of findings, through the application of a mutual critical correlation strategy (including theological reflection) in chapters 15–18 and linking to Osmer's fourth core task (the normative task) in practical theological interpretation, asking the question, "What ought to be going on?"[4]

---

4. Osmer, *Practical Theology*.

15

Acceptance

> Jesus' uniqueness consists, therefore, in his being "the unambiguous manifestation of God's unconditioned empathic acceptance at the level of finite beings."[1]

As is clear in the substantive theory, *acceptance* is a key attribute of the program, the core category of the theory. It contributes to the mystery of My Group and with the whole *Leadership* community, across all stages, particularly the acceptance leading to brotherhood with groupmates and staff. But the acceptance goes much deeper; it goes to self-acceptance, as illustrated in these focus group participants' comments:

> I think part of that therefore is that as the boys, young men, find acceptance from others, they can finally put to rest the unacceptance they find in themselves and come to that acceptance of themselves . . . who they are as a person.

> I wonder if the acceptance there, of themselves, goes back to their first opportunity to play with their attitudes. It's their first real opportunity from outside of maybe their family, to realise, oh, there's other people that are messed up too. When you're 15, you're the only one who could possibly be as ruined as you are, even when you're not; even when you're just the average person. You recognise, oh, there's some stuff in my head that's not nice. And when you realise there's another group of fellas there and we're all like

---

1. James, "Theology of Acceptance," 379.

that, you're all like, ah, I'm alright, I'm normal.... Maybe that's the problem, not what other people are saying but what they're saying to themselves. And we're telling them, you're okay.

Finding out that they are *normal* and hearing from peers, older *brothers*, and God that they are *okay*, facilitates the self-acceptance that also speaks to them of a personal and spiritual freedom; a freedom *to be*, a freedom *to be me*. Finding freedom and acceptance in God, leads to the unique response of transformation, celebration, and worship that participants describe.

Similarly, in HSTPs, Proffitt and Young record the comments from participants:

> The best feeling I can think of is that this is a place that has no shame and you don't have to be shamed to say anything.
>
> I feel like [the leaders] create safe environments for us, and that we can open our minds up to anything and they are not going to laugh at something.[2]

Throughout the findings and coding processes in the study of *Leadership*, the category of acceptance continually gained strength and was identified as the core theoretical category or central phenomenon, interacting actively and continuously with the identified subcategories, imperfection, freedom and empowerment, and with the contextual category, spiritual dimension. Acceptance was the most identified characteristic of the *Leadership* program, of their group, and of staff. Being accepted paves the way to the transformational moment of self-acceptance. The findings of the experiences of *Leadership* participants referred to are mirrored in the HSTP, as recorded by Proffitt and Young, one example being: "I found a place where I was heard, where I was seen, and where all my kooky weird stuff was not only accepted, but welcomed, encouraged, and loved."[3] Acceptance is a key concept in theological, psychological (developmental theory), and other social science theory, a selection of which is now considered.

Adopting a social ontological approach, James draws on social science to provide an example that "having less experience with human acceptance naturally decreases [one's] ability to accept."[4] The example used is children from broken homes. This is relevant for *Leadership* in groups when

2. Proffitt and Young, "Catalyzing Community," 66–67.
3. Proffitt and Young, "Catalyzing Community," 66–67.
4. James, "Theology of Acceptance," 383.

facilitators and group members are offering acceptance to a participant who has had family or other non-accepting life experiences. Adding to this observation is a further comment from James that "a theology of acceptance must imply an all-out attack upon basic human problems such as hunger and loneliness,"[5] to which might be added topics dealt with during *Leadership* such as discrimination based on certain personal attributes, including a contemporary challenge to consider apparent male disrespect of women. In his concept of a theology of acceptance, James includes acts of "acceptance and brotherly love."[6]

An experience at *Leadership* that has been noted, is that acceptance of diversity is enhanced when one of their group identifies as belonging to a different category of people or having a personal link with a particular attribute (e.g., issues to do with mental health, age, disability, criminal activity, alternate lifestyle, and sexuality). These relationship dynamics impact and are impacted by the experiences of My Group, *communitas*, lack of criticism of their own group, and identification as *brothers/family*. Diversity provides teaching/learning opportunities related to personal growth and interactive skills development, deeply challenging stereotypes, in people they have come to know as *brothers/family*. In chapter 20, the question is asked whether other attributes of contemporary concern, such as those associated with the #MeToo Movement and concern for respect for women, should be considered in the context of acceptance of others and self. For now, it is noted that in reviewing extensive scholarship that has been brought to the fore in theological debate by the #MeToo Movement, Jayme Reaves and David Tombs focus on the naming of Jesus as a victim of sexual abuse.[7] They adopt two approaches, the first, dealt with comparatively quickly, a vicarious linking through the Matthew 27:26–45 Scripture passage where whatever is done to or not done for "the least of these" (the hungry, thirsty, stranger, unclothed, sick, or incarcerated) is done or not done to Jesus, or that Jesus is being accepted or not accepted. Reaves and Tombs extend the examples to include the sexually abused. Then, and more extensively, these authors focus on the actual sexual abuse of Jesus as part of the cross and crucifixion, citing compelling historical evidence and scholarship, in particular from Australian theologian Michael Trainor, who

---

5. James, "Theology of Acceptance," 385.
6. James, "Theology of Acceptance," 385–87.
7. Reaves and Tombs, "#MeToo Jesus."

concludes that physical and sexual abuse "was integral to crucifixion,"[8] suggesting that such contemporary issues should be included in a program such as *Leadership*.

Although in thirty years, practice in human services and other social sciences and the focus in sociology has changed dramatically, a 1987 article by Bogdan and Taylor captured a historical position in what they refer to as a sociology of exclusion, that examined deviance and difference using dimensions such as stigma, labelling, and rejection.[9] They argue for a turn in the study of deviance (encompassing difference because of physical or intellectual disability, criminality, etc.) to develop a sociology of acceptance, suggesting even that "sociologists have regarded acceptance as a form of deviance."[10] They employ a grounded theory methodology to develop a "systematic grounded theory" of a sociology of acceptance, examining relationships between persons with atypical attributes and typical persons, suggesting that "no attribute of a person, no matter how atypical, precludes accepting relations."[11]

Bogdan and Taylor express insights that have relevance for *Leadership*.[12] "People who are involved in accepting caring relationships eventually take them for granted." (Example: a participant in a Stage 1 *Leadership* who said, "I don't see my [disabled] sister as disabled. She's just my sister.") Those drawn to accepting typical/atypical relationships because of religious sentiment readily see that "all people are imperfect" and "all are equal in the mind of God." (Example: Reinforcing the imperfection theme and subcategory in this study; reinforcing equality before God, even despite imperfection.) "Accepting relationships can start with a feeling of pure obligation toward the person because of family membership and then evolve to affection." (Example: accepting someone because they are in the same group, then the evolution towards seeing the person as a *brother*, as *family*.)

In developing a sociology of acceptance, Bogdan and Taylor[13] describe a series of possible steps in the evolution of accepting relationships. Their theory helps explain the apparent success of *Leadership* because their

---

8. Trainor, *Body of Jesus*, 405.
9. Bogdan and Taylor, "Sociology of Acceptance."
10. Bogdan and Taylor, "Sociology of Acceptance," 35.
11. Bogdan and Taylor, "Sociology of Acceptance," 35.
12. Bogdan and Taylor, "Sociology of Acceptance," 36.
13. Bogdan and Taylor, "Sociology of Acceptance," 38–39.

steps are observable in the program (though Jesus's examples of acceptance are more immediate and spontaneous):

- "Accepting relationships are formed in stages" (similar to the development in a new *Leadership* group)
- The "initial encounter . . . tends to focus on the difference" (before they share and realize there is more sameness than difference between them)
- Contact becomes more regular, leading to greater "at ease" feelings in the "typical" person (group members wanting to spend more time with their group, even free time)
- Trust and shared understanding develop; difference becomes less central to the relationship (as above, sameness is highlighted; difference is irrelevant)
- Shared feelings of "contempt" towards negative remarks of outsiders (non-criticism of own group; defending their group against *outside* criticism)
- Empathy towards rejection and discrimination suffered by an atypical person (protection of someone who is a group member)
- "Typical" person de-emphasizes the negative and emphasizes the positive and "unique value" of the other person (acknowledging strengths and contributions of all).

While in the study it is acceptance between people that is the focus, there is also the dimension of acceptance of one's situation. Acceptance of one's lot reduces stress. One of the contributions of the social sciences is their knowledge and practice experience, through their focus on the negative impacts of non-acceptance and their role in ameliorating stress. This is readily able to be turned upside down to focus on the positives (e.g., the positive impact of real acceptance).

Taking the discussion on a theology of acceptance a little deeper, Krueger, writing an abstract for Schroeder, points out what is generally known in theology and social science, that "the human personality reveals a core hunger for acceptance"[14] and therefore that a theology of acceptance is important. In presenting his theology of acceptance, Schroeder makes several points, including that "man cannot make himself acceptable before God"; that "I become acceptable finally when someone [outside of me]

14. Schroeder, "Theology of Acceptance," 1.

accepts me;" and that "only when the other person accepts me do I have acceptance." This latter statement is consistent with the insights from the research. Participants have first to experience acceptance from others (e.g., in their group and despite their imperfection) and be able to accept others (and their imperfection) before they can truly accept themselves (and their imperfection), a discussion we will return to later. Ultimately though, humans are unacceptable, and in that state are accepted by God. Jesus reflects God's acceptance in these words, "All those the Father gives me will come to me, and whoever comes to me I will never drive away" (John 6:37). Acceptance cannot be demanded; it must be bestowed. As put by Schroeder, "unacceptable man is accepted by God" and "the man of faith . . . is the man who 'courageously' (from Paul Tillich) accepts himself as accepted in spite of his being unacceptable."[15] Schroeder makes a link between acceptance and reconciliation: Christ having reconciled us to himself and we having been given the ministry of acceptance; of reconciliation[16] (2 Cor 5:11–21). People are acceptable to God because of Jesus's sacrifice (Rom 8:3–4; Heb 3:14, 26).

Christ's standard of acceptance of others is contrasted with a worldly or human acceptance that is clouded in "an aroma of judgement" where "achievement precedes acceptance."[17] Christ's example of acceptance is illustrated in Paul's instruction to the Romans to "Accept one another, then, just as Christ accepted you" and the extension of this acceptance to the Gentiles, just as Paul did as a "minister to the Gentiles" (Rom 15:7, 9, 16). The expectation from Jesus's teaching is that we are instructed to accept those who Jesus accepts and that acceptance of others is accepting Jesus, for example, the "least of these" identified in Matthew 25:26–45; "Anyone who welcomes you welcomes me, and anyone who welcomes me welcomes the one who sent me" (Matt 10:40); "whoever accepts anyone I send accepts me; and whoever accepts me accepts the one who sent me" (John 13:20). Jesus exampled acceptance of children (Matt 19:13–15) and gave the extreme instruction to love our enemies (Matt 5:43), which leads to verse 48, "Be perfect as your heavenly Father is perfect," a statement interpreted in the next chapter on imperfection.

Concerning self-acceptance, Paul accepted himself (by the grace of God) despite what he once was (1 Cor 15:9–10). When we become

---

15. Schroeder, "Theology of Acceptance," 7.
16. Schroeder, "Theology of Acceptance," 18.
17. Tchividjian, *One Way Love*, 149.

overdemanding of ourselves, "we become our own personal taskmasters, perfectionistic and inflexible," we hide who we really are, and we may have "a great level of success" in one area of life (e.g., in business) but be a "train wreck" in other areas (e.g., family relationships)."[18] Our lack of self-acceptance colors our relationships with others. Theologically and psychologically, there is debate over which comes first, self-acceptance or acceptance of others. Does the instruction to "Love your neighbor as yourself" (Matt 22:39; Gal 5:4) mean to love yourself first, then your neighbor? The practical evidence from *Leadership* is that finding acceptance from others, leads to confident self-acceptance. These two interpretations, from the theological and the practical, correlate through interpretation of the Matthew/Galatians instruction. It is not so much a question of which comes first, but of the quality or level of acceptance (or love) required towards one's neighbor—no less than one's self-acceptance or self-love.

An example of full and unconditional acceptance is found in the Acts 8:26–40 account of the encounter between Philip and the Ethiopian eunuch. After acknowledging ethnicity and color, Bock (2007) highlights the impact of this example of total acceptance, commenting that "His [the eunuch's] condition (being castrated) would not allow him full participation in Jewish worship," but now, "all barriers are down."[19] Polhill extends the impact with the comment: "A eunuch, a Gentile, a black, was baptized and received into full membership in the people of Jesus Christ."[20]

Familial Characterization of Acceptance

The concept of *family*, along with *brothers*, is frequently used by *Leadership* participants in describing their My Group experience. This is extended to encompass and describe a broader group such as a stage group or the whole *Leadership* community as "family" or "brothers." The Research Collaboration Group[21] discussed how difficult it is to determine when this transition occurs, and like many aspects, it is part of the unspoken mystery of *Leadership*. There is evidence that the whole community becomes *family* to participants very quickly in Stage 1, perhaps almost simultaneously with

18. Tchividjian, *One Way Love*, 150.
19. Bock, *Acts*, 341, 343.
20. Polhill, *Acts*, 226.
21. As referred to earlier—a specific focus group developed during theoretical sampling.

the feeling of acceptance which many describe. This explains the assumption of this ethos as they return for other stages.

As the key theme of acceptance emerged, it was noted in chapter 2 that in a cluster of trust, connection, and belonging, friendship/brothers/family/mateship were also common descriptors used. Respondents offered further observations of their experience: they became "completely comfortable with one another" and experienced "peace in sharing"; "knowing each other deeply"; "by the end of the week we were more than just a group; we were family; we were brothers" (Stage 1, 2013).

A link between acceptance and brotherhood was noted in chapter 2—that acceptance led to brotherhood. Once participants encountered a My Group level, they realized that they were accepted as they, in turn, accepted others, even others who initially appeared very different and are still diverse. Then the descriptions of *brother* emerged. Unconditional acceptance incorporated unconditional brotherhood, without any need to prove oneself or earn the status. They freely gave one another the status out of the experience of acceptance.

As noted in chapter 2, during interviews two referred to the brotherhood formed as, "the brother I never had," seeing *Leadership* as filling that void.

Exploring the brotherhood concept further, it does reflect Paul's instructions to "Be devoted to one another in brotherly love. Honor one another above yourself" (Rom 12:10). It also reflects Peter's instructions to leaders to "love one another deeply, from the heart" (1 Pet 1:22) and his progression from faith to love, justified because we have been given the knowledge of Jesus Christ. We are to "make every effort to add to your faith goodness . . . knowledge . . . self-control . . . perseverance . . . godliness . . . brotherly kindness . . . love" (2 Pet 1:5–7). This theological insight assists in articulating a deeper understanding of the *Leadership* experience.

Hebrews 13:1 is a call to "keep on loving one another as brothers and sisters." Commenting on this passage, Lane refers to brotherly love as "clearly represent(ing) the quality of love that binds the community together as brothers and sisters within the family of faith."[22] The Hebrews instruction contributes to a theology of brotherly love. As an aspect of working out of such love, the writer continues to exhort us to show hospitality to strangers, those in prison, and those who are suffering (Heb 1:2–3), linking with the Matthew 25 "least of these" passage. Showing hospitality and brotherly

---

22. Lane, *Hebrews 9–13*, 510.

love to others is showing hospitality and brotherly love to Jesus. Jesus is not ashamed to call us brothers and sisters, members of his family (Heb 2:11–12). These further theological insights inform and positively critique the brotherly love and acceptance insights generated from the research data.

Based on the data, it is observed that while the *Leadership* experience provides a good base, it does not overtly take the experience of brotherliness, even brotherly love to the final step of this theological understanding, though it would be a simple step to make that link and is something that has been observed to staff.

Summary of Chapter

In summary, it is established that acceptance, the core category in the theory, is important from a theological perspective, and that theology informs the insights generated, including from social science. This perspective assists in understanding the hunger humanity has for acceptance, that a person cannot make themselves acceptable but can find acceptance because of Jesus's sacrifice. God's acceptance backgrounds the *Leadership* experience of acceptance by others and of self. Jesus is the essence of acceptance, as in the reported *Leadership* experience; acceptance and no judgment, regardless of what one has done or one's apparent lack of ability. Jesus did, however, challenge to strive, grow, and examine one's attitudes, for example, with the Pharisees. Pure unconditional love and acceptance is only found in God. So, at *Leadership*, the love and acceptance can never be pure unless it is in God that it is offered and received. Staff mirroring God's acceptance, even that bestowed through Jesus's sacrifice, will always be imperfect, though it may be good. Staff can exercise a ministry of reconciliation; a ministry of acceptance. The theology of acceptance and brotherhood clarifies that the experience at *Leadership* can be offered as a steppingstone towards accepting God's acceptance and familial status. Even as *Leadership* participants freely extend brotherhood to one another based on the mutual and unconditional acceptance experienced, only God can bestow acceptance, sonship, and therefore brotherhood, that is true and lasting and able to be taken with them by participants when they are not in the face-to-face *Leadership* community.

The opportunity for further theological teaching on brotherly love within the *Leadership* program is noted.

16

Imperfection

> We weren't all perfect and had similar struggles and goals.

IMPERFECTION IS A SUBCATEGORY in the grounded theory of what factors contribute to the apparent success of *Leadership*. An example of realization of imperfection being a profound and freeing enlightenment for *Leadership* participants was cited in chapter 2 in the comment of one participant when discussing the impact of the Overnight Expedition on teamwork. Elsewhere (e.g., chapter 14) there is reference to the acknowledgment of imperfection in relation to worship. They sing and play instruments without having to put on a *perfect* show; they worship enthusiastically, recognizing their own imperfection and its acceptance by themselves, by others, and by God.

The excitement of acknowledging, even celebrating, imperfection in oneself and finding it in others, links with acceptance. *Leadership* staff acknowledge their own imperfection; that they have made and do still make mistakes; that they are still learning and hopefully growing. You don't have to wait until you are perfect to lead; you can lead *now*. You don't have to wait until you are perfect to come to God; you can come to God *now*. The imperfection dilemma, striving for personal, relational, emotional, and spiritual wholeness, yet accepting this as a life-long impossible task, is exposed to theological reflection later.

Realization that neither they, nor their parents, their fellow group members, their group facilitators, nor any other staff at *Leadership* are perfect, neither do they pretend to be, is one of the most powerful insights that participants experience and articulate, leading often to a transformational experience. Even the highly regarded spontaneous arrival of *communitas* in a group is likely to encounter power relations within the liminal phase and therefore be imperfect, or not *pure*.[1] Understanding a theology of imperfection enhances the realization, for the present and the future.

Peter Nelson asks the question of how to "fashion a theology of imperfection that is, at one and the same time, honest about Christian struggles (the kingdom is future) and yet hopeful about the potential for Spirit-empowered living (the kingdom is present)." He identifies as "a pressing dilemma," "expecting too little in the way of life transformation" and "expecting the overly triumphal."[2] A biblical and practical theology of imperfection acknowledges that "The life of discipleship is a life in tension; there is always a gap between our actual realization of holiness and the goal of God-like holiness to which we are called."[3] The Christian experience is one of growth rather than "absolute attainment"; it is about "being transformed" (2 Cor 3:18) and "moving towards maturation" (1 Cor 3:1–4); it is about being on "the journey but not yet at the destination; forming but still not fully formed."[4] These understandings provide confidence for both staff and participants at *Leadership*; longing for wholeness but accepting the reality of imperfection.

In addition, Nelson points to the paradox of spiritual growth where "the more progress you make, the more you realize how far there is to go,"[5] and, drawing on Bridges,[6] he discusses the "continually expanding gap" between the "knowledge [and] practice of holiness." With application for supporting young men dealing with self-harm, even suicidal ideology, Nelson draws the contrast between being "content to be 'in process' as disciples grappling with sin rather than living under the unbearable expectations of attaining the perfect holiness of heaven." In a blunt but helpful statement, he adds, "Believers need to plan to be sinners for the rest of their lives, and yet do so without planning to sin," possibly what Paul was referring to when he declared his imperfection and that he was pressing on "to take hold of that for which Christ Jesus took hold of me" or that he was pressing on

1. Carson, *Crossing Thresholds*, 24.
2. Nelson, "Discipleship Dissonance," 63.
3. Nelson, "Discipleship Dissonance," 80.
4. Nelson, "Discipleship Dissonance," 81–82.
5. Nelson, "Discipleship Dissonance," 82, 85.
6. Bridges, *Pursuit of Holiness*.

"toward the goal to win the prize" (Phil 3:12, 14), acknowledging imperfection in the midst of a forward momentum.[7]

In striving, Christians become "sensitive and humble soul[s]"[8] who seek out help from other struggling Christians by sharing their struggles (a picture of the *Leadership* experience that participants report).

Continuing with Nelson's discussion, he offers a further helpful analogy. We can learn from artists who strive for perfection that is unattainable (the "impossible vision"), which along the way leaves "monuments of greatness."[9] The *Leadership* "monuments of greatness" happen at particular turning points or in shared and celebrated transformations in the lives of participants.

What Nelson labels as *discipleship dissonance* or *a theology of imperfection* leads to humility and personal (spiritual, relational, and emotional) growth. It leads to hope and contentment and an authentic *acceptance* of self, by self and by others, and *acceptance* of others. It becomes "the path for growth in grace by which we aim at Christ-like holiness while resting in the Lord's forgiveness and transforming power";[10] it offers a "balanced biblical and practical theology," sitting at the intersection of theology and psychology.[11] Here too, the phenomena of acceptance and imperfection also intersect and are recognized as key components of the substantive theory. The relevance of this concept for young men is reinforced through Hernandez's writings on the spirituality of theologian Henri Nouwen. Hernandez suggests that Nouwen's personal brand of spirituality was trademarked by imperfection and that it "connects deeply to a generation that places such a high premium on authenticity, transparency, and a sense of 'realness,'" the quality of authenticity also having been identified as valued by *Leadership* participants.[12] It could be claimed that Nouwen's spirituality or theology of imperfection, which is dealt with in a more expansive way by Hernandez in his earlier work,[13] breaks through the barrier of twenty

---

7. Nelson, "Discipleship Dissonance," 85–86.
8. Nelson, "Discipleship Dissonance," 84.
9. Nelson, "Discipleship Dissonance," 86.
10. Nelson, "Discipleship Dissonance," 92.
11. Hernandez, *Soul Care*, 70–71, expands this in his observation that Nouwen "smoothly combined the critical elements of practical theology, spiritual formation, psychological concepts and techniques, redemptive counselling, and pastoral care."
12. Hernandez, *Soul Care*, 3.
13. Hernandez, *Spirituality of Imperfection*, 3, 75.

years since Nouwen's death to prophetically speak through the postmodern era to today's young adults, who value Nouwen's identified hallmarks of *authenticity* and *integrity*. One insight is that "Nouwen keenly recognized the spiritual journey to perfection as a journey through imperfection, along with the realities of struggle, weakness, and incompleteness."[14]

Louw brings a *spirituality of imperfection* into his experience of pastoral theology (as did Nouwen, who Louw draws on, when he linked pastoral care with other lenses, including practical theology and spiritual formation).[15] Louw presents and examines his own theological and emotional development from pressure to achieve, to acceptance of imperfection. He was influenced by Nouwen's classic work, *The Wounded Healer*,[16] and by his own pastoral reflection towards the poor, the suffering, the marginalized, the hungry, the homeless, and others who require compassion and confrontation of imperfection. Louw's conceptualization of a "Christian spirituality of imperfection" implies "spiritual movements of the human soul"; "from having to sharing; from possession to communion; from competition to compassion; from withdrawal to solidarity; from estrangement to enjoyment; from hostility to hospitality,"[17] all influenced by Nouwen's *The Wounded Healer*, contrasting a "theology of ascent" with a "theology of descent."

Nouwen's theology of imperfection continues to resonate with contemporary youth as represented by *Leadership* participants, that "real, earthy spirituality does not obsess over perfection but willingly confronts reality as it is, with its ugly sides—including all traces of imperfection. Strangely enough, it is a spirituality that seems particularly alien to our present culture and is both counterintuitive and countercultural."[18] However, this is not so in the experience of participants at *Leadership* as they understand and take in the concepts of *acceptance* and *imperfection* and apply them through psychological and theological lenses. This may be summarized and applied through the words of Hernandez: "The focus is not so much on measurable progress or spiritual advancement but more on the experience of inner transformation despite—and perhaps because of—imperfection."[19]

---

14. Hernandez, *Spirituality of Imperfection*, 2, 88.
15. Louv, "Christian Spirituality."
16. Nouwen, *Wounded Healer*.
17. Louv, "Christian Spirituality."
18. Hernandez, *Spirituality of Imperfection*, 133–34.
19. Hernandez, *Spirituality of Imperfection*, 91.

So, perfection is an unattainable goal; an arrival never reached; a practical reality accepted in oneself and for the sake of others, particularly those dealing with the harshnesses of their lives. We remain, and it's okay to remain or even set as a goal to be as Hernandez described Nouwen, a "restless seeker, wounded healer, faithful struggler."[20] The "willingness to confront imperfection [is found] in the light and power of the Gospel."[21] Imperfection is not necessarily a goal, but a reality to be accepted and be comfortable with, even to celebrate as we see in imperfection a struggling humanness and commitment to be like, but never fully like, Jesus. A summary statement is found in this insight of Kurtz and Ketcham:

> The core paradox that underlies spirituality is the haunting sense of incompleteness . . . For to be human is to be incomplete, yet yearn for completion . . . to be imperfect, yet long for perfection . . . All these yearnings remain necessarily unsatisfied . . . because we are imperfectly human—or better, because we are perfectly human, which is to say humanly imperfect.[22]

One needs then to deal with the apparent instruction in Matthew 5:48 to "Be perfect, therefore, as your heavenly Father is perfect." Consistent with this dealing with a theology of imperfection, commentators, for example, Blomberg, offers: "'Perfect' here is better translated as 'mature, whole,' i.e., loving without limits . . . Jesus is not frustrating his hearers with an unachievable ideal but challenging them to grow in obedience to God's will—to become more like him,"[23] "being transformed into his image with ever-increasing glory . . ." (2 Cor 3:18)—the "results of freedom all believers have."[24]

The *good enough* concept[25] developed by pediatrician and psychoanalyst Donald Winnicott, was liberating to many mothers, and led to other applications such as the "good enough" pastor.[26] One might equally apply this concept, with liberating impact, to the *good enough Leadership* group facilitator, or participant, or Christian young man. This is consistent with

---

20. Hernandez, *Spirituality of Imperfection*, 91.
21. Hernandez, *Spirituality of Imperfection*, 94.
22. Kurtz and Ketcham, *Spirituality of Imperfection*, 2, 18–19.
23. Blomberg, *Matthew*, 115.
24. Baker, *2 Corinthians*, 167.
25. "Good enough," not meaning poor, but not so perfect it encourages unhealthy dependence; rather, good enough, yet supportive enough, to encourage growth, development, and independence.
26. Carson et al., *Crossing Thresholds*, 28.

the teaching of Paul in 2 Corinthians 3:18, that transformation into the image of God is a progressive endeavor—with "ever-increasing glory." *Good enough* is good, but it is not and cannot be perfect.

Grace is a continuing blessing offered by God and is always sufficient—at any time and in any situation, including in weakness, as testified by Paul (2 Cor 12:9–10) and in imperfection, as acknowledged by *Leadership* participants and staff. Some specific situations of imperfection needing grace that young men acknowledge are dealt with by John Piper, including anxiety in all its manifestations, e.g., over the COVID-19 pandemic or stress; pride; shame (of self or others—e.g., family/parents); impatience (Jas 5:7–11); or lust.[27] A realization of the liberation and freedom that comes from an understanding of and relationship with the God of the imperfect and acceptance of his grace, transfers to life post-*Leadership*. It is important for the church to realize that youth and young adults will often not be perfect, but then, neither will their parents, youth leaders, mentors, nor even church leaders be perfect either. What is more important is that youth and young adults are invited into a community where they are accepted and offered authenticity, honesty, and grace, as God did with Joseph, Daniel, David, and Timothy, as Barnabas did with Mark, and as Jesus did with the young men he called to be his disciples, recognizing that it was not perfection that was called out, but rather potential. In all relationships, particularly in family relationships, grace is the key. Tchividjian cites a practical theological example of grace, of God at work in the world of family relationships, that will resonate with young men. A sixteen-year-old young man recalled the actual moment when he became a Christian. In his words, "My father spoke grace to me in a moment when I knew I deserved wrath . . . and I came alive." (He and his mates had become drunk, and he wrote off his car.) "God's grace became real to him in the moment of forgiveness and mercy."[28]

Community is the critical place for unashamedly realizing and acknowledging imperfection, in self and all community members. Through living in communion with a perfect God, the only perfect one, we, like him, can accept and live in community with the imperfect, including in our own imperfection.

Two respected theological thinkers are drawn on to add further insights on the importance of community for youth and young adults, on the mystery and the incarnational. Henri Nouwen speaking to an audience, shared:

27. Piper, *Future Grace*.
28. Tchividjian, *One Way Love*, 165.

> Only when I live in communion with God can I live in community that is not perfect, and kind of love the other person and create space in which we might be quite distant or very close, but we can still allow something new to be born ... This is the mystery of the spiritual life. It starts precisely there in the heart, and then we can live in the community.[29]

Drawing on Bonhoeffer, Proffitt and Young provide this insight:

> Because community is a reality already created by Christ, we do not need to be ideal people before we can be in community, nor are we permitted to demand that others fit our ideal—or that which our culture labels as ideal—before we enter into relationship with them, rather, in Christian community, we set others free to be what they are in *Christ*, and we honor the true image they bear as Christ's own.[30]

They add that "It takes an 'incarnational' community to nurture the gifts of young people ... and help them share their unique gifts with the world."[31]

Summary of Chapter

Imperfection is an important theoretical category—a subcategory of acceptance. A theology of imperfection is recognized in examples cited and as an element contributing to the apparent success of *Leadership*, linking imperfection with acceptance, the core category of the developed theory. Imperfection gives full meaning to God's grace and makes *good enough* acceptable, indeed celebrated. Liberation from the bondage of perfection, and acceptance of life as a work continually in progress, means God is accessible and approachable, through Jesus who accepted the imperfect, or in the words of Tchividjian, "the Gospel ... liberates us to be okay with not being okay."[32] A community like *Leadership* is the context where the realization of acceptance of imperfection most occurs and is profitable for living in the mystery and encountering the incarnational.

---

29. Ford, *Lonely Mystic*, 108.
30. Proffitt and Young, "Catalyzing Community," 66.
31. Proffitt and Young, "Catalyzing Community," 64.
32. Tchividjian, *One Way Love*, 148.

17

Freedom and Empowerment

ACCEPTANCE AND FREEDOM WERE linked very early in the emerging themes, particularly in the self-acceptance that also speaks of a personal and spiritual freedom; a freedom to be; a freedom to be me, empowering one with confidence to act, to lead *now*, to find one's vocation and mission. *Empowerment* was one of the eight characteristics of servant leadership selected for the research. As reported in chapter 10, empowerment (believing in others and enabling others' development) was the most selected servant leadership characteristic noted in staff by survey participants (see tables 26 and 27).

The subcategory of *freedom and empowerment* was found to be a critical factor in the apparent success of *Leadership*. The experience of acceptance opens the door to empowerment. Similar to *Leadership*, with the US HSTP, Proffitt and Young ask and answer: "What empowers . . . young people in HSTPs is the presence of a community through which Christ takes human form, accepting young people fully so they no longer need to pretend to be anything but the wildly promising human beings God made them to be."[1]

Being empowered to make their own decisions was noted with pleasure by *Leadership* participants referring to the Stage 1 Overnight Expedition (see chapter 2). Though not confined to the wilderness experiences, the concept of freedom was expanded in the contribution of a focus group participant when reflecting on the Stage 1 Overnight Expedition:

---

1. Proffitt and Young, "Catalyzing Community," 78.

PART IV: THEORY DEVELOPMENT

> I was really excited to see [recognition that] leadership offers freedom, and specifically to make one's own decisions. Obviously, the leadership course isn't at its core about learning how to lead; it's about Christian manliness and about becoming better followers of Christ and therefore bolder leaders and so on. I'm really stoked to see that we're getting across with people taking responsibility and understanding that freedom and the responsibility that goes with it.

There are varying categories of and limits to freedom. The freedom *Leadership* participants are claiming is a freedom to say, ask, be, or do something they previously have not felt free to say, ask, be, or do.

In discussing the benefits of solitude in chapter 9, two categories of freedom were identified, termed *freedom from* (from constraints—with negative benefits) and *freedom to* ("to engage in activities . . . because of the presence of necessary resources," with positive benefits).[2] The freedom to/freedom from dichotomy is taken further by Gascoigne, applying a political/ethical lens, freedom from constraints being a negative freedom and positive freedom being related to human rights. The "positive freedom" category of Gascoigne[3] is not explored further here, though it is acknowledged and is a challenge for the church (and for *Leadership*) into the future, as has already been identified in relation to the global #MeToo movement, to which could be added the BLM[4] movement.

The reported experience of *Leadership* participants encompasses both Long and Averill's categories of freedom,[5] the first of which mirrors the first of the Gascoigne categories.[6] *Freedom from* relates to constraints such as shyness, embarrassment, reticence to share, or past history, though labelling this as "negative freedom" grates a little. *Freedom to* relates to being able to engage in activities with resources available, even the resources of invitation and opportunity. As some would simplify, it is a freedom to be myself and to be different to what I normally am like. One focus group member offered: "that freedom is different to what we're hearing the world say. Freedom to be me means that anyone will accept me for who I am."

As well as what one might call personal freedom, there is a spiritual freedom, a gift from the Spirit of the Lord. God's boundaries are designed

2. Long and Averill, "Solitude."
3. Gascoigne, *Freedom and Purpose*.
4. Black Lives Matter.
5. Long and Averill, "Solitude."
6. Gascoigne, *Freedom and Purpose*.

for freedom. They are not designed to be seen as bondage, but as we pursue other kinds of freedom, whether it be sexual, money, fame, or power, we actually find they do not lead to freedom. This is contrasted with the words of Jesus recorded by the apostle John: "If you hold to my teaching, you are really my disciples. Then you will know the truth, and the truth will set you free . . . If the Son sets you free, you will be free indeed" (John 8:31, 32, 36).

The acceptance and freedom that Jesus gave to those he met, most obviously his disciples, but also the powerless and marginalized, was empowering. Dean and Foster suggest that God "seems especially fond of calling upon the most unlikely suspects," (including youth). "Young people—impetuous, inexperienced, improbable choices by all accounts—figure prominently among God's 'chosen' in both the Hebrew Scriptures and the New Testament."[7] God chose them, and he empowered them.

From a psychological perspective, "True freedom is primarily a state of mind, not a physical condition, therefore the study of the mind is central to an inquiry into freedom."[8] There is debate between different schools of psychology concerning freedom and self-determination. Hassed summarizes the views of several well-known psychologists on freedom, commencing with James (1842–1910), followed by Freud (1856–1939), Jung (1875–1961), and Frankl (1905–1997).[9] According to Hassed, "The bottom line is we do not have to be trapped by the mind. If we train and use it well the mind resembles a faithful servant rather than a tyrannical master. That, however, requires some wisdom, patience, perseverance, careful guidance, courage, and more than a little self-compassion."[10]

Psychology and theology are dealing with two different concepts when considering freedom. Psychologists are referring to the capacity or lack of capacity for self-determination. From a theological perspective, Baker considers the passage from 2 Corinthians 3:17: "Now the Lord is the Spirit, and where the Spirit of the Lord is, there is freedom" (2 Cor 3:17); freedom "from the law of sin," adding, and "freedom to boldly radiate the glory of God in spreading the Gospel."[11] Barnett adds that "Spirit-empowered freedom" is freedom from condemnation, not to lawlessness,

---

7. Dean and Foster, *Godbearing Life*, 17–18.
8. Hassed, "Psychology of Freedom."
9. Hassed, "Psychology of Freedom."
10. Hassed, "Psychology of Freedom."
11. Baker, *2 Corinthians*, 167.

but moved to follow God.[12] Blending the theological and the psychological in the *Leadership* context, the freedom that participants recognize and celebrate is a freedom from the negative impacts of past experiences or choices, a freedom to be a new self (in themselves, in their family, in God), and a freedom that is empowering.

In Maslow's hierarchy of needs,[13] after physiological and safety needs, one needs love and belonging, incorporating friendship, intimacy, and a sense of connection, which includes acceptance. When *Leadership* contributes to the fulfillment of these needs, it prepares participants to move to the higher-order need areas of esteem and self-actualization. Freedom has been related to the second top rung (esteem) of Maslow's hierarchy of needs, while empowerment has been related to the top rung (self-actualization), incorporating creativity, problem-solving, and spontaneity. Empowerment is motivational, for example, motivation to fully participate in *Leadership* and, after Stage 1, to return for subsequent stages. Empowerment includes being given the invitation to exercise leadership *now* and to make one's own decisions—individually and in their group. The motivational value of empowerment is recognized in business:

> Employee empowerment has become increasingly common as a motivational approach to management. The idea is that front-line employees are given authority and decision-making responsibilities in areas once reserved for managers . . . Maslow suggested that employees cannot move to the next level of the hierarchy until the lower-level needs have been satisfied. The highest-level needs, self-actualization and peak experience, are closely tied to empowerment. Empowered employees feel that they can exercise their independent judgment in their pursuit of success for themselves and their organizations.[14]

Freedom and empowerment often come from a realization that one is not and cannot be perfect, nor can anyone else, and nor does God expect them to be perfect, illustrating the link between the various categories of the substantive theory. Being chosen or being given the opportunity is empowering. One interviewee linked the empowering, or equipping, from *Leadership* to being able early afterwards to respond to an opportunity given: "I think I've been very fortunate. Leadership equipped me very well.

12. Barnett, *Second Epistle*, 203.
13. Maslow, "Human Motivation."
14. Kokemuller, "Empowerment."

After Leadership to have had the opportunity of taking on two leadership positions." (Stage 1, 2019)

Summary of Chapter

Freedom and empowerment are highly regarded by *Leadership* participants. They recognize that staff empower them. They are empowered by the unique worship experience, by being given the authority to make decisions on the Stage 1 Overnight Expedition (chapter 2), and particularly when they are affirmed as men in Stage 2 (chapter 3). Empowerment for ministry post-*Leadership* is also highlighted as a desired goal. Freedom and empowerment together are recognized as comprising a subcategory in the developed substantive theory of what contributes to the apparent success of the program. Linking to the previous two categories considered, being accepted, and living in the full understanding of imperfection, is freeing and empowering—for action and for mission. Freedom and empowerment are important from a theological perspective. A key understating is knowing that the truth (of Jesus's teachings) will set you free (John 8:31–32), with added emphasis, "free indeed" (John 8:36). There is freedom in the Spirit, sufficient to encompass the mystery of the work of the Spirit at *Leadership* and in individual lives (often acknowledged as mystery; see chapter 14). God liberates and empowers. Jesus empowered young men to lead; he empowered the powerless; the marginalized. These theological insights add to our understanding of why the factors of freedom and empowerment are important for the apparent success of *Leadership*.

18

Spiritual Dimension (Mystery)

THE SPIRITUAL DIMENSION (OR the overarching presence of God described as a characteristic of the uniqueness of *Leadership*) is recognized as the contextual category of the substantive theory. It also incorporates transformation, celebration, and mystery. In the theory narrative it is described in the *Leadership* context as being young-man appropriate, God-attractive, transformative, celebratory, and community invoking, and that it explains the mystery.

The spiritual dimension of *Leadership* is not just the daily activity called *worship*, or even adding in the optional morning devotions, which attracts a significant number pre-breakfast. Christian teaching is embedded in the range of program activities, including the overall ethos of acceptance and servant leadership. It is drawn from lessons on non-discrimination because of personal attributes, from caring for others, through the quiet times of reflection. The spiritual dimensions are evident in each of the lenses employed: *communitas*, liminality, servant leadership, rites of passage, masculine spirituality, and wilderness. The spiritual dimension of rites of passage, mirroring that of Jesus, is particularly relevant. The Spirit is part of the mystery of transformation that occurs in the lives of participants and the times of celebration, often linked into the worship experience.

Worship

Worship, within the broader spiritual dimension, emerged as a significant experience in all stages, commanding a high level of engagement and recognition that *Leadership* provides for young men a worship experience, different from and something they are more able to connect with than any other worship experience they have encountered. Transformation occurs and this is celebrated, the theme of feasting, celebration, and worship being linked—this three-phase theme being related to the parable of the prodigal son, Isaiah's vision, and the example/teaching of Jesus.

The research data indicated that worship was one of the most significant aspects of *Leadership*. Interestingly, the worship format is similar to what they are used to in church and other contexts—songs, prayer, message, song. The uniqueness of the worship at *Leadership* was explored further in interviews, with responses confirming the views of survey participants. The first two were also quoted in chapter 13 when considering worship as a theologically integrated unique characteristic of *Leadership*:

> For me, the worship would be up in there as well. It was unlike anything I've ever done.

> I would say it's some of the most significant worship ever in my life. The worship at leadership feels like we're not singing for ourselves. We're singing to God. Like, I can't sing. A lot of the boys next to me can't sing. You can really lean into that and not worry about anyone else. It's all worship when we all sing together, there's something really beautiful about that. It feels intentional and from God.

> I was able to interact with it myself, being someone who is incredibly touched by music. I just love being able to be involved in that and not be blocked out of it and not be told that you can't do it. Just having boys worship as well alongside the leaders. The worship and the relationships; it's just amazing.

In focus groups, the worship experience was interpreted:

> The power of worship lies in the authenticity of it and how it's only men doing it. The impact is not in the skill of the band, or in any individual.

> It's different from where everything is mint and you just sit in your seat and watch it go.

PART IV: THEORY DEVELOPMENT

The evening worship appears to take on a special meaning when related to celebration of a major course event—for Stage 1, the day they come back from Overnight Expedition; for Stage 2, the day they return from Solo; for Stage 3, the day they return from Duo, but even more so, after they have shared their mission statements and realize it is their last night.

It was unknown exactly what survey respondents included in worship. One focus group, in discussing the final night, merged the formal dinner with the worship and celebration, specifically adding the sharing of communion in groups. They added: "The most significant part of the night for me is always the worship; and the Communion; always when the facilitators get to pray for their group"; "the most memorable time for me in Stage 1 is worship with the Communion in the group because it's so unique."

A theoretical sampling strategy was employed to explore this point further, targeting those who had participated in interviews and focus groups. One detailed response was received, indicating that in referring to worship, he was referring to the whole daily evening sessions, incorporating songs, message, and prayer. In relation to the final worship service, he commented:

> I think that the final service would be one of the most significant for almost everyone, some more than others obviously, but it is still a very eye-opening experience. Having your group facilitator, someone who has likely become a friend and something of a mentor, go around to each guy, solidifying them in their faith, and even validating them in the eyes of God (from their perspective, some guys may need to be reminded that God does actually accept them, speaking from experience) is a very profound experience, and I think really embodies one of the core elements of Leadership. (Stage 2, 2019)

There is a high level of engagement in worship, something unusual for fifteen- to nineteen-year-old boys. *Leadership* participants are attracted to the worship because it is different, authentic, and appropriate to them. The evidence of the significance of worship at *Leadership* and this contributing to the apparent success of the program is substantial.

It is of interest that in the HSTP, Edie reports a similar experience, relating it as well to the impact that youth at worship has on staff. "Worship is, I think, the most important space at YTI [a HSTP]."[1] "In my own experience, it is impossible to worship with these students and not be filled with

---

1. Edie, "Formative Power," 174.

wonder and hope."[2] Edie expands on the significance of worship to link it with identity formation and meaning-making: "worship becomes generative for their [students'] Christian *identity*, their sense of inner coherence, their claim to belong to a people—to God's people."[3]

Transformation and Celebration

Change, insight development, commitment to something new—sometimes small, sometimes transformational—is celebrated in groups. As is acknowledged, the transformation of a group of individuals and the change in individual lives is often difficult to explain in human terms and can only be seen as the work of the Spirit—the mystery identified.

Celebration on return from the Stage 1 Overnight Expedition, or as part of the Stage 2 Solo return day, or after Stage 3 Duo and the delivery of the mission statement merges and is only completed in the eyes of participants in the evening worship of that day. Formal occasions like graduation at the end of the course increase in significance as Stage 3 is celebrated. One of the events that is important in every stage is the formal dinner and particularly in Stage 3, is incorporated into the experience of the final celebration evening. All celebrations are joined with acknowledgment that they are being experienced with mates, with *brothers*. Response to the formal dinner has been outlined and because there was an element of surprise in the level of significance it is accorded, it is further explored here.

Formal Dinner

To include the formal dinner in a chapter on the spiritual dimension may seem strange. However, evidence is documented to conclude that the formal dinner is a key event towards the end of the course each year, significant to all stages, with particular significance to Stage 3 in their final course and in the experience of participants on that night, is merged into worship. Through its newness for some, it contributes to the uniqueness and apparent success of *Leadership*. The comments of two interviewees are cited and these confirm the difference of this formal dinner, enjoying the event with *brothers* and the particular significance for Stage 3 participants at their last dinner.

2. Edie, "Formative Power," 175.
3. Edie, "Formative Power," 191.

PART IV: THEORY DEVELOPMENT

> I have been to other formal dinners, and it didn't feel the same. At Leadership you sit around with others having a very very nice meal with brothers, brotherly men.
>
> I agree with it being important for Stage 3 because it's a lot bigger. You get to see them in every stage. I agree. It seems a lot bigger then; you get to the middle table.

This activity was raised in interviews, and responses included:

> I've been to a lot of formal dinners in my life, but some of the people I encountered at leadership I could definitely say with certainty that that was their first one and, I think it does have much significance because in a way that it is a very rite of passage and people don't necessarily do that anymore . . . No one puts on a dinner suit and goes out to have dinner very much anymore; no one puts on a dinner suit to go to the opera anymore, it's just t-shirt jeans which is terrible. So I think it has immense connotations.

Other expanded explanations offered by interviewees were that it's fun, it's one of the last events, and it's a celebration with those one has shared the experience with; it's "celebrating we (all these blokes) are still together"; formal dinners are "steeped in tradition" and have "significance throughout history"; the formal dinner signifies a "change in one's life"; "something is no longer what it was"; a "clearly defined change"; and it's the whole course together—making some notable links with having been in and now emerging from liminal space.

Reflection on the Spiritual Dimension

One of the lenses used to view the program was the lens of masculine spirituality. Though contested space, it was concluded that such a concept does exist, the key elements of which correlate with the characteristics of servant leadership, and that these elements are acknowledged and adopted by *Leadership* participants. The overarching presence of God has been discussed in chapter 13 as a property of the uniqueness of *Leadership*. Though dealt with as a separate property of uniqueness for the purposes of discussion and theory formation, all other uniqueness properties: servanthood exampled, group(s), staff, context, and strategies and ethos in practice are absorbed by and contribute to the spiritual dimension. The following explanation from the narrative of the final substantive theory in chapter 14 is repeated:

> So accepted and embedded throughout the program is the spiritual dimension, that participants say they assume this and see it particularly in servant leadership. The most common reference to the spiritual dimension is through the worship experience at *Leadership*—its uniqueness and its spontaneous engagement of young men who rarely become or even feel motivated to become so enthusiastically engaged in worship. They draw other concepts into their spiritual engagement, particularly Jesus' example of servant leadership and importance of solitude, and the example of staff. Yet there remains a mystery with only the Spirit as an explanation of community and transformation.

These words raise three key observations. The first again highlights the significance of worship and this has been dealt with. The other two, the unspoken and the mystery, are further explored.

The spiritual dimension is also characterized by the appreciation of celebration at *Leadership*—a theme linked into the contextual category of the substantive theory through its identified importance by participants, where they celebrate completions, *successes*, discoveries, and changes. In his reflection on the parable of the prodigal son, Nouwen states that "celebration belongs to God's Kingdom."[4] He continues to highlight the rejoicing of God and the invitation "to rejoice with him,"[5] citing the other lost/found parables—the sheep and the coin. Perhaps the celebration times at *Leadership* are also reflecting the finding of joy in finding new hope; finding that I am not bad, I am returning home to the Father and finding my mission—celebrating a new understanding that the kingdom is near.

The Unspoken and the Mystery

There are certain elements that were only spoken about to a limited extent in survey responses. They include the spiritual dimension and related topics within that dimension, such as the expression of altruism as an outcome of *Leadership*, the operation of liminal space as a vehicle for transformation, and *sacred* sites and symbols. Elements that may be identified by participants but are not specifically spoken about by staff in specific sessions include *communitas*, liminality, and brotherhood. But these elements are strongly present, which is part of the *Leadership* mystery.

---

4. Nouwen, *Prodigal Son*, 113.
5. Nouwen, *Prodigal Son*, 114.

PART IV: THEORY DEVELOPMENT

The operation of altruism is not articulated, but it is there. This was clarified by a focus group participant: "Altruism is strange—is a mundane thing throughout Leadership (like someone taking your porridge bowl). Not everyone says anything about it because everyone does it at some point." Other explanations as to why this was not often articulated in survey responses included that it is not a common word, that some boys (culturally) do not like bragging about doing good and that if you are brought up with altruism as what you (and your family) do, it is not new or unique enough to mention. A similar explanation was that you just do it in your exercise of leadership.

Liminality and *communitas* have been dealt with adequately in chapter 9. The point is that they are vital understandings for staff, are vital components of *Leadership*, and are lenses to examine the program, but it is not vital that participants have full understanding of or are able to articulate the concepts. A similar conclusion is drawn in relation to sites and symbols. Where these are spoken of by participants, they often have a spiritual significance for the individual, but they do not necessarily have to. An example is the reference to their Solo site as sacred to them—possibly because that is where they had a significant encounter with God.

The concept of *family*, along with *brothers*, was extensively dealt with in chapter 15, as a factor within the key category of *acceptance*. As identified by the Research Collaboration Group, the timing of the transition from just fellow group members to *brothers* is difficult to determine, and like many aspects, it is part of the unspoken mystery of *Leadership*.

A further insight and warning from the Research Collaboration Group which is heeded is that what is unspoken should remain unspoken because, as soon as one attempts to change this and incorporate sessions in the program specifically addressing these elements, their impact is compromised, as participants think they must demonstrate them and talk about them. It was observed in chapter 2 that the strength of the "brotherhood of *Leadership*" (or "the tribe or whatever we want to call it") is that it is not pushed, and "because we don't have to push it, means it's the real thing."

The concept of *mystery* raised in a focus group was then taken up by a second group, who were asked: "How do we unravel and understand the mystery, particularly the mystery of boys coming and changing so much in one week and the mystery of how the groups work, develop *communitas*, and the lasting impact that has? What is the understanding of the mystery?" Their response was:

SPIRITUAL DIMENSION (MYSTERY)

> The mystery is that God's doing work and the Spirit is moving and maybe we are uncomfortable in naming those things sometimes like it's clear that that's what's happening.

On the question of transformation, an observation from Carson et al. is pertinent to this discussion: "[transformation] cannot be planned for in some kind of cause-and-effect straight line or even accessed on demand. All we can do is cooperate as far as possible with the conditions in which we are likely to be open to God's transformative work."[6] The mystery of how boys become *brothers* and experience *communitas* so quickly, deeply, and long-lastingly; how boys change so substantially in one week, can only be explained through recognizing that this is the space where the Spirit moves. It is God in action in the world of younger and older men together, in the community that is *Leadership* leading to life change/transformation—spiritually, relationally, and practically.

Summary of Chapter

The spiritual dimension of *Leadership* is the contextual category within which other categories theologically coalesce. It surrounds other categories with a theological perspective, incorporating the drawing of participants into worship, transformation, and celebration. It explains that no matter what one feels about oneself, either in imagination or reality, God is present in the struggle as he is with those who are marginalized. Worship is the focus of the spiritual dimension of *Leadership* and is a key component for participants. They participate enthusiastically and frequently contrast it with their worship experience elsewhere (e.g., in their home churches), as exampled in chapters 2 and 3, where their voices are noted, describing worship at *Leadership* as different, uplifting, encouraging, amazing, most significant ever, and focused on God. They incorporate in worship, the whole evening experience, particularly on the final night, where a formal dinner and communion are included. But the mystery of the work of the Spirit in participants' lives remains.

---

6. Carson et al., *Crossing Thresholds*, 6.

Part V

Implications, Conclusions and Contextualization

HAVING DEALT WITH THE rationale for the research into the *Leadership* program and considered the research findings leading to the articulation of a grounded theory, the question is asked, "What are the implications for the program and for youth ministry practice?" Questions, including what the carry over impacts for participants may be, are explored in chapter 19 (Beyond *Leadership*).

In chapter 20 (Conclusions and Youth Ministry as Context), findings are summarized, and conclusions are drawn. *Leadership* and the research findings are located in the context of youth ministry generally. A consolidated review of contemporary approaches to youth ministry is provided and where *Leadership* sits in this context is considered. Limitations to transferability are acknowledged and suggestions that have emerged for future research are offered.

19

Beyond *Leadership*

Introduction

AFTER *LEADERSHIP* IS OVER, what do participants retain of the experience, and does it continue to impact their lives? This was able to be measured for those who completed the survey up to ten years after completing *Leadership*. Several questions were asked that assist in ascertaining this: what they remember was most taught; how they were impacted; whether they have exercised leadership in their home situations (e.g., Was the leadership *now* opportunity pursued?); and the impact of who they continued to *hang out* with—either from *Leadership* or from their home situations. Another experience for some is joining the *Leadership* staff.

Most Remembered Concepts from *Leadership*

Participants were asked to select up to three of the topics listed in table 34 that they most remembered being taught at *Leadership*.

	ALL RESPONDENTS (%)	PARTICIPANT RESPONDENTS (%)	STAFF RESPONDENTS (%)
Working in teams	67.1	68.0	66.7
Self-reflection	56.5	57.7	54.6
Decision-making	43.5	45.4	36.4

	ALL RESPONDENTS (%)	PARTICIPANT RESPONDENTS (%)	STAFF RESPONDENTS (%)
Critical thinking	26.0	19.6	45.5
Authentic self	24.4	22.7	30.3
Conflict management	19.9	21.7	12.1
Ethical aspects of leadership	19.1	20.6	15.2
Mentoring	18.3	19.6	15.2
Responsible morality	13.7	17.5	3.0
Transforming influence	13.0	12.4	15.1
Voluntary subordination	8.4	6.2	15.1
Covenantal relationships	7.6	7.2	6.1
Transcendental spirituality	6.9	6.2	9.1
Encouragement to practice altruism in the community	6.1	6.2	6.1

Table 34. What Participant Respondents and Staff Respondents Consider Was Most Taught at *Leadership*

Given the emphasis in *Leadership* of their group and teamwork, it is not surprising that *working in teams* was the most remembered (68%) by participant respondents. More than half of them (57.7%) also remembered *self-reflection*, followed by *decision-making* (45.4%), *authentic self* (22.7%), *conflict management* (21.7%), *ethical aspects of leadership* (20.6%) *critical thinking* (19.6%), and *mentoring* (19.6%). The strength of these reported choices is heightened when considering that they were only able to select three options. While this demonstrates those topics most remembered, it does not mean that the other topics were not remembered. In chapter 4 there is a reference to participants from Stage 3 remembering the *7 Habits* up to ten years later and still finding this useful, for example, in their approach to life, including university. They actually name the habits, the most remembered being *Be Proactive*.

Eva and Sendjaya pointed to the "research-practice gap" in youth leadership development and as a contribution to addressing this gap, they set out to "examine the effectiveness of leadership development in Australia."[1] The focus of these researchers was on leadership development programs in schools for student leaders. They noted the following skill deficiencies in

---

1. Eva and Sendjaya, "Creating Future Leaders," 584.

program outcomes: "leadership, critical thinking, self-reflection, conflict-management, and decision-making." They also reported that there was "little exposure to ethics training throughout their leadership programs."

Leadership can be contrasted with these findings, where participants remembered *critical thinking* skills development, *self-reflection*, *conflict management*, and *decision-making*. Critical thinking skills was highlighted, an example given by one interviewee being that this was enhanced by receiving frequent appraisal of one's activity in a positive way, rather than as cynicism. *Self-reflection, conflict management,* and *decision-making* skills are topics that are taught, commencing in the Stage 1 program. Similarly, *ethical aspects of leadership* was reported as being remembered by 20 percent of participant respondents, reflected in their adoption of a servant leadership approach, the framework for the Eva and Sendjaya research.[2]

Eva and Sendjaya found that there was "a significant gap between perceptions of the students and those of the teachers/facilitators on what was being taught and what is required in youth leadership development programs."[3] Contrary to the Eva and Sendjaya study, in this study of *Leadership* there was a high level of agreement between participant respondents and staff respondents that *working in teams* was the most remembered topic taught, followed by *self-reflection*. Although there are other trends, the main significant differences of opinion are that 45.5 percent of staff respondents believed *critical thinking* was taught but only 19.6 percent of participant respondents (something that seems to have been corrected during in-depth interviews); 45.5 percent of participant respondents believed that *decision-making* was taught compared with 36.4 percent of staff respondents; 21.7 percent of participant respondents believed that *conflict management* was taught compared with 12.1 percent of staff respondents; 17.5 percent of participant respondents remembered that *responsible morality* was taught, as compared with 3.0 percent of staff respondents.

What is important to note is that some respondents completed the survey up to ten years after they completed the program and were indicating what they still remember. This justifies a conclusion that the items they selected are significant and have a lasting impact.

---

2. Eva and Sendjaya, "Creating Future Leaders," 585.
3. Eva and Sendjaya, "Creating Future Leaders," 584.

PART V: IMPLICATIONS, CONCLUSIONS AND CONTEXTUALIZATION

How They Were Impacted

Survey respondents were invited to share anything else they would like to about their *Leadership* experience. Twenty-nine participant respondents and ten staff respondents responded to this invitation. Respondents took up the invitation in different ways. The most common words used by respondents were experience, helped, amazing, good, and learn, indicating a dynamic within their lives of a growth promoting nature. The most common response was to talk about the positive impact on their lives. See table 35 for a broad characterization of responses.

CHARACTERIZATION	NUMBER	%
Positive	28	71.8
Negative	6	15.4
Neutral[4]	2	5.1
Suggestions	3	7.7

Table 35. Categorization of Additional Comments

Four different ways the invitation was taken up were, with examples:

1. *To share their views on the impact that Leadership had and continues to have on their lives.* Three staff respondent comments, reflecting on their experience as participants, though having then had the opportunity of continuing the *Leadership* experience as staff, are offered as examples:

   > Without the encounter I had with my God whilst doing Solo in the bush desperately seeking the reality of him for me, I don't know if I would have stayed in the faith for the years that followed. Instead I have grown immensely in my faith and relationship with my heavenly father. I am forever grateful to the course and staff for helping me in this journey! (Stage 3, 2012)

   > Leadership defined my life. It will always have a special place in my heart and is something I hope my own kids will be a part of in the future. As a participant, it was life changing and I still feel the effects from it to this day—particularly with the connections and friendships I have made. As a staff member, it shaped me further

---

4. The responses characterized as neutral were to do with unique personal attributes.

(almost like a 4th stage). It is even something I hope to come back and serve on God-willing. (Stage 3, 2013)

Leadership is what has helped form me into the man I am today. Honestly without Leadership I don't know where I would be. For the past 3 years my favourite moments of the year have come from my time serving in Leadership and seeing the change and the same affect it had on me done to others, and that brings me such joy and happiness. It truly is a fantastic course, and I will continue to be a part of it until I cannot. (Stage 3, 2015)

While staff have the opportunity of continuing to be refreshed annually, the following participant respondent views reinforce the impact and that it continues:

Leadership experience is something that I most certainly appreciated and remembered in many ways at the time. The atmosphere of just being able to be you while being supported unconditionally, being able to be open, and be with a group of boys from very different backgrounds, and the various opportunities to grow in maturity and as a Christian were wonderful and crucial. However, I believe I appreciate what leadership has done for me even more now than it did back then, and I believe I will continue to appreciate it more and more the years I experience and the older I get (am 24 now). (Stage 3, 2013)

It made my faith real for me, and gave me many brothers to share Christ with. I think it's one of the best things I have ever done, I also really appreciated the influence of [J] as the Chaplain. He is an inspiring source of wisdom and encouragement to us all. (Stage 3, 2018)

It was the most amazing and worthwhile thing I've ever done. I am so grateful to have been a part of such an amazing experience. (Stage 2, 2019)

2. *To affirm their view of the positive nature of Leadership.* Terms used include: "incredible experience," "love the transformation," "absolutely life-changing," "great experience and well thought out plans," "I gave my life to the Lord in Stage 2 during Solo," "Solo, Solo, Solo. Amazing," "thank you so much for the work you did in my life," "don't change it, it's fantastic the way it is."

3. *To share their experience when this was not as positive as reported by a majority of respondents.* Small though this group was, and that is significant in itself, nevertheless, their views are important. One was disappointed with his Solo. The other comments all related to individualization of the program, including one who said he had a "fragile ego" at the time and another that adventure/camping does not suit everyone. They need a greater level of acceptance and care (especially when someone else made the decision for them to attend).

4. *To suggest changes in Leadership into the future.* Suggestions made were to update teaching styles and materials; stay up with current youth issues; and put the course material on-line for ease of ongoing access.

The weight of evidence is that the experience was positive for most and the impact is ongoing.

Leadership *Now*—At *Leadership* and at Home, Church, School

Participants are invited to exercise leadership at any time during *Leadership*, something they frequently comment is an unusual invitation compared with what they are used to. While this is a recognition that young men are capable of exercising leadership *now*, not waiting until later when they are *mature*, there is a challenge to continue this recognition beyond *Leadership*.

The exercise of leadership *now* (not sometime in the future) enhances transferability and implementation of learning. One described *Leadership* as "an anchor point." Another positive example, referenced in chapter 17, comes from an interviewee who immediately after Stage 1 was appointed to a school leader role and a leader role in the ADF Cadets. He said:

> I think I've been very fortunate, Leadership equipped me very well, After Leadership to have had the opportunity of taking on two leadership positions . . . Leadership equipped me well in the roles I was placed in. (Stage 1, 2019)

Seventy-nine percent reported (see chapter 10) that they were able to exercise leader roles at *Leadership*. Whether this continues in their home circumstances is problematic. The evidence is that some do, though often in a minor way that is automatic with age. Others say they went home and were not given any responsibility in their local groups or churches—a critical ingredient of best practice in youth ministry that is explored in chapter 20. Those who said they exercised leadership roles post-*Leadership* in their local BB groups numbered 56.8 percent. This would likely occur regardless of *Leadership* as the local BB program is designed to appoint those of fifteen plus years to leadership roles with younger boys. As an extension of this if they are attending church, 17.1 percent exercised leadership in youth ministry and 14.4 percent in kids' ministry. In another area of interest for youth—worship, music, creativity, or technology, 17.1 percent had exercised leadership roles. There were 17.4 percent who indicated that they exercised leadership roles in their schools or universities; 26 percent in their work/business/management roles. What is of concern is that few, given that some were by then aged in their late twenties, indicated that they had exercised leadership roles in their churches (beyond BB, kids ministry, youth ministry)—only 2 percent in leadership within their church (e.g., church council or deacon) and only 4.5 percent as pastor/preaching/prayer.

In Stage 3, proactivity is taught. One young staff member took this concept up in his comment, placing responsibility on participants:

> Boys' Brigade companies and the church should be wanting to help and assist people in more leadership roles. I think what Leadership does well is that it takes some of the power away from the church and puts it on the boy and says, hey, is there some opportunity you can see at your church. Don't wait for them. You go to them and actively seek those leadership roles. It doesn't matter if they're at a Boys' Brigade company or their school, they're the ones with the onus on them for them to go out, take a step.

While *Leadership* makes a positive contribution and statement about being given real roles and responsibilities, or running their own programs, there is work to do in bridging the gap with the ongoing church experience for participants beyond *Leadership*, some of whom have no real link into a church community other than their local BB group meeting through the week—a challenge highlighted in chapter 20. The work of Lukabyo[5] and the revival of understanding and advocacy of capacity of youth for leadership introduced in chapter 1 could be a stimulus to revitalizing this momentum. Youth are ready, capable, and respond well to being given leadership roles—for example, a comment noted in chapter 2 (putting learning into practice), when there was surprise "at being given the responsibility" for leading their own Stage 1 Overnight Expedition. The evidence indicates not

5. Lubakyo, *Ministry for Youth*.

only their capacity, but also their readiness for this freedom and empowerment, with support. The challenge is to work with others at home base to extend beyond *Leadership*.

Dean raises the possibility of offering theological education in stages—working with congregations—staged vocational formation/discernment.[6] The idea is that confirmation becomes the beginning of discernment to Christian discipleship and Christian leadership within the congregation, where gifts are named and allowed to be used in ministry. Confirmation would "become an occasion for experiences of liminality, competence, deep belonging, and holy struggle, and for honing their leadership through service, witness, and stewardship." Could this model fit for *Leadership*, the ongoing BB ministry program, and the church?

The *Leadership* emphasis on vocational formation may have to be considered earlier, because although participants may consider the question of where/what is God calling them to learn for Christian leadership, in Stage 3, if vocational formation is linked to developing a mission statement, this may be too late as many by then are in university and are at least pursuing a tentative career path preparation, or are in full-time employment.

Dean reports that:

> Many students we talked to openly wondered what it would be like to go back to "real life" in their churches and schools, now they had tasted theological reflection with equally interested others, and now that they thought of themselves as potential leaders in the Christian community. They wondered whether the church as they know it has room for them, or whether God might best use their leadership elsewhere.[7]

This highlights the risk of creating and encouraging entrepreneurship without the backing of mentors.

Horn captures the *going home* dilemma faced in such intense and focused programs that involve close community: "for some, going home is the hardest part of their pilgrimage." "The [HSTP] journey is in some way designed so our youth never do go home again [not suggesting literally]." The hope is that they are "now more theologically reflective," deal with distractions differently, not just be like they were before, are transformed, are community-dependent, have developed habits of the heart (Bible study,

---

6. Dean, "Hitting It Out," 278.
7. Dean, "Hitting It Out," 287.

silence, journaling), have memories (including of God), and have a mentor (including serving at home).[8]

Expecting youth "to return home as confident servant leaders who can engage in theological and personal reflection with their mentor, we help them continue as pilgrims who seek God, rather than tourists who simply recall a fun trip"[9]—or, do we?

Hearlson injects a youthful wildness into the discussion: "When the wild God of elsewhere sends us home to the here and now, reintegration is never simple." "People come home bearing gifts." This does not ensure welcome or acceptance of the gifts, or "integration."[10] On return home, it is easy to slide into old ruts. Participants may face apathy (even from youth ministers) or active resistance (in which case they give up, change churches, or leave church),[11] again highlighting the challenge for program and home to grow together.

Different orientations noted in HSTPs approach to returning home,[12] and how these impact effectiveness are important to note. Clearly, a partnership approach between program and the home church/family, with a high level of mutual trust and involving sponsorship, prayer, mentorship, and financial support, is the most effective. Orientations that are not helpful are a substitution or compensation approach (where the program substitutes for church or family), a transformational approach (where participants go home thinking they can change the world and may get out of their depth), and an oppositional approach (opposition to family or church). However, there is a reality described by Hearlson that needs to be addressed: "For some participants, their program becomes the first place they have encountered life-giving Christian community that deals with conflict constructively, honors their hard questions, and equips them for leadership." Family language abounds in this approach. There are problems with return home—when the resources are not available. A risk is that participants "become judges and critics rather than gift-bearers."

There is plenty of room for *Leadership* to develop essential partnerships between the program and home bases. Continued revisiting of the material mentioned in these comments from participants—the naming of

---

8. Horn, "Prepare Me," 207–8.
9. Horn," Prepare Me," 209.
10. Hearlson, "Taking It Home," 125.
11. Hearlson, "Taking It Home," 125–26.
12. Hearlson, "Taking It Home," 127–34.

identified fruit of the Spirit in one participant's life and the value of a lifelong mission statement provide good fodder for post-*Leadership* mentoring relationships and for participants being honored as *gift-bearers*.

Hanging Out in Local BB Company, Youth Group, School

What happens pre-*Leadership*, between stages, and post-*Leadership* is of importance. For Stage 1 in particular, key people in the local group are significant motivators to attend and to continue to subsequent stages.[13] This is further illustrated by a comment made during a focus group meeting:

> Boys' Brigade definitely helps. People go because of Boys' Brigade, because of the emphasis Boys' Brigade puts on it and the encouragement they see in other men. The young boys see the impact it has on other boys and then they say I would like the impact on me and so they go and experience that and then they're the ones that influence the younger kids going to go in the next few years.

It is of benefit if the local group has a number of boys attending *Leadership* together, not necessarily in the same stage. One interviewee spoke of those from his BB company forming a group they call "The Leadership Boys," a group that hangs out together. Because of numbers, that is not the experience for every local group. At a consultation session for BB company ministry leaders, one leader reinforced the partnership, speaking of knowing boys who go to *Leadership*, seeing them after *Leadership*, and observing the difference. The value of having a group to *hang out* with is reinforced by this comment:

> When you return from the camp, you're not just returning to a group of strangers. You are returning to your Boys' Brigade company where your captains and your other leaders there are wanting you to take the next step in the program and help out and then a couple of weeks later you've got the reunion which definitely helps instil the community.

For those who have never been BB members or are no longer members, choices for *hanging out* are limited to church, youth group, school, or a decision to keep in contact with their *Leadership* group or a particular person, most commonly their Stage 3 Duo partner. This seems critical, at least for the initial post-*Leadership* phase.

13. Smith, "Leadership Development Program," 79.

Serving on the *Leadership* Staff

One of the marks of apparent success in *Leadership* is the regular (every year) recruitment of new graduates from Stage 3 to join the staff team. In 2021, for example, even after a COVID-19 gap year in 2020, six 2019 Stage 3 graduates joined the staff to do whatever they were asked to do. These roles are highly sought after, prioritizing the organization of one's life around this annual opportunity to serve as servant leaders to the next group of participants. The commitment is strong with many continuing to serve over many years and, as identified as a characteristic of the uniqueness of *Leadership* (chapter 13), seamlessly transitioning into a staff role. One of the realities of *Leadership* that surprises participants is that staff return year after year, paying their own way, taking leave from their employment, supported by their families, to clean toilets, do the washing up, or as one Research Consultation Group member put it, "do other crappy jobs." Participants see this and often relate it to observing servant leadership in action.

Summary of Chapter

What happens beyond *Leadership* is important to assess the value of the program and what makes it apparently successful. Survey respondents' views on aspects of post-*Leadership* are significant to reveal their importance to bridging the gap. Some responding were doing so up to ten years later, being themselves now in their late twenties.

The key aspects they most remembered, the ways *Leadership* impacted them, whether they have exercised leadership since (have become reproduced leaders), and who they keep in contact with (are influenced by) are all relevant to the beyond *Leadership* considerations and ongoing reinforcement of the positive experience. Partnership with the sending group (e.g., BB Company or church) or person is essential at both initial sponsorship and follow-up phases. Those who join the *Leadership* staff have a regular opportunity to reflect and be engaged annually in the *Leadership* community, which continues to impact them.

20

Conclusions and Youth Ministry as Context

Introduction

THE STRUCTURE OF THIS chapter is to present a broad summary of the findings, followed by a review of youth ministry, and a bringing of these two focus points together as the point of contextualization, concluding with recommendations and suggestions for further research.

Summary of Findings

Conclusion statements relating to the research question occur throughout the book. These include steps towards theory development presented in part IV. Findings were discussed, applying a mutual critical correlation strategy (bringing together theological and social science insights). The final substantive theory identified the key categories of acceptance, imperfection, freedom and empowerment, within the context of a spiritual dimension (or mystery).

The findings of the research study confirm that *Leadership* can be regarded as an effective intense period of training, in the pattern of Jesus's training of his disciples, in an atmosphere of full acceptance, even through *failures* and seeming slowness to reach understanding and commitment. Jesus did not wait for full maturity or seek perfection. He saw potential in his disciples and provided training and mentoring *now*, where they were at. *Leadership* contributes to the church fulfilling its responsibility to provide youth with training and encouraging them to find their role in ministry, as leaders *now*, not as leaders-in-training for some ill-defined future. They should not be regarded as *adults-in-waiting, waiting for their turn* or just receivers of the culture, beliefs, and so on, of the church, but as connected contributors.[1] The involvement of youth in real ministry, in a mutually respectful partnership is advocated, a valuable context being an intergenerational community, such as *Leadership*, where all can serve together, irrespective of age, maturity, or experience—*doing it together*.

This research makes further contributions to Christian (youth) ministry:

- It reinforces the power of personal story sharing.
- It establishes liminality as an organizing concept; a space for God's Spirit to work; a space where God meets people on the margins of life and people imperfectly living on the edge.
- It makes links between *communitas*, liminality, rites of passage, and wilderness (solitude).
- It identifies with a paradoxical claim that solitude calls one into community.
- It promotes Jesus's servant leadership.
- It tackles with some risk and some courage the concept of masculine spirituality.
- It highlights the power of uniqueness in youth ministry; something participants experience that no one else experiences: the particular kind of group, the relationships with staff, the wilderness location for some activities, the freedom and encouragement to serve *now*, and the overarching presence of God.
- It identifies and describes a unique worship experience.
- It presents a unique combination of acceptance (that is unconditional), imperfection (that is recognized in all), freedom and empowerment (that give release and confidence at a time when Christian ministry is criticized for being the opposite), and the spiritual dimension (incorporating worship that they have never experienced in any other place).
- Its intergenerational leadership model contributes to the ongoing discussion in youth ministry desiring a return to an intergenerational/

1. Cannister, "Thinking Ecclesiologically."

family-based approach, involving the youth's family and the youth's church family.[2]

The findings challenge a view that boys/young men from age fifteen are not vitally interested in their futures, are not ready or keen to respond to the challenges of relationships, leadership, and manhood, and do not have a strong interest in the spiritual.

Youth Ministry

How children and youth are regarded and the state of youth in the world may be a litmus test of the state of the world. And the state of youth ministry in the community of the body of Christ, the church, may be a litmus test for the state of the body. While youth are treated as people in waiting and their potential is not recognized and acted upon, so too, youth ministry, treated as an appendage and not as a vital and equal cog in the wheel, will remain in an adolescent waiting game, that even the most patient participants may reject.

To set the tone and recognize the challenges, claims, and uncertainty about youth ministry, reference is made to the 2016 Dean and Hearlson[3] edited work on the US HSTP, in which they make the claim that "youth ministry can change theological education, if we let it." The very title of this publication raises three preliminary theological and contemporary youth ministry issues:

- The position of youth in the world and in the church.
- Acknowledgment of youth; listening to their voices.
- The interface between youth ministry and theology.

In the last twenty years, responding to the loss of youth from the church, there has been criticism of youth groups or youth ministry that is primarily focused on pizza, entertainment, and numbers. Academics, resource providers, and practitioners have grappled with the issue. As well, the separation of youth, or siloing[4] that has isolated youth from their families and the adult church into youth-specific programs has come under

---

2. DeVries, *Family-Based Youth Ministry*; Clark, ed. *Adoptive Youth Ministry*; Diaz, "Call to Adoption"; Fritz, *Art of Forming*.

3. Dean and Hearlson, *How Youth Ministry*.

4. DeVries. *Family-Based Youth Ministry*, 21, 35, 38.

fire when it is the only involvement of youth with the church. However, despite many different youth ministry program approaches being adopted, the outflow of youth from the church has continued.

This section visits some historical and developmental trends of youth ministry and considers the youth ministry scene today, including the theological setting. This is the context in which the program, *Leadership*, is offered.

In many ways, there emerges something of a cyclical pattern in youth ministry, with the new (or is it the old?) being introduced with dramatic challenge, as in the literature, with titles that include revolution,[5] new directions,[6] purpose driven,[7] starting right,[8] postmodern,[9] timeless,[10] family-based,[11] revisiting,[12] doesn't last,[13] reinventing (again),[14] together—transforming the church,[15] theological turn,[16] by teenagers,[17] youth ministry changing theological education,[18] adoption as a model,[19] from for, to of,[20] wide-awake,[21] and the end of youth ministry.[22]

Illustrating the cyclical pattern, Rice, promoting his emphasis, noted:

> It's taken youth ministry almost fifty years to get where we are today. Perhaps we can, in a somewhat shorter amount of time, back things up and restore the intergenerational quality of the church that we have lost . . . What I am calling for as a new way of doing

5. Senter, *Coming Revolution*.
6. Rice et al., *New Directions*.
7. Fields, *Purpose Driven*.
8. Dean et al., *Starting Right*.
9. Jones, *Postmodern Youth Ministry*.
10. Vukich and Vandegriff, *Timeless Youth Ministry*.
11. DeVries, *Family-Based Youth Ministry*.
12. Root, *Revisiting*.
13. DeVries, *Sustainable Youth Ministry*.
14. Rice, *Reinventing*.
15. Baxter, *Together*.
16. Root and Dean, *Theological Turn*.
17. McKee and Smith, *Ministry by Teenagers*.
18. Dean and Hearlson, *How Youth Ministry*.
19. Clark, *Adoptive Youth Ministry*.
20. Lukabyo, *Ministry for Youth*.
21. Stanton, *Wide-Awake*.
22. Root, *End of Youth Ministry?*

youth ministry or doing church isn't new at all. For hundreds of years the church was intergenerational and family-based." [It is not turning the clock back but making] "course correction."[23]

A sample of models and approaches is now considered.

Family-Based Youth Ministry

More than twenty years ago, it was being proposed that "traditional youth ministry hurts families."[24] Family-based youth ministry was strongly promoted by Mark DeVries in 2004.[25] There are two identified models of family-based youth ministry, a family-ministry model—strengthening and equipping families (parents), and a youth-ministry model; not ignoring parents, but widening this to include other adults, with the church as an extended family. DeVries[26] promotes intergenerational ministry structures—the extended family of the church—as family-based youth ministry. They are not *either/or* models. Whichever model is adopted, it builds on "a foundation of parents providing intentional Christian nurture for their children" and "youth connecting to an extended Christian family of faith–full adults."[27] DeVries challenges that "the church, the one place where teenagers could logically be linked to the world of adults, has missed the opportunity"[28] and a family-based youth ministry can contribute to remedying this.

Relational Youth Ministry

DeVries voiced criticism of relational ministry "done by a few enthusiastic, inexperienced, short-term, early-twenties youth leaders who stay around only long enough to 'wow' our kids."[29] His real point is the question of who the young person is in relationship with. Is it young inexperienced leaders or mature Christian adults in the church? Subsequently, Root

23. Rice, *Reinventing*, 191–92.
24. Clark and Ewen, "Reconstructing Family Life."
25. DeVries, *Family-Based Youth Ministry*.
26. DeVries, *Family-Based Youth Ministry*, 83, 85.
27. DeVries, *Family-Based Youth Ministry*, 174–76.
28. DeVries, *Family-Based Youth Ministry*, 42–43.
29. DeVries, *Family-Based Youth Ministry*, 56.

revisited relational youth ministry, acknowledging its negative reputation, but extending the profile of relational youth ministry. He promotes it to a new sphere where incarnation is a key component and introduces his concept of "place-sharing."[30] In summary, Root's thesis is that Jesus Christ is concretely present to us in our relational lives, in our person-to-person encounters. Christ is encountered *in the relationship*. "Relational ministry [is] participation in the person of Christ in the world . . . Relationships in youth ministry . . . are seen . . . as the place where we experience God's presence in the world."[31] "Relational ministry, then, is not about a strategy of influence but about persons being conformed to the person of Jesus as incarnate, crucified, and resurrected, and going into the world to join the *who* of Christ as incarnate, crucified, and resurrected."[32]

Youth-Focused Youth Ministry

As noted in chapter 1, McGarry reminds us that "Jesus could have called any group of people to become His disciples, but He choose a group of teenagers and young adults who were overwhelmingly ordinary. Jesus spent time with His young apostles and empowered them for significant ministry, entrusting them with the mission of the church."[33]

It is becoming uncontested ground that children and youth should be involved in leadership for their own development and as members of the body of Christ—the church. This is good theory, that is often not what one observes or experiences in practice. Questions arise, as to how and when and how much youth should be involved in leadership of their own ministry. One question is how to balance a family-focused adult—youth together ministry with ministry for, to, of, or with youth.

Taking a historical look, during the 1930s and 1940s, "in university ministries, the schools ministry, and the local church fellowships, young people were encouraged to lead and take initiative in ministry to their peers."[34] Lukabyo continues, "the empowerment of young leaders had been wonderfully productive for youth ministry, but this movement displayed the potential for destructive behaviour by charismatic leaders who were

30. Root, *Revisiting*.
31. Root, *Revisiting*, 102–3.
32. Root, *Revisiting*, 103.
33. McGarry, *Biblical Theology*, 55.
34. Lukabyo, *Ministry for Youth*, 220.

PART V: IMPLICATIONS, CONCLUSIONS AND CONTEXTUALIZATION

unconstrained by adult mentors or denominational disciplines."[35] In the history of Anglican youth ministry, Lukabyo acknowledged the importance of supporting adults,[36] often of some status. Empowerment and ownership were key markers of successful youth ministries.[37]

Various authors have cited examples and debated the respective roles of youth themselves as leaders and the role of adult mentors, some being highly critical of the role and ability of youth.[38] Without adult mentoring, there is a warning that youth, left to their own devices, may have difficulty in taking the lead. On the one hand, DeVries states, rather harshly, that "We can expect that any system run by children or teenagers (including youth ministry) will be dysfunctional."[39] However, DeVries later offers a balanced view: "Youth programs that emphasize student leadership without connecting those teenagers to an ongoing community of faith deprive the young people of the very relationship that can most effectively lead them to Christian maturity."[40]

Nel suggests that:

> the question at stake here is especially who they [youth] are as co-workers in Youth Ministry and how they are involved. Youth Ministry is, according to our definition, a ministry *to*, but also *with* and *through* (by means of) the youth. The departure point behind this is that children and older youth are included in God's dealings with people. He is not only dealing with them, but also comes through them to each other and to the world.[41]

An Australian study of models of youth ministry in Melbourne found that youth ownership of the program, with "youth to be under the pastoral guidance of faithful adults" was a key element of effectiveness.[42]

So, is youth ministry for youth, to youth, of youth, with youth or through youth, or Nel's reference to youth being co-workers? It is some of all these descriptions, each offered at times to balance an overemphasis of

---

35. Lukabyo, *Ministry for Youth*, 221.
36. Lukabyo, *Ministry for Youth*, 225–26.
37. Lukabyo, *Ministry for Youth*, 224.
38. DeVries, *Family-Based Youth Ministry*, 55; Senter, *Coming Revolution*, 177; Fritz, *Art of Forming*, 48.
39. DeVries, *Family-Based Youth Ministry*, 55.
40. DeVries, *Family-Based Youth Ministry*, 142.
41. Nel, "Youth Ministry," 245.
42. Webber et al., "Models," 204–15, 209, 212.

one and neglect of the other and the addition of the balance and pastoral guidance offered by faithful supporting adults who do not wrest ownership from the youth but provide the intergeneration links into the ongoing faith community. A further insight offered by Henri Nouwen through his work with people with severe disabilities adds to our practical understanding of best practice in youth focused youth ministry—*doing it together*.[43]

Culturally Driven Youth Ministry

Amy Jacober, blending her experience in theology and social science, adopts an interdisciplinary approach to youth ministry, reminding us that context and culture are important and that it is important for youth workers to understand the spheres of adolescent development, enabling them to explore the surface and deeper levels of an adolescent's life.[44] A further helpful insight offered by Jacober, from her understanding of groups and community is that "transformation occurs when the social group, as the Body of Christ, can come and say, 'we, not we, but the *koinonia* of Christ.'"[45]

Theologically Centered Youth Ministry

Neither better training nor greater resources have decreased the disengagement of youth from the church or from Jesus. The challenge for those in youth ministry is "to make the pursuit of Jesus the central, consuming, desperate focus" of their ministry. "*Only* a deeper attachment to Jesus has any chance of stopping the church's slide towards the abyss."[46]

In the interface between youth ministry and theology, there is a primary thrust to recognize the necessity of specific, directional, and intentional inclusion of theology (not just entertainment and pizza parties) in youth ministry or the call for youth ministry to experience a theological turn.[47] This has become a consistent call and one for application to the program under review.

---

43. Nouwen, *Name of Jesus*, 76–81; see Appendix III for full outline of "Doing it Together."
44. Jacober, *Adolescent Journey*.
45. Jacober, *Adolescent Journey*, 72; Drawing on Haitch, "Trampling Down," 48.
46. Lawrence, *Jesus Centered*, 6, 17, 19.
47. Root and Dean, *Theological Turn*.

Within the scope of theologically centered youth ministry, but not limited by it, is the Jesus-centered youth ministry thrust of Rick Lawrence. He presses his point with terms such as "the intoxicating presence of Jesus."[48] Lawrence acknowledges the identity-forming phase of youth and stresses the precedence of answering "who I am" (in Jesus), not "what I know" (about Jesus). The only two questions that matter are "knowing Jesus and "knowing ourselves in the light of Jesus."[49]

Dean and Hearlson add the following observation: "many congregational youth ministries do not include deep intellectual engagements of theological texts as part of their program . . . teenagers are far more capable, and far better theologians, than we expect them to be."[50] Further on respect and readiness, with a contrast to their usual church experience, one participant in a HSTP said: "I wanted to ask all my questions—that was taboo in my church . . . It was the first time I'd heard someone in the church say, 'Yeah, faithful people have questions and they're hard questions and we're going to talk about that for as long as you'd like.'"[51] Seventeen-year-old Brian, also contrasting the learning at HSTP said: "My youth group is more about everybody having fun. Maybe small lessons where you learn something about the Bible, but you don't really have discussions. I swear I don't remember what I learned last week."[52]

In the approach of Nel, doing youth ministry is doing theology.[53] Most leading thinkers and writers in youth ministry have turned the corner from the problems with the traditional youth group, to recognize that the theological component, including the incarnational factor, is what has been missing. Many have recognized this, for example, beginning in 2001 with Dean et al.,[54] consolidated by Andrew Root and Kenda Creasy Dean,[55] and developed further by Root in the 2020 provocatively titled work: "The End of Youth Ministry? Why Parents Don't Really Care about Youth Groups and What Youth Workers Should Do about It."[56]

48. Lawrence, *Jesus Centered*, xvi.
49. Lawrence, *Jesus Centered*, 41, 84.
50. Dean and Hearlson, Creative Process, 53.
51. Dean and Hearlson, Creative Process, 52.
52. Dean and Hearlson, Creative Process, 53.
53. Nel, *Youth Ministry*, 19.
54. Dean et al., *Starting Right*, 19.
55. Root and Dean, *Theological Turn*.
56. Root, End of Youth Ministry?

Purpose-Centered Youth Ministry

Commencing with Doug Fields in 1998,[57] purpose has featured in discussion of youth ministry. Purpose-centered youth ministry adds a gloss to theologically centred youth ministry. In his latest work, Andrew Root[58] asserts that "youth ministry is for joy because youth ministry invites young people to focus on the Good, and only God is Good. Joy is when you find the Good as an end."[59]

Youth Ministry Summary and Extension

Just as youth search for identity—a feature of adolescence—so too, youth ministry continues to search for its identity in the church. This appears to be a repeating generational experience as youth ministry moves through repeating cycles. As each generation of youth, or individuals, experience their own adolescence or identity search, so too youth ministry seems to continue the generational pattern.

Various approaches and foci have been promoted, including the recognition of the need for youth ministry to be intergenerational; to be family focused and integrated (meaning within both the youth's family and the church family). But the strongest thrust is a call to include meaningful and relevant theological (Christian) teaching, in an intentional way, not just the weekly devotion on top of pizza parties and the like. This provides respect and recognition for youth and acknowledges their desire to engage with meaty personal, life, and spiritual questions. So, intergenerational ministry, family-centered, and theologically strong youth ministry, is advocated, along with a current challenge to listen to the voices of youth and of doing ministry *with* youth, not to them, for them, or even by them in isolation.

This review of aspects of youth ministry provides a best practice check. Key attributes are:

- Appreciation of the desirability of basic, authentic, and gutsy theological inclusion
- Adoption of the best of relational youth ministry, not as a means to an end but as an end

---

57. Fields, *Purpose Driven*.
58. Root, *End of Youth Ministry?*
59. Root, *End of Youth Ministry?*, 111.

PART V: IMPLICATIONS, CONCLUSIONS AND CONTEXTUALIZATION

- Adoption of a fully functional family-based approach, including recognition of the significance of youth's families, but essentially, also the inclusion, even adoption, of youth in the intergenerational body of Christ; the church
- Recognition that youth are not people-in-waiting, but fully fledged partners in ministry *now*
- Doing youth ministry with youth (*doing it together*), with pastoral care from supporting adults who do not seek to take it over. This conveys ownership and inclusion of the voices and capacities of youth
- Recognizing that youth can be teachers of those who teach them.

The recognition that youth are not only learners, but teachers, including being teachers of those in the role of youth workers (and staff of *Leadership*) is put with some firmness by Corrie:

> They [young people] appear to be the weakest parts [of Christ's Body], and yet if we honor them as we are called to do, we find they are the most necessary parts. As a result of this core commitment, staff members must allow themselves to be taught by teenage scholars, even as they lead them. Clothing young people with honor as the most necessary of Christ's Body pushes those in ministry with them to be self-reflective, humble, and welcoming of the distinctive voices of young people.[60]

This approach should not be surprising in considering the ways of Jesus, exemplified by Henri Nouwen who is reported as acknowledging that truths can be uncovered, lessons learned, and gifts received (including gifts of faith and hope) from those who many consider the most unlikely; those experiencing great suffering.[61] In his experience, this included:

- "The despised and rejected of the Third World [of Latin America]"[62]— "their great faith, hope, and renewal of spiritual life that was taking place amid all forms of suffering"[63]
- People in the Daybreak community (a L'Arche community for severely disabled and their assistants) in which he lived.

60. Corrie, "Christ's Hands and Feet," 242.
61. Ford, *Lonely Mystic*, 38.
62. Ford, *Lonely Mystic*, 35.
63. Ford, *Lonely Mystic*, 38.

Ford adds that "Vanier [the founder of L'Arche] understood that we discover how we can be healed by those who are most vulnerable. It was not a matter of going out and ministering to *them* but recognizing that receiving the gift of their presence transforms us,"[64] and, concerning Nouwen, "He [Henri] came to learn that the very people to whom he had been sent were, in fact, his guides. This was the mystery of the mutuality of true ministry most visible among the poor."[65] It should not be surprising then, that youth can teach us and be gift-givers to us too. So, in our approach to youth ministry, those who work with youth, even those who teach them, will benefit, grow and be taught by youth if we are open and allow them to give us those gifts. And, broadening this to the church, "Youth ministry ultimately is not limited to what the church has to offer youth. It includes what youth offer us as well; a way of being 'church' that takes seriously the search for God that is so acute during adolescence but so necessary for us all."[66]

Then, youth will find their rights of passage in the intergenerational church and youth ministry will experience its rites of passage in the church.

Contextualization and Application of Youth Ministry to *Leadership*

Placing *Leadership* in the context of youth ministry, table 36 sets out an application of *best practice* criteria to the findings about *Leadership*.

YOUTH MINISTRY *BEST PRACTICE* CRITERIA	EVIDENCE FROM *LEADERSHIP*
Appreciation of the desirability of basic, authentic and gutsy theological inclusion.	Recognition of the spiritual dimension (the mystery); the significance of worship; voluntary participation in morning devotions. Discussion of the theology of various needs/interests of youth (e.g., family, sexuality, vocation) are welcomed.
Adoption of the best of relational youth ministry—not as a means to an end but as an end.	Relationships are a key aspect of *Leadership*—the community, My Group, Duo, staff-participant interactions. Sharing of personal story is practiced.

64. Ford, *Lonely Mystic*, 44.
65. Ford, *Lonely Mystic*, 47.
66. Dean and Foster, *Godbearing Life*.

PART V: IMPLICATIONS, CONCLUSIONS AND CONTEXTUALIZATION

YOUTH MINISTRY *BEST PRACTICE* CRITERIA	EVIDENCE FROM *LEADERSHIP*
Adoption of a fully functional family-based approach, including recognition of the significance of youth's families, but essentially, also the inclusion, even adoption, of youth in the intergenerational body of Christ—the church.	This is the model of *Leadership*, including amongst staff and participants—an intergenerational and ever-renewing community. Family is highly regarded and key interactions are programmed. However, there are sometimes weak links with local groups and churches, into a mentored, intergenerational, family-based youth ministry at church level.
Recognition that youth are not people-in-waiting, but fully fledged partners in ministry *now*.	This is a key aspect, where participants are invited to exercise leadership at any time during the program.
Doing youth ministry with youth (*doing it together*), with pastoral care from supporting adults who do not seek to take it over. This conveys ownership and inclusion of the voices and capacities of youth.	*Doing it together* and listening to the voices of youth are included in the primary ethos of *Leadership* and as a major focus of this book.
Recognition that youth can be teachers of those who teach them.	Permission is given and participants are encouraged to become the leader and exercise leadership at any time. Commitment to listen to the voices of youth, including through hearing their shared stories.

Table 36. Comparison of Elements of *Leadership* with *Best Practice* in Youth Ministry

Leadership meets some of the criteria for *best practice* in youth ministry. There is theological inclusion and relational commitment. It is intentionally intergenerational and *doing it together* with youth in leadership *now* and listening to the voices of youth is practiced. However, maintaining and strengthening links with local groups and churches is an ongoing challenge.

Contributions to Theory and Practice

The review of *Leadership* sits in a neglected space, where research and the literature concerning young men and leadership development is limited.[67]

---

67. Mortensen et al., "Leadership"; Karagianni and Montgomery, "Developing Leadership Skills."

The research makes several contributions. It adds to the literature on leadership development for youth. *Leadership* is identified as a program with differences from other leadership programs. While teamwork is commonly recognized across programs, including *Leadership*, in contrast with other programs, *Leadership* participants recognize that they are also taught critical thinking, self-reflection, conflict management, decision-making, and ethical aspects of leadership. Certain concepts may not be overtly recognized or spoken about by youth, but this does not mean they are not present. For example, altruism, though recognized as the essence of the servant leadership promoted at *Leadership*, is assumed by participants to not need to be articulated. *Leadership* provides an example of responding to the call of Eva and Sendjaya to develop leadership attributes early in the lives of young adults as a contribution to developing ethical mindsets and values, using former students (*Leadership* graduates) as mentors/facilitators and combining classroom/academic teaching with practical experience initiatives outside the classroom, reinforcing the value of these approaches in theory and practice.[68]

This research makes further contributions to Christian (youth) ministry, as outlined in the summary of findings above.

In the substantive theory presented, the core category, acceptance, is understood as important in both theory and practice in youth work and in interventions for youth and young adults. However, one learning is that giving lip service only to *unconditional* acceptance and not backing this up with authenticity and integrity is likely to be *seen through* by young men and is not likely to contribute to effective, respectful, and lasting relationships or ministry. Acceptance must be lived, not just spoken. The emphasis on the subcategory, imperfection, is a fresh aspect to consider for youth work—an enhancement of current theory and practice. Youth workers need not to fear acknowledgment of their own imperfection, though they need to recognize boundaries. It is similar with the subcategory of freedom and empowerment. Taken together, these two concepts extend the understanding of their importance in working with youth. The spiritual and the mystery surrounding it is recognized by young men as an overarching dimension for life and purpose.

The collaborative approach used in this research is consistent with contemporary insights and developing understanding in youth work practice. For example, among the themes that emerged from an International

---

68. Eva and Sendjaya, "Creating Future Leaders."

Association for the Study of Youth Ministry International Colloquium in January 2021 was that the voice of youth needs to be heard and that the approach to youth ministry should no longer be *to you* or *for you*, but *with you*—not just connection, but fellowship. Reference is also made to the recognition that this is not a new approach and that the effectiveness of ministry *of youth* approach was demonstrated frequently in the 1900s.[69] Combining ministry *of* and ministry *with* youth is a helpful marriage of ethos. Youth workers need to take on a posture of vulnerability and share an equal leadership terrain with young people. Programming should be collaborative. Within *Leadership*, participants can ask the questions they cannot ask anywhere else and their (sometimes very personal and emotive) issues and concerns are listened to without judgment. The nonhierarchical nature of the staff team; the adding of young adults to the staff team every year in a constant renewal process; the welcoming of all new participants as equal members of the *Leadership* community; and that they are invited to become the leader and exercise leadership at any time, confirms the value of listening to the voice of youth and reinforces the need to empower youth for *now*, not for the future only.

The research also models participatory practical theological and critical grounded theory approaches that may be of interest to other researchers.

The main limitation is that *Leadership* is a unique and one-off program,[70] so the transferability of findings and conclusions to youth work more generally may be questioned. The complexity and wide-ranging nature of this study may lead to criticism about lack of depth in some areas. However, this research is viewed as a positive contribution as it establishes a base line and sets the scene for future research.

General and Specific Application/Transferability

Because of its uniqueness, some findings may be specific to this program. However, the general application and transferability of findings to youth ministry generally, especially for young men, are considered. The findings embodied in the substantive theory are transferrable, as are the identified program elements, strategies, and contextual features (e.g.,

---

69. Lubakyo, *Ministry for Youth*.

70. Although there is a similar program for young women in Queensland and partly similar programs for young men interstate and in New Zealand and the US.

acknowledgment of *communitas*, use of liminality, exploration of rites of passage, and wilderness location).

It is not suggested that *Leadership* itself as a whole is replicable, though some success has been achieved with taking the program to the US. One difficulty in immediate replication is that the program has been conducted for many years and has a number of staff with many years' experience. It would be very difficult to simply pick up the manuals and run the program. However, there are elements of the research findings that can be replicated in other youth ministry modes. This includes the unique composition of the small group, particularly in Stage 1, with new participants (as clean slates) and their facilitator (often not much older) becoming an operational peer group and together exercising a ministry *of* youth. Another area to consider, offered with humility and respect, is a suggestion that the elements of the substantive theory—acceptance, imperfection, empowerment and freedom, and spiritual context might be helpful criteria to examine a particular youth ministry.

Suggestions for Future Research

It was suggested in chapter 2 that a contemporary youth ministry such as *Leadership* should expect to encounter youth who have experienced abuse and family breakdown and their consequences. The data and practice confirm that disclosure of these and other personal issues are made during *Leadership* and that the immediate response of acceptance is beneficial. However, further research would be useful to study whether the disclosure and strategies for dealing with the issues between stages and post-Stage 3 are effective.

Given the Mission Australia youth survey[71] indicating a fall in youth group and church involvement amongst youth, further research could be carried out to support the indication here that participation in *Leadership* enhances maintenance of youth group and church involvement—and through this, commitment to long-term leadership. This may assist youth ministry generally given that there is an often-repeated concern over the loss of youth to the church and the ineffectiveness of youth group programs.[72]

Accepting that *Leadership* is apparently successful on measures investigated and that this extends into the long-term for participants,

---

71. Tiller et al., *Youth Survey Report*.
72. DeVries, *Family Based Youth Ministry*; Root, *Revisiting*; Fritz, *Art of Forming*.

further research could be carried out on whether this also includes ongoing faith commitment.

In the light of the comparisons participants made between *Leadership* and church or other Christian youth groups, a pilot action research project could be considered with one or two churches to develop strategies and share learning in relation to the effectiveness of the positively regarded *Leadership* staffing model: *multigenerational, nonhierarchical, and servant-led, not placing a high value on differentiation of status*. One could add to this, the worship style. A focus of such new research may be developing a partnership between *Leadership* and the local church (using a broad definition of *church*) as the location for ongoing discipleship and exploration of the role and importance of parents in discipling teens rather than the *church* or the temporary *Leadership* community; how they can be informed that this is what their youth want (though they may not say so and in fact may say the opposite), and how to equip parents for the role.

There is increasing interest in each of the lenses employed in this study in theological and social science literature, spurred on in part by the current state of the world, so can *Leadership* respond to this opportunity and be at the forefront of the further development of relevant programs for youth in today's world? This study has been complex and wide-ranging. Often examples have been used rather than attempting to fully cover the field, and some lenses and theory categories have been examined in greater detail than others. Each of the lenses employed could give rise to a substantial study and that is a possibility for future research.

The emerging literature on desert, mountain, and wilderness as a place for solitude and exploration of spirituality could be further investigated, with particular reference to the Stage 2 Solo experience.

The identified *mystery* of spontaneous *communitas*, significant, observable, and lasting transformation in the lives of young men could be further explored.

Though small in number, further research could be carried out in a respectful and collaborative manner with those who do not return to a subsequent stage of *Leadership*, to investigate at greater depth the possibly superficial reasons given, and with any who report a negative experience.

Summary of Chapter

This final chapter summarizes and contextualizes the research. A summary of findings is presented. From a review of youth ministry approaches—academic and practical—over the last twenty years, a *best practice* checklist is distilled and then applied to *Leadership*. The value of the research, its contribution to theory and practice, its limitations, general and specific application and transferability of findings, and recommendations for the future are considered. Finally, an extensive range of suggestions for future research is offered, including examining specific program aspects in greater depth, sharing and testing learnings, collaborative research with churches, and consideration of whether and how to respond to contemporary and still developing global issues that are impacting the world, including youth.

Appendix I

Excerpts from Reports of Three Participants

Josh on Stage 1

I ARRIVED AT STAGE 1 as a quiet, reserved yet thoughtful boy who had no idea of his identity and with a lack of self-worth. I was very awkward at first because I barely knew anyone there and had to sit with a group of total strangers that I would be living and learning with over the next eight days. As the first day progressed, I sat back and listened and after a little while, I noticed that most of the others in my group were in the same boat. I slowly began chatting with people and realized that I knew one person in the group from my old company. From there, I gained confidence and started getting to know the others. As the days went by, I found myself opening up and really enjoying the activities as well as learning a lot from the lessons. I found I didn't enjoy the more sporty activities as much but I really enjoyed the team building programs such as the problem-solving, milk crate stacking, and blindfold mazes.

Mitch on Stage 1

When I arrived at Stage 1, it was very daunting, because there were all of these men that I had hardly ever seen before, and all of these boys that I had never seen before, and I was going to be put in a cabin for a week with nine of them. It all started off slowly, we talked to each other only a little bit, and our team/group problem solving activities weren't going too well, because we were all too shy to take the lead. But being the loud person that I am, I started to take the lead a bit, and then everyone else's confidence grew along with mine. Our problem-solving skills increased throughout the week until we were basically an unstoppable team. . . . I learnt a lot about myself over the week, especially that I was stubborn and need to listen to everyone else more. I learnt a lot more about God, and how I can communicate with him more. Also, how to be an effective team member, how to communicate better, and that listening is more important than talking, how to set more specific goals that are actually achievable, and how to deal with bad influences, like peer pressure, when entering the real world again.

Sam on Stage 1

I arrived at the gates of Leadership a shy, timid, and confused young boy but while at the end I may not have been perfect, I certainly returned home determined to change for the better. While on this course I attended all worship times available and started seeing God truly for the first time. It was as if my eyes had been open. Additionally, through group activities such as handball, problem-solving, and milk crates, I was able to see myself as part of the group caring for one another. Other activities such as group time and overnight expedition proved to me that this group could truly be trusted but yet I was still hesitant. I had my personal struggles . . . finally had the courage to share part of my story with adults that I could trust . . . by the time of graduation I was not quite ready to go home but I was glad when they told the parents not to "pressure anything about the week from the boys." That year I kept on climbing and decided that it was time to get baptized. I did so and also decided to take the plunge and return to Leadership this year.

Josh on Stage 2

Some major changes occurred in the time between Stage 1 and 2. . . . I went back to Stage 2 with a new determination and eagerness to be challenged, especially with regards to Solo. We had a goal setting session quite early on in the program where I set myself a list of six goals to complete over Solo. Some of my goals included fasting, reading sections of the Bible, and also spending time to reflect on my relationships with those closest to me. I found that the sessions we did on relationships were very helpful and I learnt skills that I have since been able to apply in my everyday life. I can certainly say that my time on Solo pushed me to my limits in every way possible and was an experience that I will never forget. I was physically challenged with my fasting for most of Solo, mentally challenged from being alone for three days and nights, and spiritually challenged in my search for God's voice and answers. The only way I can describe how I was feeling by the last day is that I felt very raw and bare. It was just me, without any layers or masks to hide behind. I discovered a lot about myself, and I also had an amazing encounter with God that left me feeling giddy with joy. After returning from Solo, we had a group debrief session where we could share our experiences, both funny and serious. That same night, we had a Solo celebration that affirmed us on our completion of Solo. For me, this night was a rite of passage from boyhood into manhood. Stage 2 has left a lasting impact on my life in the way that I relate with others and in my relationship with God.

Mitch on Stage 2

When I arrived back at "Leadership Development Course" for Stage 2, I was slightly nervous, as I didn't know what to expect that year, but I was looking forward to seeing my group and finding out how they had been over the past year. The sharing in cabin time got off to a way quicker start than it had the previous year, as we already trusted each other. Throughout the last year between Stage 1 and 2, I had started to drift away from God, and Stage 2 really helped me get back on track with him, especially by doing another emotional bank account. I found out who I was again and developed myself more as a Christian leader. The solo was a very intimidating experience; it was a challenge for me, as I am a very social person. However, it was a really good thing for me, because I became a lot closer to God through reading the bible and listening to him. I also found out a lot about myself whilst being alone with myself for four days. Learning about dealing with relationships was also a great thing, as I learnt about how to express my feelings, how to deal with anger, and also how to forgive and work through problems together. I also became better at goal setting and using what I learnt in the real world.

APPENDIX I

Josh on Stage 3

After such a high on Stage 2, I was incredibly eager to go the next step with Stage 3. It was a big change moving from the tight knit group to a much larger group, but it was great being able to create new relationships. We kicked off the course by starting with "The Seven Habits of Highly Effective People." Over the week, the habits that really stood out to me were being interdependent (cooperating to achieve a goal together), being proactive, and thinking of ways to achieve win-win situations. Duo took up the other part of the course. This was also very challenging, as Solo was, but in a very different way. There weren't the problems like loneliness or shelter. The big challenge was opening up to someone else about personal issues and sharing on deeper topics than just your average chat about the footy. Some of the things that came up were confronting and challenging to talk about but were very beneficial to the both of us as we could relate on certain things and help each other. During our time on Duo, my partner and I spent some time reading through sections of the Bible, both together and alone. We also spent time in prayer together, praying for the other duos and also for the other stages and staff. It was also during my time on Duo that I wrote my mission statement. This statement portrays the man that I will endeavor to become. During the graduation ceremony at the end of Leadership 12, I was given the opportunity to state publicly my mission statement in front of my family and peers. This was another moment I will never forget.

Mitch on Stage 3

When I arrived back again for Stage 3, my last year, I was really excited to get back and see all the guys. By this year I created a great friendship with all of my group members. This year were put in together as one big group. This was daunting at first because we had to share with people that we weren't used to sharing with, like Stage 1. However, it soon became easier and everyone became great mates throughout the week. This year the best things that I learnt are that I need to be proactive, take my consequences as they come and not make excuses, put first things first in my life, as I am a very busy person. Sometimes I concentrate way too much on my music, sport, and school, and I concentrate less on God, my family, and other important things. I also learnt that I need to keep my mind alert, keep exercising, read the Bible, and continue working on my mission statement.

EXCERPTS FROM REPORTS OF THREE PARTICIPANTS

Mitch on After the Course

I believe that now after having completed the "Leadership Development Course" I know a lot more about myself; I am a lot closer to God; more about relationships and how to cope in different situations; I can work in an effective team with whoever I need to be in a team with; how to communicate better; I can survive four days by myself; how to be proactive; how to put first things first in my life, for example, God; how to continue the path to become the best Christian man of faith that I can possibly be. I have also left the "Leadership Development Course" with lifelong mates that I will continue to talk to for hopefully the rest of my life.

Josh on Joining the Staff Team

In early 2013, I was contacted in relation to my being a part of the support staff team for Leadership 2013. I happily agreed; eager to give back to the course that had been such an amazing blessing to my life. I was contacted again not long after, inviting me to assist with the facilitation of one of the Stage 2 groups. At first, I was very unsure, worried that I wasn't ready to take on this responsibility. I felt more confident when I was told that I would be working alongside another facilitator, L, an experienced group leader. We arrived at the course and met the group, a mixed bunch from the previous year's Stage 1 cohort due to a big drop in some of the group's numbers. This caused some issues as two of the guys wanted to be with the rest of their group from the year before. One young man in particular was quite upset and resistant to the new group at first. But over the next few days, as he realized he was accepted by the group, he softened and began to fit in. Solo came around and I was again able to go out by myself for three days, although with a tent and flat ground this time. This time was significantly different from the first as I was able to enjoy my own company a great deal more, I had visitors occasionally, and I had a deep awareness of God's presence the entire time. It was amazing being able to see the changes in some of the group after Solo. Seeing some choose to use this experience as a rite of passage into manhood for themselves was deeply moving as I know how much of an impact this had in my own life. By the end of the week the changes I could see in each young man was wonderful. The originally resistant member had a very significant encounter with God on the final night and it changed his entire outlook on a number of things in his life.

APPENDIX I

This opportunity was an overwhelming experience. Having the chance to invest into young men's lives and make an impact that they can then use to impact others.

Appendix II

Research Methodology and Methods

THE RESEARCH ADOPTED A participatory practical theological approach and critical grounded theory[1] methodology. The methods adopted were document analysis, survey, interviews, focus groups, and a research reference group. Though the research is not completely a collaborative practical theological[2] research project, there is a move in this direction with youth participants, listening to their voices through interviews and focus groups.

In a grounded theory methodology such as is employed in this study, the desirability of establishing boundaries around pre-study review of the literature is acknowledged. As put by Strauss and Corbin, "It is impossible to know prior to the investigation what the salient problems will be or what theoretical concepts will emerge. Also, the researcher does not want to be so steeped in the literature that he or she is constrained and even stifled by it."[3] This creates a dilemma for grounded theory research as to how far one should proceed with a review of the literature prior to gathering research-related data. The issue is well put by El Hussein et al.:

> The issue of the literature remains a conundrum and a controversy within the discourse of grounded theory methodology. Grounded theory researchers are expected to minimize preconceptions to ensure the concept of interest is grounded in data, yet at the same

1. Hense and Mcferran, "Critical Grounded Theory."
2. De Roest, *Collaborative Practical Theology*.
3. Strauss and Corbin, *Basics*, 49.

time are required to evaluate existing literature to support institutional ethics and scientific review of the research proposal.[4]

El Hussein et al. identify the challenge for a grounded theory researcher in dealing with a review of the literature: "We believe that just reporting about the literature is an academic flaw and unless the reviewer challenges his own assumptions trying to find a unique interpretation of the literature, then the review is just 'more of the same' and does not amount to a critical review of literature."[5] This requires the striking of a balance between critically reviewing the literature, yet not extending its application prematurely into the arena of theory development before the research data is collected and systematically examined.

Accepting the conundrum and challenge, the literature pertinent to the key research question was examined, leading into the development of the research methodology, including informing the framing of survey questions. The literature is returned to in Parts I and II and the scope expanded, the directions determined by the findings and the developing theory, and the application of a mutual critical correlation approach between theology and the social sciences.

Some of the theories canvassed have been applied to *Leadership* intuitively before program leaders were aware of their existence. While such theories are identified, their application, even drawing an assumption as to their significance, was, however, *bracketed* before data collection, acknowledging the grounded theory methodology being employed.

Hense and Mcferran[6] acknowledge texts such as Strauss and Corbin that offer "specific strategies for approaching data collection and analysis" but claim that "grounded theory is far from a rigid methodological procedure,"[7] with Charmaz encouraging "flexible engagement."[8] The more flexible approach of Charmaz, placing emphasis on "the views, values, beliefs, feelings, assumptions, and ideologies of individuals,"[9] and the recognition by Charmaz of "the role of the researcher" throughout the research process as participant and decision-maker, are valuable insights. However, the systematic approach of Strauss and Corbin was adopted as the general

4. El Hussein et al., "Grounded Theory," 1199.
5. El Hussein et al., "Grounded Theory," 1201.
6. Hense and Mcferran, "Critical Grounded Theory," 8.
7. Strauss and Corbin, *Basics*.
8. Charmaz, *Constructing Grounded Theory*.
9. Creswell, *Qualitative Inquiry*.

organizational scaffold in this study. While acknowledging the pioneering work of Strauss and Corbin and others in developing grounded theory, the methodological guidelines offered by Birks and Mills[10] have guided this research process, with the adoption of the insights of critical grounded theory to ensure an authentic participatory focus.

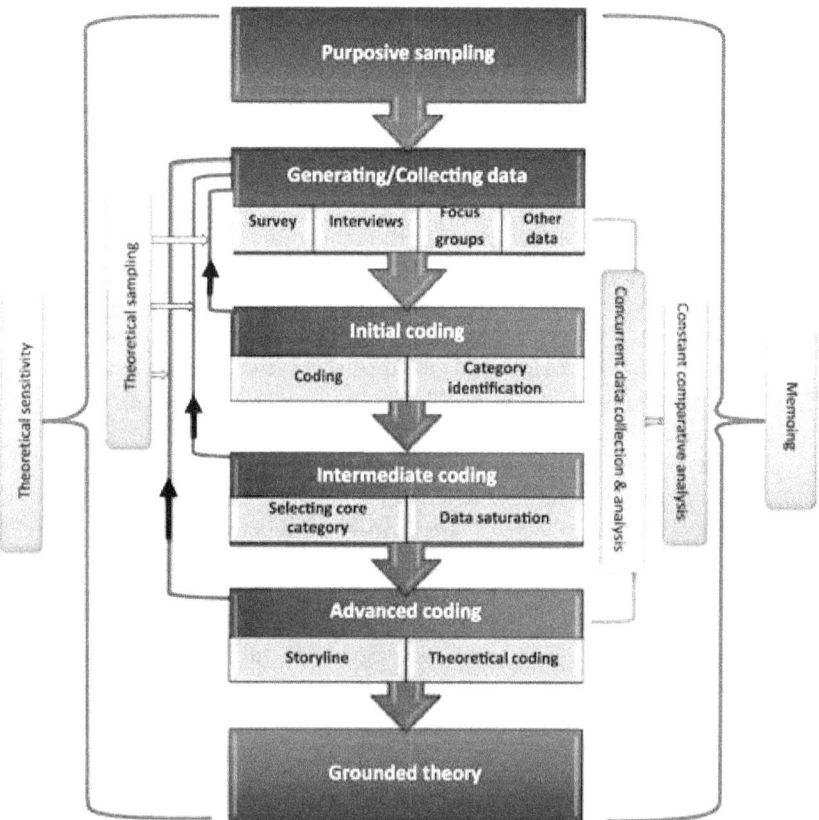

Research design framework: summary of the interplay between the essential grounded theory methods and processes.

Figure 9. Grounded Theory Design Framework

Consistent with a grounded theory approach, the methodological steps described and implemented did not follow a strict linear trajectory. There was constant back and forth movement between phases. For example, in the analytical phases, following purposeful sampling through the

10. Birks and Mills, *Grounded Theory*.

APPENDIX II

survey, analysis and theory development moved back and forth between data generation, coding at increasingly sophisticated levels, theoretical sampling, constant comparative analysis, and memo generation phases. This approach is illustrated in figure 9, a diagram offered by Tie et al.,[11] illustrating their comment that "the process of doing a GT research study is not linear, rather it is iterative and recursive."

Accompanying the diagram is a narrative explanation which was adopted:

> Grounded theory research involves the meticulous application of specific methods and processes. Methods are "systematic modes, procedures or tools used for collection and analysis of data." While GT studies can commence with a variety of sampling techniques, many commence with purposive sampling, followed by concurrent data generation and/or collection and data analysis, through various stages of coding, undertaken in conjunction with constant comparative analysis, theoretical sampling, and memoing. Theoretical sampling is employed until theoretical saturation is reached. These methods and processes create an unfolding, iterative system of actions and interactions inherent in GT. The methods interconnect and inform the recurrent elements in the research process as shown by the directional flow of the arrows and the encompassing brackets in [the diagram]. The framework denotes the process is both iterative and dynamic and is not one directional.[12]

One hundred and thirty-five completed the survey—participants who commenced *Leadership* (Stage 1) between 2006 and 2019. All years were represented in the sample, with recent years more highly represented. Of the sample of 135, 114 continued to complete Stage 2 of *Leadership* and 75 to complete Stage 3, though 16 who only did Stage 1 in 2019 and 20 who only did Stage 2 in 2019 had not yet had the opportunity of progressing to the next stage. Responses from those who subsequently served on staff were kept separate and where relevant, the difference between participant responses and staff responses are highlighted.

Osmer's practical theology tasks and related questions[13] can be linked to the framework of this book.

---

11. Tie et al., *Grounded Theory Research*, 6. Used with permission of Sage Publications.
12. Tie et al., *Grounded Theory Research*, 6.
13. Osmer, *Practical Theology*.

INITIAL QUESTION	CORE TASK	FOCUS OF TASK	BOOK FRAMEWORK
What is going on?	Descriptive-empirical task	"Gathering information that helps us discern patterns and dynamics in particular episodes, situations or contexts"	Parts I and II
Why is this going on?	Interpretative task	"Drawing on theories of the arts and sciences to better understand and explain why these patterns and dynamics are occurring"	Commenced in parts I and II; continued in parts III and IV
What ought to be going on?	Normative task	"Using theological concepts to interpret particular episodes, situations or contexts, constructing ethical norms to guide our responses, and learning from 'good practice'"	Commenced in parts I and II; continued in parts III and IV
How might we respond?	Pragmatic task	"Determining strategies of action that will influence situations in ways that are desirable and entering into a reflective conversation with the 'talk back' emerging when they are enacted"	Part V

Table 37: The Tasks of Practical Theology and Book Framework

The final part, part V, addresses the fourth and final core task in Osmer's[14] framework for practical theological interpretation: the pragmatic task, which asks the question, "How might we respond?" Answering this question involves a focus on "determining strategies of action that will influence situations in ways that are desirable and entering into a reflective conversation with the 'talk back' emerging when they are enacted." "Strategies of action" included in *Leadership* are the subject of analysis in the research, which then considers how they influence situations, in particular, the lives of young men. The research methodology and methods have enabled "reflective conversation" through survey, interviews, and focus groups, including opportunity to listen to the voices of youth. This was extended during the process of theory development and discussion of findings, adopting a mutual critical correlation approach in linking theological and social science insights. Part V extends the "reflective conversation" further, in particular, locating the study within practical theology and contextualizing it within a discussion of youth ministry.

---

14. Osmer, *Practical Theology*, 4.

Appendix III

Doing It Together

HENRI NOUWEN WAS A priest and an academic, on the faculty at three prestigious US universities: Notre Dame, Yale, and Harvard. He gave up his academic career to move into Daybreak, a L'Arche[1] community in Toronto, Canada, living with people with disabilities and other assistants. Some have severe disabilities, needing assistance with all aspects of daily life.

Henri continued to receive invitations to speak at important gatherings. He accepted a request to speak on Christian leadership to a large gathering in Washington DC. While preparing, he was reminded that Jesus sent his disciples out, not alone, but two-by-two, and realizing no one was travelling with him, he invited Bill, one of the men with a disability with whom he lived at Daybreak, to accompany him. Bill, who had limited language, accepted the invitation, and kept saying, "We are doing this together." At the gathering, after Henri was introduced to bring his address, he introduced Bill. Then, he recalls:[2]

> I took my handwritten text and began my address. At that moment I saw that Bill had left his seat, walked up to the podium, and planted himself right behind me. It was clear that he had a much more concrete idea about the meaning of *doing it together* than I

---

1. "The Identity Statement of L'Arche is: "We are people with and without intellectual disabilities, sharing life in communities belonging to an International Federation. Mutual relationships and trust in God are at the heart of our journey together. We celebrate the unique value of every person and recognise our need of one another." See L'Arche, "Identity and Mission." There are 138 communities in over thirty countries.

2. Nouwen, *Name of Jesus*, 76–81.

did. Each time I finished reading a page, he took it away and put it upside down on a small table close by. I felt very much at ease with this and started to feel Bill's presence and support. But Bill had more in mind. When I began to speak about the temptation to turn stones into bread as a temptation to be relevant, he interrupted me and said loudly for everyone to hear "I have heard that before!"

Bill's intervention created a new atmosphere in the ballroom: lighter, easier, and more playful. Somehow Bill had taken away the seriousness of the occasion and had brought some homespun normality. As I continued my presentation, I felt more and more that we were indeed *doing it together*.

When I came to the second part and was reading the words, "the question most asked by the handicapped people with whom I live was, Are you home tonight?" Bill interrupted me again and said, "That's right, that is what John Smeltzer always asks.". . . It was as if he drew the audience toward us, inviting them into the intimacy of our common life.

[As Henri finished his address] Bill said to me, "Henri, can I say something now?" My first reaction was, "Oh, how am I going to handle this? He might start rambling and create an embarrassing situation," but then I caught myself in the presumption that he had nothing of importance to say and said to the audience, "Will you please sit down. Bill would like to say a few words to you." Bill took the microphone and said, with all the difficulties he has in speaking, "Last time, when Henri went to Boston, he took John Smeltzer with him. This time he wanted me to come with him to Washington, and I am very glad to be here with you. Thank you very much." That was it, and everyone stood up and gave him warm applause.

As we flew back together to Toronto, Bill looked up . . . and said, "Henri. Did you like our trip?" "Oh yes," I said, "it was a wonderful trip, and I am so glad you came with me." Bill looked at me attentively and then said, "And *we did it together* didn't we?" Then I realized the full truth of Jesus' words, "Where two or three meet in my Name, I am among them" (Matthew 18:19). In the past, I had always given lectures, sermons, addresses, and speeches by myself. Often I wondered how much of what I said would be remembered. Now it dawned on me that most likely much of what I said would not be long remembered, but that Bill and I doing it together would not easily be forgotten. I hoped and prayed that Jesus who had sent us out *together* and had been with us all during the journey would have become really present to those who had gathered . . . As we landed. I said to Bill, "Bill, thanks so much for coming with me. It was a wonderful trip and what we did, *we did together* in Jesus' name." And I really meant it.

On reading this story, I decided that whenever I am asked to make a presentation, I will take someone with me, and in a youth ministry setting, that would be an emerging young leader. I was also reminded that Jesus, from his many followers, chose twelve to invest a lot of time and teaching into. And, from the twelve, he chose only three to invest into in a fully targeted way. So, with BB and *Leadership* I should be realistic and see that I can and should only invest into a small number.

Putting these two ideas together, when an invitation came to facilitate an open workshop session for experienced youth workers on issues important to them, I thought, who should I invite to *do it together* with me? Nineteen-year-old Levi accepted my invitation, bringing together a young man commencing his leader role and training, with experienced leaders. I shared the story of Henri Nouwen and Bill to explain why Levi and I were *doing it together*. As the group shared their concerns, it was Levi who kept the focus of why we are doing it—the primary *theological* focus: advancing Christ's kingdom . . . *and* discipling boys into mature and true Christian men. Levi contributed his own ideas. His insights were valuable and he made copious notes of what the older adult leaders were saying. He commented later on how he valued listening to the concerns and wisdom of older men. Most importantly though, *we had done it together*. In other situations we have shared since, he has continued to say, "We did it together."

This theme resonates with *Leadership* where the intergenerational community of older and younger men *do it together*.

Appendix IV

The Theory as a Symphony Metaphor

ONE OF THE PARTICIPANTS in the research suggested that *Leadership* is like a symphony. Inasmuch as a symphony is a coming together of many parts—into a unique and united whole, the three stages of *Leadership* are the three symphonic movements. Themes from the first movement (Stage 1) are continued into the subsequent movements, incorporating new emerging themes as they develop. Each movement has a beginning (sometimes tentative) and an ending (climatic and celebratory). Then, after the climax of the third movement comes the unfolding impact of the whole symphony as it continues.

Movement 1

Stage 1 participants arrive and tentatively join the *Leadership* community. As a section of an orchestra, they are divided into percussion, strings, woodwind, and brass. For a time and periodically, each group operates independently, sometimes comparing themselves with other groups and thinking they are doing better—the first violins thinking they are the most important and not taking second place to the second violins.

They are diverse; yet they are all the same. As they read and play the music, they begin to work collaboratively. *My Group*, the violins, play a passage on their own; then they join with the cellos next door.

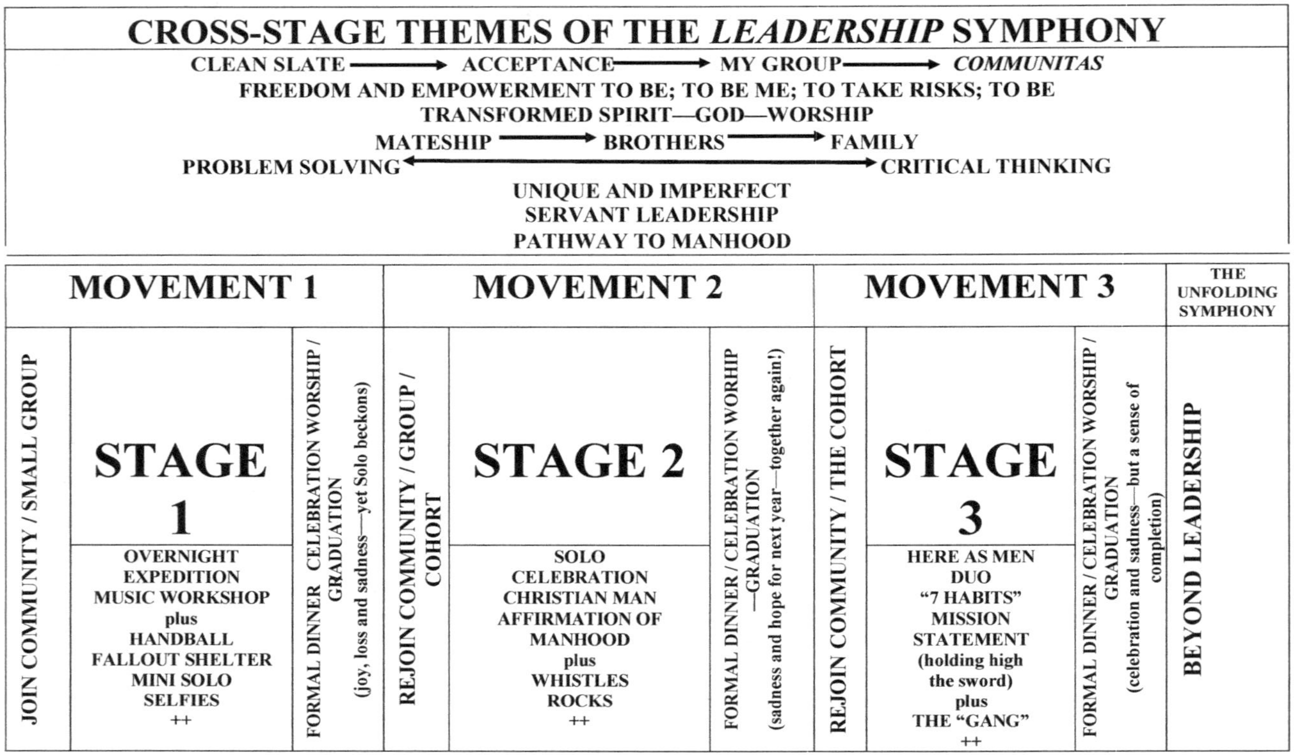

APPENDIX IV

CROSS-STAGE THEMES OF THE *LEADERSHIP SYMPHONY*

CLEAN SLATE → ACCEPTANCE → MY GROUP → COMMUNITAS

FREEDOM AND EMPOWERMENT TO BE; TO BE ME; TO TAKE RISKS; TO BE

TRANSFORMED SPIRIT—GOD—WORSHIP

MATESHIP → BROTHERS → FAMILY

PROBLEM SOLVING → CRITICAL THINKING

UNIQUE AND IMPERFECT
SERVANT LEADERSHIP
PATHWAY TO MANHOOD

	MOVEMENT 1	MOVEMENT 2	MOVEMENT 3	THE UNFOLDING SYMPHONY
	JOIN COMMUNITY / SMALL GROUP	REJOIN COMMUNITY / GROUP / COHORT	REJOIN COMMUNITY / THE COHORT	
	STAGE 1 OVERNIGHT EXPEDITION MUSIC WORKSHOP plus HANDBALL FALLOUT SHELTER MINI SOLO SELFIES ‡‡	**STAGE 2** SOLO CELEBRATION CHRISTIAN MAN AFFIRMATION OF MANHOOD plus WHISTLES ROCKS ‡‡	**STAGE 3** HERE AS MEN DUO "7 HABITS" MISSION STATEMENT (holding high the sword) plus THE "GANG" ‡‡	
	FORMAL DINNER CELEBRATION WORSHIP / GRADUATION (joy, loss and sadness—yet Solo beckons)	FORMAL DINNER / CELEBRATION WORSHIP—GRADUATION (sadness and hope for next year—together again!)	FORMAL DINNER / CELEBRATION WORSHIP / GRADUATION (celebration and sadness—but a sense of completion)	BEYOND LEADERSHIP

Figure 10. *Leadership* as an Orchestra/a Symphony

292

Sometimes, the whole orchestra is together—together, but different—the violins now playing with the flutes and trumpets. The strings, woodwind, and brass play together.

Back in their own group, group members get to know each other, and they gain confidence. Tensions within groups ebb and flow, but they will move in the direction of becoming a well-functioning team, producing sweet music: *communitas* happens; they have nailed that part of the music.

Sometimes they play just for the enjoyment of *My Group*—not needing to be perfect; just playing. For an individual, the apparently small or insignificant may emerge as critical, for example, an hour spent alone, in silence and solitude, with God and the trees in the wild, a lone instrument with an apparently minor role in a new orchestra now being heard above the rest, like a lone bird singing in the trees.

The first movement is traditionally fast, like the speed of developing *communitas*, spurred on through liminal experiences—things new and unique. They return from the wild, having tasted a new freedom of action, voice and confidence—they play stronger; they play louder. They weave through their music the themes of servanthood; a liberating acceptance; empowered and freed to be; free to be me; free to be a man and to be masculine, yet spiritual; free to serve and be a servant leader; uniqueness, imperfection, spirit, and mateship.

They are ready to present the first movement. The coming together of the whole orchestra is celebrated in the feast and celebration worship service, then recognized at the graduation—a build-up of crescendo, a pause, and then the final high notes. The end of the first movement is a climax and anticlimax—the farewells, a mixed sense of pleasure and sadness; a sense of having much still to celebrate, process, understand, and share. The immediate sadness gives into emotion—a sadness of farewelling new mates, yet a desire, sometimes a commitment, to return and be back together in a year's time for the second movement.

Movement 2

Stage 2 participants arrive and though they have continued all year in absentia to be part of the *Leadership* symphony, they now rejoin and again in person begin playing in a more intense way. The violins, cellos, and drums each back together, and identify as a cohort, as they watch new orchestra members arrive and wonder how they will play.

The expectation of the traditional slowness of the second movement of the symphony begins to excite and haunt—contemplative and silent, solitude and all that means takes center stage, like the drumbeat permeating the sound from the orchestra; like the distant, then nearer, drumbeat of many indigenous cultures calling boys to manhood.

Solitude is all-consuming; seemingly alone in the bush for three nights. The trees, the wind, and the birds provide the background music, then the individual music of the arriving souls. They meet with God. The slowness of the second movement is relaxing, yet it makes one anxious. And it is about to speed up.

They burst out of their solitude and celebrate, playing their instrument with the first person they see, then with their group, then the cohort, an ever-increasing gathering of the orchestra. Silence. Then like flutes playing together, but separately, they blow their whistles as in a chorus of birds or instruments, in an explosion of sound, before the *heroes* return to be greeted by the community. The microscopic dimension gradually recognizes the cosmic dimension, as they become aware of what is happening with the first movement.

The crescendo slows again as they take all day processing what they have experienced.

Slowly the music begins to speed up and get louder. Not knowing whether to be serious or to party, they embark on a journey, symbolic of the journey to manhood, with individual recognition of *having what it takes*. Again, for an individual, the apparently (to most) small or insignificant will emerge as critical, for example, picking up a rock, carrying it up the hill, and adding it to the pile created by others over the years. It's now more serious and they are playing a solo part in the symphony, yet still with their mates—and never the perfect symphony.

The coming together of the whole orchestra is again celebrated in the feast and celebration, then recognized at the graduation. The anticlimax is again the farewells, a mixed sense of pleasure and sadness; but this time, looking forward to the third movement.

Movement 3

Stage 3 participants arrive and are excited to again be playing in the *Leadership* orchestra, which they rejoin in a more intense way. In particular, they gather to play familiar tunes with *old mates* from the last two years.

The tempo of Stage 3 speeds up. They quickly become a single, united cohort as a company of men, having been so recognized a year ago—men on a mission or grappling with their mission.

Duo is a primary focus, two instruments playing a duet. But they also have bigger aspirations to share and check out.

They return from their duet, eager to again be a united cohort—back with the full orchestra. A primary tune now is focusing on their futures and the eagerness to be able to share it, with sword in hand, in front of their mates. The sword, like the conductor's baton, gives them center stage, at least for their moment.

The coming together of the whole *Leadership* community, again celebrated in feast, celebration, and graduation, takes on a whole new meaning, as this is their last time together at *Leadership*. They are sitting in the center of the orchestra. They are now more aware of the cosmic dimension; they have practiced well and are now more able to listen to and hear the other movements. And so, the music takes them to other places. The climatic section of the symphony is deafening. But, the celebration and sense of completion is tempered by mixed emotions, including sadness, yet hope in the future and confidence in themselves and their mission. The symphony has concluded, or has it? They have done their best; still imperfect and part of the symphonic journey that continues to unfold.

The Unfolding Symphony

A post-*Leadership* euphoria is as a musician's post-performance of a deeply profound piece of music. The impact that a musician feels following their performance of a work that moved them is incredibly spiritual and lasting. Likewise, *Leadership* participants who perform this *Leadership* symphony are left deeply affected by it and they carry those memories and emotions with them for the rest of their lives, recognizing that God is maturing them, together and with Jesus, their voices and their very lives becoming a harmonious anthem to God.

> May our dependably steady and warmly personal God develop maturity in you so that you get along with each other as well as Jesus gets along with us all. Then we'll be a choir—not our voices only, but our very lives singing in harmony in a stunning anthem to our God and Father of our Master Jesus! (Rom 15:5–6 MSG)

Bibliography

Anderson, Craig L., et al. "Awe in Nature Heals: Evidence from Military Veterans, At-Risk Youth, and College Students." *Emotion* 18, no. 8 (2018) 1195–202.
Arnold, Patrick M. *Wildmen, Warriors, and Kings: Masculine Spirituality and the Bible*. New York: Crossroad, 1991.
Australian Institute of Family Studies. "Families in Australia Survey" (2017). https://aifs.gov.au/cfca/publications/prevalence-child-abuse-and-neglect.
———. "Parenting Arrangements after Separation" (2018). https://aifs.gov.au/publications/parenting-arrangements-after-separation.
Ayres, Michale. "Toward a Theology of Leadership." *Journal of Biblical Perspectives in Leadership* 1, no. 1 (2006) 3–7.
Baker, Mandi. "Welcome to the Bubble: Experiences of Liminality and Communitas among Summer Camp Counsellors." *Journal of Youth Development* 13, nos. 1–2 (2018) 24–33.
Baker, William R. *2 Corinthians*. The New College Press NIV Commentary. Joplen, MO: New College, 1999.
Barna. *The Connected Generation: How Christian Leaders around the World Can Strengthen Faith and Well-Being among 18–35-Year-Olds*. Ventura CA: Barna, 2019.
Barnett, Paul. *The Second Epistle to the Corinthians*. New International Commentary on the New Testament. Grand Rapids: Eerdmans, 1997.
Baxter, Jeff. *Together: Adults and Teenagers Transforming the Church*. Grand Rapids: Zondervan, 2010.
Beckwith, Ivy. *Postmodern Children's Ministry: Ministry to Children in the 21st Century*. Grand Rapids: Zondervan, 2004.
Best, Jonathan L. "Liminality, Communitas, and Hope (Transition, Fear, and Humanity: Part II)." *Liminal Theology*, September 9, 2020. https://liminaltheology.org/2020/09/09/liminality-communitas-and-hope/.
Beyond Blue. "Ways to Look after Your Mental Health amid the Coronavirus Pandemic" (2021). https://coronavirus.beyondblue.org.au/Managing-my-daily-life/Coping-with-isolation-and-being-at-home/ways-to-look-after-your-mental-health-amid-the-coronavirus-pandemic.

BIBLIOGRAPHY

Bialeschki, M. Deborah, et al. "Camp Experiences and Developmental Outcomes for Youth." *Child and Adolescent Psychiatric Clinics of North America* 16, no. 4 (2007) 769–88.
Bilezikian, Gilbert. *Beyond Sex Roles*. Grand Rapids: Baker, 1985.
Birks, Melanie, and Jane Mills. *Grounded Theory: A Practical Guide*. London: Sage, 2011.
Blomberg, Craig L. *Matthew*. The New American Commentary: An Exegetical and Theological Exposition of Holy Scripture 22. Nashville: Broadman, 1992.
Bly, Robert. *Iron John*. New York: Addison-Wesley, 1990.
Bock, Darrell L. *Acts*. Baker Exegetical Commentary on the New Testament. Grand Rapids: Baker, 2007.
Bogdan, Robert, and Steven Taylor. "Toward a Sociology of Acceptance: The Other Side to the Study of Deviance." *Social Policy* 18, no. 2 (1987) 34–39.
Bridges, Jerry. *The Pursuit of Holiness*. Bucks: Scripture Press Foundation, 1985.
Bruce, F. F. *The Epistle to the Ephesians*. London: Pickering and Inglis, 1961.
Buber, Martin. *Between Man and Man*. Translated by R. G. Smith. London and Glasgow: Fontana Library, 1961.
Campbell, J. *The Hero with a Thousand Faces*. Princeton, NJ: Princeton, 1972.
Carson, Timothy, et al. *Crossing Thresholds: A Practical Theology of Liminality*. Cambridge, UK: Lutterworth, 2021.
Carter, Danon, and Timothy Baghurst. "The Influence of Servant Leadership on Restaurant Employee Engagement." *Journal of Business Ethics* 124, no. 3 (2014) 453–64.
Charmaz, Kathy. *Constructing Grounded Theory: A Practical Guide through Qualitative Analysis*. 2nd ed. London: Sage, 2014.
Clark, Chap, ed. *Adoptive Youth Ministry: Integrating Emerging Generations into the Family of Faith*. Grand Rapids: Baker, 2016.
Clark, Chap, and Pamela J. Ewen. "Reconstructing Family Life: Family-Based Youth Ministry." In *New Directions in Youth Ministry*, by Wayne Rice et al., 47–63. Loveland, CO: Group, 1998.
Cohnick, Lynn H. *Ephesians: A New Covenant Commentary*. Eugene, OR: Cascade, 2010.
Corrie, Elizabeth W. "Becoming Christ's Hands and Feet." In *How Youth Ministry Can Change Theological Education—If We Let It*, edited by Kenda Creasy Dean and Christy Lang Hearlson, 231–46. Grand Rapids: Eerdmans, 2016.
Corvig, Duane M. "Lessons in Leadership Development from the Master Student." *The Journal of Applied Christian Leadership* 4, no. 1 (2010) 12–16.
Covey, Stephen. *The 7 Habits of Highly Effective People*. New York: Simon and Schuster, 1989.
Cox, Lawrence J. "How Old Were Jesus and His Disciples?" https://www.academia.edu/30309277?How_old_were_Jesus_and_his_disciples.
Creswell, John W. *Qualitative Inquiry and Research Design: Choosing among Five Approaches*. Thousand Oaks: Sage, 2007.
Dalbey, Gordon. *Healing the Masculine Soul*. Nashville: Thomas Nelson, 2003.
Davis, John E. *Extreme Pursuit: Winning the Race for the Heart of your Son*. Colorado Springs: Navpress, 2007.
Dawes, Nickki Pearce, and Reed Larson. "How Youth Get Engaged: Grounded-Theory Research on Motivational Development in Organized Youth Programs." *Developmental Psychology* 47, no. 1 (2011) 259–69.
De Roest, Henk. *Collaborative Practical Theology: Engaging Practitioners in Research on Christian Practices*. Leiden: Brill, 2020.

Dean, Kenda Creasy, and Ron Foster. *The Godbearing Life: The Art of Soul Tending for Youth Ministry*. Nashville: Upper Room, 1998.

Dean, Kenda Creasy, and Christy Lang Hearlson, eds. "Calling as Creative Process: Wicked Questions." In *How Youth Ministry Can Change Theological Education—If We Let It*, edited by Kenda Creasy Dean and Christy Lang Hearlson, 31–62. Grand Rapids: Eerdmans, 2016.

———. *How Youth Ministry Can Change Theological Education—If We Let it*. Grand Rapids: Eerdmans, 2016.

———. "Taste Tests and Teenagers: Vocational Discernment as a Creative Social Practice." In *How Youth Ministry Can Change Theological Education—If We Let It*, edited by Kenda Creasy Dean and Christy Lang Hearlson, 3–30. Grand Rapids: Eerdmans, 2016.

Dean, Kenda Creasy, et al., eds. "Fessing Up: Owning our Theological Commitments." In *Starting Right: Thinking Theologically about Youth Ministry*, edited by Kenda Creasy Dean et al., 27–39. Grand Rapids: Zondervan. 2001.

———. "Hitting It Out of the Park: Why Churches Need Farm Teams." In *How Youth Ministry Can Change Theological Education—If We Let It*, edited by Kenda Creasy Dean and Christy Lang Hearlson, 265–87. Grand Rapids: Eerdmans, 2016.

———. *Starting Right: Thinking Theologically about Youth Ministry*. Grand Rapids: Zondervan, 2001.

Dever, Mark. *9 Ways to Raise up Leaders in Your Church* (2017) *TGC*, June 5, 2017. https://www.thegospelcoalition.org/article/9-ways-to-raise-up-leaders-in-your-church/.

DeVries, Mark. *Family-Based Youth Ministry*. 2nd ed. Downers Grove: IVP, 2004.

———. *Sustainable Youth Ministry: Why Most Youth Ministry Doesn't Last and What Your Church Can Do About It*. Downers Grove: IVP, 2018.

Diaz, April L. "A Call to Adoption: Integration of Youth Ministry in the Church." In *Adoptive Youth Ministry: Integrating Emerging Generations into the Family of Faith*, edited by Chap Clark, 335–46. Grand Rapids: Baker, 2016.

Douglass, Katherine M. "Holy Noticing: The Power of Nomination and Commissioning for Missional Formation." In *How Youth Ministry Can Change Theological Education—If We Let it*, edited by Kenda Creasy Dean and Christy Lang Hearlson, 100–120. Grand Rapids: Eerdmans, 2016.

Douglass, Katherine M., and Kenda Creasy Dean. "Research Methods of the High School Youth Theology Program Seminar." In *How Youth Ministry Can Change Theological Education—If We Let it*," edited by Kenda Creasy Dean and Christy Lang Hearlson, 288–93. Grand Rapids: Eerdmans, 2016.

Dykstra, Craig. "Foreword." In *How Youth Ministry Can Change Theological Education—If We Let It*, edited by Kenda Creasy Dean and Christy Lang Hearlson, x–xvii. Grand Rapids: Eerdmans, 2016.

El Hussein, Mohamed T., et al. "Grounded Theory and the Conundrum of Literature Review: Framework for Novice Researchers." *The Qualitative Report* 22, no. 4 (2017) 1198–210.

Eldredge, John. *Epic: The Story God Is Telling*. Nashville: Thomas Nelson, 2004.

———. *Fathered by God: Learning What Your Dad Could Never Teach You*. Nashville: Thomas Nelson, 2009.

———. (Padre). "Momentum." *And Sons Magazine*, September 2015. https://archive.andsonsmagazine.com/special-issue-1/momentum.

———. *The Way of the Wild Heart*. Nashville: Nelson, 2006.

BIBLIOGRAPHY

———. *Wild at Heart: Discovering the Secrets of a Man's Soul*. Nashville: Nelson, 2001.

Elmer, Duane. *Cross-Cultural Servanthood: Serving the World with Christlike Humility*. Downers Grove: IVP, 2006.

Eva, Nathan, et al. "Servant Leadership: A Systematic Review and Call for Future Research." *The Leadership Quarterly* 31, no. 1 (2019) 111–32.

Eva, Nathan, and Sen Sendjaya. "Creating Future Leaders: An Examination of Youth Leadership Development in Australia." *Education and Training* 55, no. 6 (2013) 584–98.

Farrar, Steve. *King Me: What Every Son Wants and Needs from His Father*. Chicago: Moody, 2005.

Fields, Doug. *Purpose Driven Youth Ministry: 9 Essential Foundations for Healthy Growth*. Grand Rapids: Zondervan, 1998.

Ford, Michael. *Lonely Mystic: A New Portrait of Henri J. M. Nouwen*. New York: Paulist, 2018.

Fowl, Stephen E. *Ephesians: A Commentary*. Louisville: Westminster John Knox, 2012.

Free Dictionary. "Epic." http://www.thefreedictionary.com/epic.

Fritz, Everett. *The Art of Forming Young Disciples: Why Youth Ministries Aren't Working and What to do about it*. Manchester, NH: Sophia Institute, 2018.

Galanaki, Evangelia. "Are Children Able to Distinguish among the Concepts of Aloneness, Loneliness, and Solitude?" *International Journal of Behavioural Development* 28, no. 5 (2004) 435–43.

Garst, Barry A., et al. "Growing without Limitations: Transformation among Young Adult Camp Staff." *Journal of Youth Development* 4, no. 1 (2009). https://jyd.pitt.edu/ojs/jyd/article/view/272.

Gascoigne, Robert. *Freedom and Purpose: An Introduction to Christian Ethics*. New York: Paulist, 2004.

Got Questions Ministries. "How Old Were Jesus' Disciples?" https://www.gotquestions.org/how-old-were-Jesus-disciples.html.

Graham, J. W. "Servant-Leadership in Organizations: Inspirational and Moral." *The Leadership Quarterly* 2, no. 2 (1991) 105–19.

Greenleaf, Robert K. *Servant Leadership: A Journey into the Nature of Legitimate Power and Greatness*. New Jersey: Paulist, 2002.

Grof, Christina. "Rites of Passage: A Necessary Step towards Wholeness." In *Crossroads, the Quest for Contemporary Rites of Passage*, edited by Louise Carus Mahdi et al., 9–11. La Salla, IL: Open Court, 1996.

Hage, Elias. "The Modern Boy's Rite of Passage and the Lacking Component of Transcendental Death Acknowledgement." *Journal of Humanistic Psychology* 58, no. 2 (2018) 214–33.

Haitch, Russell. "Trampling Down Death by Death." In *Redemptive Transformation in Practical Theology: Essays in Honour of James Loder*, edited by Dan Wright and John Kuentzel, 48. Grand Rapids: Eerdmans, 2004.

Hassed, James. "The Psychology of Freedom." *Welldoing.org*, July 18, 2017. https://welldoing.org/article/psychology-freedom.

Harris, W. Hall, III. "Leading through Weakness, Vulnerability and Self-Sacrifice: Leadership in the Gospel of John." In *Biblical Leadership: Theology for the Everyday Leader*, edited by Benjamin K. Forest and Chet Roden, 349–62. Grand Rapids: Kregel, 2017.

Hense, Cherry, and Katrina Mcferran. "Toward a Critical Grounded Theory." *Qualitative Research Journal* 16, no. 4 (2016) 402–16.
Hernandez, Will. *Henri Nouwen: A Spirituality of Imperfection*. Mahwah, NJ: Paulist, 2016.
———. *Henri Nouwen and Soul Care: A Ministry of Integration*. Mahwah, NJ: Paulist, 2008.
Hine, Thomas. *The Rise and Fall of the American Teenager*. New York: Harper Perennia, 1999.
Hirsch, Alan. *The Forgotten Ways*. Grand Rapids: Brazos, 2006.
Hoehner, Harold W. *Ephesians: An Exegetical Commentary*. Grand Rapids: Baker Academic, 2002.
Horn, David. "Prepare Me for a Worthy Adventure: Pedagogies of Pilgrimage in Adolescent Formation." In *How Youth Ministry Can Change Theological Education—If We Let it*, edited by Kenda Creasy Dean and Christy Lang Hearlson, 193–210. Grand Rapids: Eerdmans, 2016.
IgnatianSpirituality.com. "What is Ignatian Spirituality?" Loyola Press, 2024. https://www.ignatianspirituality.com/what-is-ignatian-spirituality/.
Immanuel Lutheran College. "The Rite Journey." https://www.immanuel.qld.edu.au/our-college/the-rite-journey.
Internet Slang. "Epic." http://www.internetslang.com/EPIC-meaning-definition.asp.
Jacober, Amy E. *The Adolescent Journey: An Interdisciplinary Approach to Practical Theology*. Downers Grove: IVP, 2011.
James, Ralph E., Jr. "Theology of Acceptance." *The Journal of Religion* 49, no. 4 (1969) 376–87.
Jennings, William J. "I Feel Older: Investigating the Impact of a Father and Son." *Boyhood Studies* 5, no. 1 (2011) 61–80.
Jones, Tony. *Postmodern Youth Ministry: Exploring Cultural Shift, Creating Holistic Connections, Cultivating Authentic Community*. Grand Rapids: Zondervan, 2001.
Kaethler, Andrew Brubacher. "Getting All Turned Around: Truth, Disruption, and Reorientation in High School Theology Programs." In *How Youth Ministry Can Change Theological Education—If We Let it*, edited by Kenda Creasy Dean and Christy Lang Hearlson, 139–53, Grand Rapids: Eerdmans, 2016.
Karagianni, Despoina, and Anthony J. Montgomery. "Developing Leadership Skills among Adolescents and Young Adults: A Review of Leadership Programmes." *International Journal of Adolescence and Youth* 23, no. 1 (2018) 86–98.
Karianjahi, Muhoa. "Church as Village Rites of Passage." *Journal of Youth Ministry* 14, no. 1 (2015) 5.
Kaster, Jeffrey. "Fuel My Faith: Pedagogies of Theological Reflection in High School Theology Programs." In *How Youth Ministry Can Change Theological Education—If We Let it*, edited by Kenda Creasy Dean and Christy Lang Hearlson, 63–78. Grand Rapids: Eerdmans, 2016.
Kendellen, Kelsey, et al. "Facilitators and Barriers to Leadership Development at a Canadian Summer Camp." *Journal of Park and Recreation Administration* 34, no. 4 (2016) 36–59.
Keown, Mark. "Paul's Vision of a New Masculinity (Eph 5:21–26: 9)." *Colloquium* 48, no. 1 (2016) 47–60.
Kiersch, Christa, and Janet Peters. "Leadership from the Inside Out: Student Leadership Development within Authentic Leadership and Servant Leadership Frameworks." *Journal of Leadership Education* 16, no. 1 (2017) 148–68.

King, Mike. *Presence-Centered Youth Ministry: Guiding Students into Spiritual Formation.* Downers Grove: Group, 2006.

Klamon, Virginia. 2007. "In the Name of Service: Exploring the Social Enterprise Workplace Experience through the Lens of Servant Leadership." *The International Journal of Servant-Leadership* 3, no. 1 (2017) 109–38.

Knuth, Elizabeth T. "Male Spirituality: A Feminist Evaluation." https://www.jmm.org.au/articles/11319.htm.

Kodish, S. "The Paradoxes of Leadership: The Contribution of Aristotle." *Leadership* 2, no. 4 (2006) 451–68.

Kokemuller, Neil. "Empowerment as a Motivational Method." https://smallbusiness.chron.com/empowerment-motivational-method-56050.html.

Kostenberger, Andreas J., and David Crowther. "Leading with Love: Leadership in the Johannine Epistles." In *Biblical Leadership: Theology for the Everyday Leader,* edited by Benjamin K. Forest and Chet Roden, 467–84. Grand Rapids: Kregel Academic, 2017.

Krause, Michael W. "Household: Household Code in Ephesians (Part 1)." https://krusekronicle.typepad.com/kruse_kronicle/2007/10/household-house.html#.XWcECegzZPY. *Krause Kronicle,* October 8, 2007.

Kurtz, Ernest, and Katherine Ketcham. *The Spirituality of Imperfection: Storytelling and the Journey to Wholeness.* New York: Bantam, 1994.

Kye, Jea Kwang. "Principles from Jesus Christ's Life that Inform a Biblical Perspective on Servant Leadership." *Korean Journal of Christian Studies* (2010) 73.

L'Arche. "Identity and Mission." https://www.larche.org/about-larche/identity-and-mission/.

Lane, Belden C. *The Solace of Fierce Landscapes: Exploring Desert and Mountain Spirituality.* New York: Oxford University Press, 1998.

Lane, William L. *Hebrews 9–13.* World Biblical Commentary. Dallas: Word, 1991.

Larson, Reed W. "The Emergence of Solitude as a Constructive Domain of Experience in Early Adolescents." *Child Development* 68, no. 1 (1997) 80–93.

Lawless, Chuck. "7 Reasons Young Men Raised in the Church Still Struggle with Church." February 7, 2018. http://chucklawless.com/2018/02/7-reasons-young-men-raised-in-church-still-struggle-with-church/.

Lawrence, Rick. *Jesus Centered Youth Ministry: Moving from Jesus-Plus to Jesus-Only.* Loveland, CO: Group, 2014.

Leadership Queensland. *Dear Dad: What 15-Year-Old Boys Want to Say to Their Fathers.* Brisbane: The Boys' Brigade Queensland, 2014.

———. *Goals of Leadership.* Brisbane: The Boys' Brigade Queensland, 2017.

———. *Staff Development Learning Guide, Module G.5: Debriefing.* Brisbane: The Boys' Brigade Queensland, 2018.

Lee, Bernard, and Michael Cowan. "Priority Concerns of SCCs in American Catholicism." In *Small Christian Communities Today: Capturing the New Moment,* edited by Joseph G. Healey and Jeanne Hinto, 63–770. Maryknoll, NY: Orbis, 2005.

Lee, Steve, and Chap Clark. *Boys to Men.* Chicago: Moody, 1995.

Lewis, Robert. *Raising a Modern-Day Knight.* Colorado Springs: Focus on the Family, 1997.

Lincoln, Andrew T. *Ephesians.* World Biblical Commentary 42. Dallas: Word, 1990.

Lindsay, Patrick. *The Spirit of the Digger.* Sydney: HarperCollins, 2003.

Lingard, Bob, et al. "Addressing the Educational Needs of Boys." Department of Education, Science and Training, 2002.

Lines, Andrew, and Graham Gallasch. "The Rite Journey: Rediscovering Rites of Passage for Boys." *Journal of Boyhood Studies* 3, no. 1 (2009) 74–89.

Long, Christopher R., and James R. Averill, 2003. "Solitude: An Exploration of Benefits of Being Alone." *Journal for the Theory of Social Behaviour* 33, no. 1 (2003) 21–44.

Louv, D. J. "A Christian Spirituality of Imperfection: Towards a Pastoral Theology of Descent within the Praxis of Orthopathy." https://www.proquest.com/openview/cc9f80b7f8d56961319a830fc9ddd444/1?pq-origsite=gscholar&cbl=3748033.

Lukabyo, Ruth. *From a Ministry for Youth to a Ministry of Youth: Aspects of Protestant Youth Ministry in Sydney 1930–959*. Eugene, OR: Wipf & Stock, 2020.

Marcus, Ivan G. *The Jewish Life-Cycle: Rites of Passage from Biblical to Modern Times*. Washington: University of Washington Press, 2004.

Maslow, Abraham H. "A Theory of Human Motivation." *Psychological Review* 50 (1943) 370–96.

May, Scottie, et al. *Children Matter: Celebrating Their Place in the Church, Family and Community*. Grand Rapids: Eerdmans, 2005.

McGarry, Michael. *A Biblical Theology of Youth Ministry: Teenagers in the Life of the Church*. Nashville: Random House, 2009.

McGee-Cooper, Ann, and Duane Trammell. Rev. by Matthew Kosec. *The Essentials of Servant Leadership: Principles in Practice*. Trammell McGee-Cooper and Associates Inc., 2013.

McKee, Jonathan, and David R. Smith. *Ministry by Teenagers: Developing Leaders from Within*. Grand Rapids: Zondervan, 2011.

McKenna, David L. *Christ-Centered Leadership: The Incarnational Difference*. Eugene, OR: Cascade, 2013.

McManus, Erwin. "The Servant Heart of God: We Are Most Like God When We Are Serving Others." *Preaching Today: Today's Best Sermons* 269. Christianity Today (n.d.).

McVann, Mark. "One of the Prophets: Matthew's Testing Narrative as a Rite of Passage." *Biblical Theological Bulletin* 23, no. 1 (1993) 14–20.

Merriam-Webster. "Epic." http://www.merriam-webster.com/dictionary/epic.

Molitor, Brian D. *Boy's Passage Man's Journey*. Lynnwood, WA: Emerald, 2004.

Moore, Walker. *Rite of Passage Parenting: Four Essential Experiences to Equip Your Kids for Life*. Nashville: Thomas Nelson, 2007.

Mortensen, Jennifer, et al., 2014. "Leadership through a Youth Lens: Understanding Youth Conceptualizations of Leadership." *Journal of Community Psychology* 42, no. 4 (2014) 447–62.

Nagy, Timothy, 2018. "Lens of Liminality: A Reflection on Faith Sharing in Young Adult Retreat Ministry." *Journal of Youth and Theology* 17, no. 1 (2018) 40–60.

Nel, Malan. "Youth Ministry: An Inclusive Missional Approach." HTS Religion and Society Series 1. Capetown, SA: OASIS, 2018.

Nelson, Peter K. "Discipleship Dissonance: Toward a Theology of Imperfection amidst the Pursuit of Holiness." *Journal of Spiritual Formation and Soul Care* 4, no. 1 (2011) 63–92.

Newby, Stephen M. *Worship Outside the Music Box Theology of Music and Worship in Multi-Ethnic Ministry*. Enumclaw, WA: Redemption, 2015.

BIBLIOGRAPHY

Nouwen, Henri J. *Bread for the Journey: A Daybook of Wisdom and Faith.* San Francisco: HarperSanFrancisco, 1977.

———. *In the Name of Jesus: Reflections on Christian Leadership.* London: Darton, Longman and Todd, 1989.

———. *The Living Reminder: Service and Prayer in Memory of Jesus Christ.* San Francisco: HarperCollins, 1977.

———. *Reaching Out: The Three Movements of the Spiritual Life.* New York: Doubleday, 1975.

———. *The Return of the Prodigal Son: A Story of Homecoming.* London: Darton, Longman and Todd, 1994.

———. *The Wounded Healer.* New York: Doubleday, 1972.

Nouwen, Henri J., et al. *Spiritual Direction: Wisdom for the Long Walk of Faith.* San Francisco: HarperSanFrancisco, 2006.

O'Brien, Peter T. *The Letter to the Ephesians.* Grand Rapids: Eerdmans, 1999.

Osmer, Richard R. *Practical Theology: An Introduction.* Grand Rapids: Eerdmans, 2008.

Parris, Denise L., and Jon W. Peachy. "Building a Legacy of Volunteers through Servant Leadership: A Cause-Related Sporting Event." *Nonprofit Management and Leadership* 23, no. 2 (2012) 259–75.

———. "A Systematic Literature Review of Servant Leadership Theory in Organizational Contexts." *Journal of Business Ethics* 113 (2013) 377–93.

Pettus, David. "A Concept Study: Leadership in Old Testament Hebrew." In *Biblical Leadership: Theology for the Everyday Leader*, edited by Benjamin K. Forest and Chet Roden, 29–40. Grand Rapids: Kregel Academic, 2017.

Piper, John. *Future Grace: The Purifying Power of the Promises of God.* Rev. ed. Colorado Springs: Multnomah, 2012.

Polhill, John B. *Acts: An Exegetical and Theological Exposition of Holy Scripture.* The New American Commentary 26. Nashville: Broadman, 1992.

Proffitt, Anabel, and Jacquie Church Young. "Catalyzing Community: Forming the Community as Catechist." In *How Youth Ministry Can Change Theological Education—If We Let it*, edited by Kenda Creasy Dean and Christy Lang Hearlson, 63–78. Grand Rapids: Eerdmans, 2016.

Rahn, Dave. "Focusing Youth Ministry through Student Leadership." In *Starting Right: Thinking Theologically about Youth Ministry*, edited by Kenda Creasy Dean, et al., 167–79. Grand Rapids: Zondervan, 2001.

Reaves, Jayme R., and David Tombs. "#MeToo Jesus: Naming Jesus as a Victim of Sexual Abuse." *International Journal of Public Theology* 13 (2019) 387–412.

Rice, Wayne. "Intentional Connections: Using Mentoring in Youth Ministry." In *New Directions in Youth Ministry*, by Wayne Rice et al., 64–82. Loveland, CO: Group, 1998.

———. *Reinventing Youth Ministry (Again): From Bells and Whistles to Flesh and Blood.* Downers Grove: IVP, 2010.

Rice, Wayne, et al. *New Directions in Youth Ministry.* Loveland, CO: Group 1998.

Rites of Passage Institute. "Home." https://www.ritesofpassageinstitute.org.

Rohr, Richard. *Adam's Return: The Five Promises of Male Initiation.* New York: Crossroads, 2004.

———. "Boys to Men: Rediscovering Rites of Passage for Our Times." *John Mark Ministries*, January 5, 2003. www.jmm.org.au/articles/5358.htm.

———. *From Wild Man to Wise Man: Reflections on Male Spirituality*. Franciscan Media: Cincinnati, 2005.

———. "Masculine Spirituality." www.mensfellowship.net/masculine-spirituality/.

———. "Masculine Spirituality and Why Males Need Initiation: Beloved Sons Series." Centre for Action and Contemplation, recorded 2003. Albuquerque, NM, 2007.

Rohr, Richard, and Joseph Martos. "The Wild Man's Journey: Reflections on Male Spirituality. Cincinnati: St. Andrews Messenger, 1992.

Rolheiser, Ron. "Masculine Spirituality." May 7, 1990. https://ronrolheiser.com/masculine-spirituality/.

Root, Andrew. *Christopraxis: A Practical Theology of the Cross*. Minneapolis: Fortress, 2014.

———. *The End of Youth Ministry?: Why Parents Don't Really Care about Youth Groups and What Youth Workers Should Do about It*. Grand Rapids: Baker, 2020.

———. *Revisiting Relational Youth Ministry: From a Strategy of Influence to a Theology of Incarnation*. Downers Grove: IVP, 2007.

———. *Taking the Cross to Youth Ministry*. Grand Rapids: Zondervan, 2012.

———. "What Are We Doing in These Mountains: The Outdoor Trip and the Theology of the Cross." In *The Theological Turn in Youth Ministry*, edited by Andrew Root and Kenda Creasy Dean, 174–81. Downers Grove: IVP, 2011.

Root, Andrew, and Kenda Creasy Dean. *The Theological Turn in Youth Ministry*. Downers Grove: IVP, 2011.

Ross, Richard. *Accelerate: Parenting Teenagers toward Adulthood*. Bloomington, IN: Cross, 2013.

Russell, Robert. "A Practical Theology of Leadership." *School of Leadership Studies, Regent University*. Servant Leadership Roundtable, 2003.

Schroeder, Edward H. "A Theology of Acceptance." *Proceedings of the 1964 VU Workshop and Institute of Human Relations* (1964) 24–26.

Schwarz, Gary, et al. "Servant Leadership and Follower Job Performance: The Mediating Effect of Public Service Motivation." *Public Administration* 94, no. 4 (2016) 1025–41.

Sendjaya, Sen, and James C. Sarros. "Servant Leadership: Its Origin, Development, and Application in Organisations." *Journal of Leadership and Organisation Studies* 9, no. 2 (2002) 57–64.

Sendjaya, Sen, et al. "Defining and Measuring Servant Leadership Behaviour in Organisations." *Journal of Management Studies* 45, no. 2 (2008) 402–24.

Senter, Mark, III. *The Coming Revolution in Youth Ministry: And Its Radical Impact on the Church*. Wheaton, IL: Victor, 1992.

Senter, Mark H., III, et al. *Four Views of Youth Ministry and the Church: Inclusive Congregational, Preparatory, Missional, Strategic*. Grand Rapids: Zondervan, 2001.

Slater, Thomas B. *Ephesians*. Smyth and Helwys Bible Commentary. Macon, GA: Smyth & Helwys, 2012.

Smith, Donald. "A Leadership Development Program for Young Men." *Journal of Youth and Theology* 19, no. 1 (2020) 70–94.

———. "A Theory of What Factors Contribute to the Apparent Success of a Leadership Development Program for Young Men." PhD diss., Australian College of Theology, 2022.

Snodgrass, Klyne. *The Ephesians NIV Application Commentary*. Grand Rapids: Zondervan, 1996.

BIBLIOGRAPHY

Sorenson, Jacob. "The Summer Camp Experience and Faith Formation of Emerging Adults." *Journal of Youth Ministry* 13, no. 1 (2014) 7–40.
Spears Center. "International Journal of Servant Leadership." https://www.spearscenter.org/component/weblinks/weblink/54-servant-sites/14-international-journal-of-servant-leadership?Itemid=110.
St. Vincent de Paul Society. "Two Australias: A Report on Poverty in the Land of Plenty." https://issuu.com/svdpnatcl/docs/179108_two_australias_-_a_report_on.
Stancil, David C. "Genesis 16:1–16; 21:8–21—The Uncherished Child: A 'Modern' Wilderness of the Heart." *Review and Expositor* 91, no. 3 (1994) 393–400.
Stanton, Graham. *Wide Awake in God's World: Bible Engagement for Teenage Spiritual Formation in a Culture of Expressive Individualism*. Eugene, OR: Wipf & Stock, 2020.
Steers, Judy. "Let Me Try: Experiential Learning in the Theological Formation of Young People." In *How Youth Ministry Can Change Theological Education—If We Let it*, edited by Kenda Creasy Dean and Christy Lang Hearlson, 211–38. Grand Rapids: Eerdmans, 2016.
Stone, A. Gregory, et al. "Transformational Versus Servant Leadership: A Difference in Leader Focus." *Leadership and Organizational Development Journal* 25, no. 4, (2004) 349–61.
Strauss, Anselm, and Juliet Corbin. *Basics of Qualitative Research: Techniques and Procedures for Developing Grounded Theory*. Thousand Oaks: Sage, 1998.
Tchividjian, Tullian. *One Way Love: Inexhaustible Grace for an Exhausted World*. Colorado Springs: David C. Cook, 2013.
Thielman, Frank. *Ephesians*. Baker Exegetical Commentary on the New Testament. Grand Rapids: Baker Academic, 2010.
Tidball, Derek. "Leaders as Servants: A Resolution of the Tension." *Evangelical Review of Theology* 36 (2012) 31–47.
Tie, Ylona C., et al. "Grounded Theory Research: A Design Framework for Novice Researchers." *PubMed7* (January 2, 2019). https://doi.org/10.1177/2050312118822927.
Tiller, E., et al. *Youth Survey Report 2020*. Sydney, NSW: Mission Australia, 2020.
Trainor, Michael. *The Body of Jesus and Sexual Abuse: How the Gospel Passion Narratives Inform a Pastoral Approach*. Melbourne: Morning Star, 2014.
Turner, Edith. *Communitas: The Anthropology of Collective Joy*. Contemporary Anthropology of Religion. New York: Palgrave Macmillan, 2012.
Turner, Victor. *Dramas, Fields, and Metaphors: Symbolic Action in Human Society*. Ithaca, NY: Cornell University Press, 1974.
———. *The Ritual Process*. Ithaca, NY: Cornell University Press, 2009.
Udani, Zenon A. S., and Caterina Lorenzo-Molo. "When Servant Becomes Leader: The Corazon C. Aquino Success Story as a Beacon for Business Leaders." *Journal of Business Ethics* 116, no. 2 (2013) 373–91.
Van Dierendonck, Dirk. "Servant Leadership: A Review and Synthesis." *Journal of Management* 37, no. 4 (2011) 1228–61.
Van Dierendonck, Dirk, and Inge Nuijten. "The Servant Leadership Survey: Development and Validation of a Multidimensional Measure." *Journal of Business Psychology* 26, (2011) 249–67.
Van Gennep, A. *The Rites of Passage*. Translated by Monika B. Vizedn and Gabrielle L. Caffee. Chicago: Chicago University Press, 1960.
Vukich, Lee, and Steve Vandegriff. *Timeless Youth Ministry: A Handbook for Successfully Reaching Today's Youth*. Chicago: Moody, 2002.

Webber, Ruth, et al. "Models of Youth Ministry in Action: The Dynamics of Christian Youth Ministry in an Australian City." *Religious Education* 105, no. 2 (2010) 204–15.

White, Rob, et al. *Youth and Society.* 4th ed. Melbourne: Oxford University Press, 2017.

Wilson, Stephen M. *Making Men: The Male Coming-of-Age Theme in the Hebrew Bible.* New York: Oxford University Press, 2015.

Wimberly, Ann Streaty. "Give Me Mentors: Pedagogies of Spiritual Accompaniment." In *How Youth Ministry Can Change Theological Education—If We Let it*, edited by Kenda Creasy Dean and Christy Lang Hearlson, 79–99. Grand Rapids: Eerdmans, 2016.

Witherington, Ben, II. *The Letters to Philemon, the Colossians and the Ephesians: A Socio-Rhetorical Commentary on the Captivity Epistles.* Grand Rapids: Eerdmans, 2007.

Wolfe, Richard. *The Character of Christian Leadership.* Ebook, Lulu.com, 2016.

Yates, Gary. "A Call for Faithful Servants: Leadership in Isaiah, Jeremiah and Ezekiel." In *Biblical Leadership: Theology for the Everyday Leader,* edited by Benjamin K. Forest and Chet Roden, 184–200. Grand Rapids: Kregel Academic, 2017.

Zahniser, A. H. Mathias. "Ritual Process and Christian Discipling: Contextualizing a Buddhist Rite of Passage." *Missiology* 19, no. 1 (1991) 3–19.

Zirschky, Andrew. *Beyond the Screen: Youth Ministry for the Connected but Alone Generation.* Nashville: Abingdon, 2015.

www.ingramcontent.com/pod-product-compliance
Lightning Source LLC
Chambersburg PA
CBHW070231230426
43664CB00014B/2263